An Honoured Guest

New Essays on W. B. Yeats

An Honoured Guest

New Essays on W. B. Yeats

edited by
Denis Donoghue and J. R. Mulryne

New York
St Martin's Press
1966

© Edward Arnold (Publishers) Ltd., 1965

First published 1965

Library of Congress Catalog Card Number: 66–14351

Printed and bound in Great Britain by
W. & J. Mackay & Co. Ltd., Fair Row, Chatham

Preface

' . . . a poetry which I believe is nearer the centre of our main traditions of sensibility and thought than the poetry of Eliot or of Pound'. Thus Allen Tate wrote, in 1942, of the poetry of W. B. Yeats. Large words, indeed; and to rehearse them now, a generation later, may cause us some embarrassment. The best things, Eliot tells us, are found at the centre; a living and central tradition is to be deemed a poet's first and greatest possession, and if he lacks it, or possesses it meanly, his work is bound to be eccentric or provincial, even if he lacks nothing else.

Yeats is one of those artists, Eliot himself declared, 'who are a part of the consciousness of an age which cannot be understood without them'. If this is so, we have done poor justice to the nature and scope of his achievement. On the one hand, his greatness is almost everywhere acknowledged; on the other, his place in modern literature is often considered somehow marginal, oblique. One sometimes detects, in critical opinion, the hope that Yeats may turn out to have been a special case, perhaps even an Irish case, to be disposed accordingly. Is his work of central importance in modern literature, or is it an item in the margin? We must make up our minds.

Mr. Tate in the same essay said: 'Yeats's special qualities will instigate special studies of great ingenuity, but the more direct and more difficult problem of the poetry itself will probably be delayed.' The present book is a contribution to the discussion of this problem. The ten new essays it contains, taking in the prose and drama as well as the poetry, were each editorially invited from critics who share, perhaps, nothing more than the willingness to respond afresh and directly to the challenge of Yeats's work. The editors assume responsibility for the structure of the book and for the map of Yeats's enduring work which it implies, but the individual areas, once assigned, were entrusted to the good offices of their tenants.

D.D.
J.R.M.

Contents

Abbreviations

Auto.	*Autobiographies.* London, 1955.
C.P.	*The Collected Poems of W. B. Yeats.* London, 1950.
C.Pl.	*The Collected Plays of W. B. Yeats.* London, 1952.
E. & I.	*Essays and Introductions.* London, 1961.
Letters	*The Letters of W. B. Yeats,* ed. Allan Wade. London, 1955.
Myth.	*Mythologies.* London, 1959.
P. & C.	*Plays and Controversies.* London, 1923.
A Vision	*A Vision:* A Reissue with the Author's Final Revisions. London, 1961.
Hone	*W. B. Yeats, 1865–1939,* by Joseph Hone, Second Edition. London, 1962.
Saul	*Prolegomena to the Study of Yeats's Poems,* by George Brandon Saul. Philadelphia, 1957.

Acknowledgement

The author and publishers wish to express their thanks to Mr. M. B. Yeats, to Macmillan & Company Ltd. and to the Macmillan Company of New York for their kind permission to reproduce quotations from the works of W. B. Yeats.

I

Yeats and the Practising Poet

CHARLES TOMLINSON

*

WE live in an age of demolition. If the practising poet is to record this
characteristic defilement of our time—its sacrifice of fine relationship,
and the literal and daily demolition of its inherited architecture—he will
turn to Yeats both as a custodian of value and a poet who can experience
and record the tragedy without flinching:

> Childless I thought, 'My children may find here
> Deep-rooted things,' but never foresaw its end,
> And now that end has come I have not wept;
> No fox can foul the lair the badger swept. (C.P., 369)

He is writing about Lady Gregory's house in Coole Park. He had
(despite line two) foreseen its ruin years before, when he wrote:

> Here, traveller, scholar, poet, take your stand
> When all those rooms and passages are gone,
> When nettles wave upon a shapeless mound
> And saplings root among the broken stone,
> And dedicate—eyes bent upon the ground,
> Back turned upon the brightness of the sun
> And all the sensuality of the shade—
> A moment's memory to that laurelled head. (C.P., 274-5)

Yeats's stay against this image of dereliction is the positives Lady
Gregory exemplified: 'pride established in humility', 'a dance-like
glory that those walls begot'. There is a measure and a tone for these
qualities and Yeats fleshes them, as he so often does, by filling out an
entire stanza with a single unfolding sentence that brings to bear such
calm and strong recognition as would be worthy of 'all that pride and
that humility'. He holds close to his moral exemplar with his very
syntax, in its turn the articulation of a spiritual courage that the woman
herself would have approved of:

Augusta Gregory seated at her great ormolu table,
Her eightieth winter approaching: 'Yesterday he threatened my life.
I told him that nightly from six to seven I sat at this table,
The blinds drawn up.' (C.P., 348)

Yeats did not master for his verse the spiritual poise of his exemplar
without struggle—he who portrays himself at Coole, between Douglas
Hyde with metaphorical sword and 'that meditative man, John Synge',
as 'one that ruffled in a manly pose / For all his timid heart'. The growth
was a moral growth and, in part, that of one who has brought himself
to look at the irreparable and to find a language for both the loss and
the value of the loss. Coole Park no longer exists and the swallows
that whirled upon Lady Gregory's compass-point in 'Coole Park, 1929'
are memorialised only by their initials on a tree in the grounds. Indeed,
even while Yeats was writing, his subject-matter was on the point of
disappearing. What matters is, however, that a tone adequate to that
subject-matter did not disappear with it, and it is the tone which is at
once a lesson and an admonition to the practising poet:

> How but in custom and in ceremony
> Are innocence and beauty born?
> Ceremony's a name for the rich horn,
> And custom for the spreading laurel tree. (C.P., 214)

Yeats revivifies for us the language of courtesy that we know from
the seventeenth century. His poems on great houses, and on their ruin,
stand at the end of the line of the English country-house poem, descendants of Ben Jonson's 'To Penshurst', of Carew's 'To My Friend
G. N., from Wrest', Herrick's 'Panegerick to Sir Lewis Pemberton',
Marvell's 'Appleton House' and the fourth epistle of Pope's moral
essays. The language of these poems is the language of tact and the
language of power: 'laughing Ceres' must 'reassume the land' in the
way they are written and the very existence of the houses they celebrate
is sanctioned only by the vitality such houses transmit. 'Leisure, wealth,
privilege were created', says Yeats in Dramatis Personae, 'to be a soil for
the most living.' '. . . maybe the great-grandson of that house, / For
all its bronze and marble, 's but a mouse' (C.P., 226): Yeats knows the
significance of his ideal and he knows its vulnerability. He draws
sustenance for this ideal from an aristocratic context. He speaks in
Estrangement (Auto., 474) of the analogies 'between the long-established
life of the well-born and the artist's life'. There is a silly sentence here,
in which he says, 'When we are happiest we have some little post in

the house of Duke Frederick where we watch the proud dreamless world with humility . . .' Yeats would scarcely have been content with some 'little post' in an aristocratic household: he mixed with aristocrats on a basis of equality and friendship, not service. What, indeed, properly speaking, is Yeats's 'aristocracy' but a circle of friends, centred it may be on an hereditary figure like Lady Gregory, but essentially free of the petty tyrannies of feudal dependence? One of his aristocratic ladies wrote plays and another wrote poems. The circle of friends was a circle of artists or of promoters of the arts. Yeats could speak of it with all the courtesy of *Il Cortegiano* and with something more:

> Think where man's glory most begins and ends,
> And say my glory was I had such friends. (*C.P.*, 370)

The linguistic equivalent for his ideal he arrived at as early as 'Upon a House Shaken by the Land Agitation', with

> a written speech
> Wrought of high laughter, loveliness and ease. (*C.P.*, 107)

Yeats's style of courtesy, preluded here, has, at its finest, a humour that is part of the moral poise which can survive an age of demolition. It makes for a poetry where that tact of which I have spoken consorts with a nonchalance that is never carelessness: we must prize this union now that 'the conversational' has become an unquestioned virtue and that form stands in danger of growing 'weedy and colourless', as Miss Moore has it, 'like suckers from an unsunned tuber'. The humour can appear as a gentle demur, as in

> Mancini's portrait of Augusta Gregory,
> 'Greatest since Rembrandt,' according to John Synge;
> A great ebullient portrait certainly . . . (*C.P.*, 369)

or it can, as in 'A Prayer for my Daughter', put aside gloom and storm and future years that may 'come, / Dancing to a frenzied drum', to joke about the causes of mischance:

> Helen being chosen found life flat and dull
> And later had much trouble from a fool,
> While that great Queen, that rose out of the spray,
> Being fatherless could have her way
> Yet chose a bandy-leggèd smith for man.
> It's certain that fine women eat
> A crazy salad with their meat
> Whereby the Horn of Plenty is undone. (*C.P.*, 212)

Peter Allt has remarked on 'the contemptuous strength and the strangely triumphant contempt'[1] which often accompanies Yeats's humour. This is a different thing from that rather mechanical stress on 'haughtiness' and 'pride' into which he is at times betrayed. It is a term free of all cant and, at a time when cant has invaded and eroded the language of almost every social endeavour from government to education, the younger practitioner must learn its spirit and its use. Again, this tone was an achievement difficult to arrive at, difficult not to disperse in mere back-biting or pettishness. Its attainment brings once again into English verse a note which had gone out of it with Pope:

> You say, as I have often given tongue
> In praise of what another's said or sung,
> 'Twere politic to do the like by these';
> But was there ever dog that praised his fleas? (C.P., 105)

This example, 'To a Poet, who would have me Praise certain Bad Poets, Imitators of His and Mine', is an early one, from The Green Helmet of 1910. Already a comparable note is being sounded in Yeats's prose, and in Estrangement of the previous year we read: 'I have been talking to a man typical of a class common elsewhere but new in Ireland: often not ill-bred in manner and therefore the more manifestly with the ill-breeding of the mind, every thought made in some manufactory and with the mark upon it of its wholesale origin—thoughts never really thought out in their current form in any individual mind, but the creation of impersonal mechanism—of schools, of text-books, of newspapers, these above all' (Auto., 461-2). What Yeats already recognises is the mind of England as we now have it, and he feels free to express his recognition in a way that today few of our intellectuals would dare, with their middle-of-the-way tolerance, their readiness to show an interest in the latest fad and call the result sociology. Cant would restrain a man from writing now: 'In daily life one becomes rude the moment one grudges to the clown his perpetual triumph.' Today, there are no clowns, only an indefinite number of 'honest opinions'.

Yeats's refusal of cant goes together with what he terms a 'curious astringent joy'. He is aware of this quality long before he can get it over into verse and, in defining it in this way, he is describing, in 1902, his reaction to reading Nietzsche. It is two years after this experience ('I have read him so much that I have made my eyes bad again') that

[1] Irish Writing, No. 31, p. 23.

he writes to George Russell, echoing his first formulation, but now in a criticism of 'shadowiness' in poetry: '. . . let us have no emotions, however absurd, in which there is not an athletic joy'. We have lost our sense of the more Mediterranean Nietzsche in our image of the blond beast, yet here is a genuine parallel to Yeats's aristocratic spirit and an insight which is that of a poet. There is the same courtesy of aphoristic phrasing that we find in *Autobiographies* in Nietzsche's

> In intercourse with scholars and artists one readily makes mistakes of opposite kinds: in a remarkable scholar one not infrequently finds a mediocre man; and often in a mediocre artist, one finds a very remarkable man.[2]

Nietzsche's awareness in *Beyond Good and Evil* of the 'general war against everything rare, strange, and privileged', his picture of Genoa in *The Joyful Wisdom*, its buildings 'images of bold and aristocratic men', 'built and decorated for centuries, and not for the passing hour', are very Yeatsian, and so are his words on 'Work': 'How close work and the workers now stand even to the most leisurely of us! The royal courtesy in the words: "We are all workers" would have been a cynicism and an indecency even under Louis XIV.'

In our own time the poet has thrown in his lot with the university. This doubtless has its advantages for him and for the university, but he will soon learn, in the spirit of Nietzsche's aphorism, that those who 'work' there will become suspicious of him, that those who write about literature mostly regard its production as a rather frivolous pursuit. It is here that he will find allies in Nietzsche and in Yeats and, for all their differences, they belong together, as perhaps the two most outspoken opponents of the utilitarian conscience which has robbed our day of delight in that leisure 'created to be a soil for the most living'. 'Work', says Nietzsche, 'is winning over more and more the good conscience to its side: the desire for enjoyment already calls itself "need of recreation" and even begins to be ashamed of itself.'

Yeats found in Nietzsche, he said, 'a strong enchanter'. He chose him to represent Phase Twelve in *A Vision*, and though his own phase (he insisted) was seventeen, Yeats evidently felt their similarities. Both must strive to become one with their measure of aristocratic largesse, Nietzsche being 'driven from one self-conscious pose to another . . . full of hesitation'. Just as Yeats felt himself doomed by his time 'to imperfect achievement', so Nietzsche cannot but be

---

[2] *Beyond Good and Evil*, § 137.

'fragmentary'; however, there is the possibility for him, in the awakening of 'his antithetical being', of 'a noble extravagance, an overflowing fountain of personal life'. Ultimately it is chiefly as an enemy of abstraction that Yeats prizes Nietzsche and he associates him with Blake, bringing together the Blake who 'preferred to any man of intellect a happy thoughtless person', with Nietzsche 'at the moment he imagined the "Superman" as child' (*Auto.*, 474). It is precisely this 'unabstracted' quality he finds (in *Dramatis Personae*) translated by Lady Gregory into her Irish heroic tales, a quality acquired in that world 'where men and women are valued for their manhood and their charm, not for their opinions'. Wasn't it also Nietzsche who spoke of the need for '*a new nobility* opposed to the rabble and to all tyrannies, to write on new tables the word *noble*'—as indeed it would have to be rewritten for an aristocracy that would include himself, Yeats, Lady Gregory and Duke Frederick of Urbino *and* William Blake.

The ideal here, where aristocracy of spirit and the childlike are reconciled, is central to Yeats and it brings us back from Nietzsche to his finest formulation of it in 'A Prayer for my Daughter'. It is in this poem that 'radical innocence' depends upon the soul's driving out mere opinion; and courtesy, showing the way to this, becomes a kind of secular grace:

> In courtesy I'd have her chiefly learned;
> Hearts are not had as a gift but hearts are earned
> By those that are not entirely beautiful . . . (*C.P.*, 212)

In the last line Yeats's aristocracy takes on its fullest humanity: whatever simplifying, fragmenting violence his ideal may seem in danger of, is purged away in this conception where love is something to be earned by a courtesy that is moral endeavour and by a person who may be less than a hero. Within this conception Yeats has found a poetic style for domesticity, one that never descends to the banal and one that bestows on its human subject the kind of more-than-individual importance which Jonson gives to his figure of the lady in 'To Penshurst'. Here is a courtesy towards traditions that counterbalances the individual, that reaches out through style to involve the mind of the future, to bear in upon that mind the necessity of finding what forms it may to foster and prolong its graces.

We should not 'imitate' Yeats: some of the work of F. T. Prince—take 'To a Friend on His Marriage'—and of my own earlier poems—'Monuments', for example—show that to try for this is, in a sense, too easy. What we can do is to benefit from that tact and largesse of his, confronting in its spirit the pathological repetitiveness of 'the universe of the absurd', that laziest among recent recruits to literary dullness. A nobility that would be a fountain, such as Yeats thought he had glimpsed in parts of Nietzsche—'the abounding glittering jet' of 'Meditations in Time of Civil War', 'That out of life's own self-delight had sprung'—whether this is a recoverable dimension for our poetry remains to be seen. But there are possibilities other than the poet as anti-hero ready to sink height and breadth in a worrying over personal and domestic trifles. Yeats gives us the sense of liberating scale, scale generated by—what remains for the practitioner the central and necessary miracle—the ability to remake himself and his verse.

II

The Rising of the Moon: a Study of 'A Vision'

NORTHROP FRYE

★

I

LITERATURE is one of the products of the constructive or imaginative power in the mind, and is the verbal part of the process of transforming the non-human world into something with a human shape and meaning, the process that we call culture or civilisation. In literature, particularly in poetry, the non-human or natural world is symbolically associated with the human world. The two great principles of association are analogy and identity, which are reflected in the grammatical forms of the simile and metaphor respectively: 'A is like B', and 'A is B'. Identity is found in mythology, which is concerned with gods, that is, beings in human shape identified with various aspects of physical nature. Hence mythology is a congenial language for poets, and even the more conceptual language of theology has to deal with some doctrines, such as the identity of Christ with God and Man, which can be expressed grammatically only in the form of metaphor. Another religious language, typology, is founded on analogy, and appears in Swedenborg's conception of 'correspondence', which he applies to his interpretation of the Bible. Analogy and identity are prominent in the associative cosmology of the Ptolemaic universe, where the seven planets are associated with the seven metals, the four elements with the four humours, and so on. As the sense of the objective validity of these associations waned, they became increasingly confined to occultism, in its various branches. Occult constructs, or constructs that unite occult and mythological or typological concepts, such as we find in Boehme, Swedenborg, and later Blavatsky, have played an important part in the mythopoeic poetry of the last two centuries. It is unnecessary to labour the point that Yeats had absorbed an immense amount of associative apparatus, much of it traditional, from his Rosicrucian and Golden Dawn studies.

These associative constructs, considered apart from whatever assertions they may make about the structure of the external world, become a framework of associations of imagery, in other words, 'metaphors for poetry', which is what Yeats's instructors said they were bringing him. In this context we can understand Valéry's remark that cosmology is one of the oldest of the *literary* arts. Nobody would attempt the serious study of Dante's *Commedia* or *Paradise Lost* without studying their cosmologies, and the fact that no objective validity is now attached to these cosmologies does not affect their importance as structural principles of the poems they are in. Further, every major poet has his own structure of imagery, and we soon become familiar with the way in which certain images are repeated in different contexts through his work. If we push this familiarity into a systematic study, we find ourselves creating out of the poet's total work a single and symmetrical world of images: in short, a cosmology. Yeats himself provides a brilliant and pioneering example of such criticism in his early essay on 'The Philosophy of Shelley's Poetry'. The word 'philosophy' is misleading, as he is not looking for ideas that express meaning but for images that contain it: his reason for using the word is to emphasise the consistency of structure that he finds in Shelley's work.

A further step would lead us to the more schematic elements in poetic thought which are implicit in the whole process of association. Poetic thought is inherently schematic, though some poets, of course, are more obviously schematic than others. Blake is very obviously so: there are several diagrams in his engraved poems reminding us of similar diagrams in *A Vision*, and Crabb Robinson tells us of his enthusiasm for the diagrams that William Law provided for his translation of Boehme. The study of the cosmology of the *Commedia* or *Paradise Lost*, just mentioned, would, if our commentaries provided no diagrams, soon bring us to pencil and paper, and this is even more true of Dante's *Convivio*, which, if closer to more widely accepted speculations in Dante's day, is a work not different in kind from *A Vision*. Yeats, in company with Edwin J. Ellis, made an early study of Blake, laying great stress on the schematic elements in Blake's imagery, and the second volume of their edition of Blake, whatever Ellis may have contributed to it (not much, one gathers from Yeats's letters), represents a kind of trial run for *A Vision*. The influence of Dante is also very strong, though later, and 'Ego Dominus Tuus', one of the central poems of the *Vision* period, takes its title from the *Vita Nuova*.

Analogy and identity produce, not only the two commonest figures of poetic speech, but the two major patterns of poetic imagery. One of these is the cyclical pattern, based on the assimilation of the death and rebirth of life in the human world to the natural cycles of sun, moon, water and the seasons. The other we may 'call the dialectical rhythm, the movement towards a separation of happiness from misery, the hero from the villain, heaven from hell. The two halves of this separation correspond in imagery to the two phases of the cycle, the images of the desirable world being youth, spring, morning and the like, and of the undesirable world their opposites.

In the traditional Christian pattern of symbolism, as we have it in Dante, there are, at the poles of reality, two eternally separated and opposed worlds, heaven and hell, beatitude and damnation. Heaven is symbolised by the starry spheres, now all that is left of the order of nature as God originally planned it. In between is the present order of nature, which exists on two levels. One is the level of physical nature and fallen humanity, the ordinary world of experience, Italy in 1300, which pervades the poem though it is not a setting for any part of it. The other is the level of human nature as it was before the Fall, represented by the Garden of Eden, which Dante reaches by climbing the mountain of Purgatory. This mountain is a narrowing cone or gyre in shape, a winding stair (*escalina*), and as Dante proceeds up it, shedding a deadly sin at each stage, he recovers the freedom of will and the moral innocence that man had before his fall. When he reaches Eden he is told that it is among other things a place of seed, that all forms of life on earth, except human lives, proceed from and return to it.

Dante's order of nature is, then, a cyclical movement. Christian doctrine prevents Dante from ascribing this cyclical movement to human life, but purgatory and rebirth are associated even in him. Yeats saw in the doctrine of purgatory, which in Dante is a second life on the surface of this earth, an accommodating of Eastern and Platonic conceptions of reincarnation to Christianity. Dante's mountain of purgatory, again, is directly underneath the moon, where the vision of *Paradiso* begins, and so it suggests the conception of nature as a cycle under the moon, the mountain forming a gyre narrowing to a point. An opposite gyre, though this is not explicit in Dante, would begin to broaden again for all forms of life that are reborn at that point. For Yeats the 'pern mill' whose smoke made Ben Bulben look like a burning mountain was an early source of an associating of a mountain with fire and with the spinning of double gyres.

In Spenser's *Faerie Queene*, though there are brief glimpses of a heaven and a hell, the main concern is with the two intermediate worlds: the England of Spenser's own day, which, like Dante's Italy, is present only by allegory, and the world of 'Faerie', which is a world of moral realisation, like Dante's purgatory, where the good is separated from the bad. In this world of faerie we find the Gardens of Adonis, a 'Paradise' on a 'Mount' which is also a place of death and rebirth, not said to affect only non-human lives. It is not said either to be directly under the moon, but in the *Mutabilitie Cantos* the 'sublunary' principle of change and decay, Mutability herself, thrusts her way into the moon and demands to be recognised as the ruler of the world above as well. The debate of being and becoming that results confines Mutability to the lower world, and leaves the starry spheres in their place as symbols of heaven. The trial to hear her case is held on top of 'Arlo Hill', like Ben Bulben an Irish mountain.

In Blake the main bent of symbolism is increasingly dialectical, towards the final separation of human redemption from human misery that he depicts in so many pictures of the Last Judgement. His treatment of the cycle is more complicated. Coming as he does after Newton, Blake rejects the traditional association of the starry spheres with the unfallen world. For him the starry heavens are also a projection of man's fallen state, and the unfallen world has to be sought within. The child, taking the world for granted as a place made chiefly for his benefit, lives in a state of innocence recalling the traditional unfallen life in the Garden of Eden. Blake calls this state of innocence Beulah, and associates it with the moon. As the child grows into an adult he moves into the state of experience, and his childlike wish to see the world in a better shape is driven underground into the subconscious. Beulah thus becomes an explosive, volcanic world which breaks into experience periodically in revolution, and its presiding genius is the youthful rebel Orc, as the presiding genius of experience is Urizen, the old man in the sky.

In *The Marriage of Heaven and Hell* the principles of rebellion and of conservatism are associated with 'Devils' and 'Angels' respectively, the 'Devils' being called that because they are regarded with such horror by their opponents. The two principles represent 'Contraries', and without contraries, according to Blake, there is no progression. These contraries have a close relationship to Yeats's conceptions of antithetical and primary, presently to be considered. Human life, both individual and social, tends to run in a cycle from Orc's revolt to Urizen's conservatism and back. A similar cycle is traced in the poem called 'The Mental Traveller', a major and acknowledged influence on Yeats's

Vision. In this poem the entire cycle is divided into four main phases, but another poem of Blake's, 'My Spectre Around Me', which again deals with a cycle, assigns seven 'loves' to four phases, making twenty-eight in all.

In his *Descriptive Catalogue*, written as a commentary on some of his paintings, Blake discusses the General Prologue to the *Canterbury Tales*. Considering Chaucer's constant use of astrology, including a tantalising allusion to the twenty-eight phases of the moon in *The Franklin's Tale*, and assuming his interest in combinations of the seven planetary and the four humorous temperaments, one would expect his 'Well nine and twenty in a company' to consist of twenty-eight characters plus Chaucer himself. In actual count there are one or two more, but more important than the number is Blake's suggestion that 'The characters of Chaucer's Pilgrims are the characters which compose all ages and nations: as one age falls, another rises, different to mortal sight, but to immortals only the same; for we see the same characters repeated again and again'. This sounds very like a statement of Yeats's own theory of personal archetypes, of which more later. There are echoes of the *Descriptive Catalogue* in *A Vision* and elsewhere in Yeats: compare, for example, the discussion of beauty, ugliness and the Dancing Faun in the commentary on Phase Two (pp. 106–7)[1] with Blake's commentary on his picture 'The Ancient Britons'. In Blake's later prophecies human history from Adam to Milton is divided into twenty-eight periods or 'Churches', and the twenty-eight cathedral cities of England, or 'Albion', the hero of *Jerusalem*, play a prominent role in that poem. In Blake's version of the apocalypse, Albion becomes absorbed into the body of Jesus, who is portrayed in the Book of Revelation as surrounded in heaven by twenty-eight beings, the twenty-four 'elders' and the four 'Zoas'.

In Classical literature there are two visions of recurrence and rebirth that particularly impressed Yeats. One is the myth of Er (or 'the man of Ur', as Yeats insists on calling him) in Plato's *Republic*; the other is the journey of Aeneas to the underworld, where it is foretold that 'Another Troy shall rise and set', in Yeats's echo of Virgil's words. Virgil's tendency to see the moon as the symbol of cyclical human life is recorded in his phrase *per amica silentia lunae* (*Aeneid* ii, 255), employed by Yeats as a title. The cave of the nymphs in Homer's *Odyssey*, which

---

[1] As I am dealing only with *A Vision* in its totality, having abandoned the project of tracing its development from its sketchy first edition, I am using the latest (1961) edition of it, subtitled 'A Reissue With the Author's Final Revisions', and my page references are to that edition.

has a southern gate for gods and a northern one for mortals, is the subject of an allegorical commentary by Porphyry, *De Antro Nympharum*, a source of 'Among School Children', and the same symbolism had previously found its way into Blake's *Book of Thel*. The two gates are reflected in the opposed Phases 15 and 1 of Yeats's lunar cycle, the former being a beauty too great for human life and the latter the point of mortality. Many other suggestions came to Yeats from his reading which we have no space to deal with. His debt to the Catholic poets of the later nineteenth century has perhaps not been sufficiently studied: he quotes (p. 250) from one very remarkable prototype of his Easter symbolism, an ode by Francis Thompson.

The well-known introduction to *A Vision* explains how it was dictated to Yeats by invisible spiritual instructors who worked through his wife's gift for automatic writing. Not having any explanation of my own to offer of this account, I propose to accept his at its face value. But it seems obvious that *A Vision* should be approached as a key to the structure of symbolism and imagery in Yeats's own poetry, as what Yeats calls in another connection 'the emergence of the philosophy of my own poetry, the unconscious becoming conscious'. If we did not have *A Vision*, a critic could still do with Yeats what Yeats did with Shelley: extract a poetic cosmology or created world of images from his work. Such a cosmology would have, or at least begin with, the same general outline as *A Vision*. It would lack its detail, but the detail is seldom rewarding either for the light it throws on Yeats or in its own right as part of 'a rule of thumb that somehow explained the world', in Yeats's phrase. That is, no critic could discover from Yeats's poetry that Queen Victoria belongs to Phase 24 of a lunar historical cycle, but then this does not tell us anything of much value about either Yeats or Queen Victoria. On the other hand, the cosmology that one could extract from Yeats's poetry would be more complete than *A Vision*, for the poet in Yeats knew much more about poetic symbolism than his instructors did.

To say this is to define an attitude to his instructors, so far as they may be thought of as instructing us. The great advantage of *A Vision* was that it increased Yeats's awareness of and power to control his own creative process, and so did much to provide the self-renewing vitality, the series of bursts of energy from within, like a jet engine, which is so extraordinary a feature of Yeats's development. It also emphasised certain forward intellectual developments for him, such as the sense of the poetic relevance of history and philosophy, and thus helped to make his later poetry more concrete and precise. One obvious modern parallel to *A Vision* is Poe's *Eureka*, but *Eureka* is neurotic in a way that *A Vision* is not: it hints at vast significance but expresses itself with very little precision, whereas *A Vision* at least says what it has to say. The schematic elaboration of *A Vision* was not very congenial to Yeats's temperament, and would probably never have been undertaken had it not come to him in this involuntary form: one thinks of the condescension with which, in the poem 'The Dawn', he looks down upon

> the withered men that saw
> From their pedantic Babylon
> The careless planets in their courses,
> The stars fade out where the moon comes,
> And took their tablets and did sums. (*C.P.*, 164)

But there were also disadvantages in being 'overwhelmed by miracle'. The traditions about the kind of spirits that Yeats evoked seem to suggest that they are, when separated from the mind of the person who controls them, mischievous, irresponsible, even malignant. This is doubtless why Prospero in *The Tempest* nagged and bullied his spirits unmercifully. Yeats distinguishes such spirits as 'Frustrators', but whether or not the warning 'Remember we will deceive you if we can' came from them, he subjected himself passively to his instructors, in a way that made it impossible for him to detect frustration or irrelevance until pages of it had been written. *A Vision*, as a result, is a fragmentary and often misleading guide to the structure of imagery in Yeats. It is to the student of Yeats what *De Doctrina Christiana* is to the student of Milton: an infernal nuisance that he can't pretend doesn't exist.

The analogy between human and natural worlds founded on the cycle is a central principle of symbolism, and we have seen that it is traditional to make the moon the focus of it. Structures of the same cyclical and lunar shape may be found in *Finnegans Wake*, with its twenty-eight 'Maggies', in Robert Graves's white goddess mythology, in Pound's *Pisan Cantos*. In Western cyclical symbolism the human emphasis falls on the social and historical rather than the individual. Reincarnation was never accepted in Christianity nor widely held in the West, and so it has been the cycle of nations and empires that for Western poetry is assimilated to the rotation of life and death and rebirth. Yeats's interest in reincarnation gives his cyclical symbolism an individual emphasis as well, but his instructors knew far less about this than they did about the more solidly established historical cycle. One fragment of this part of the construct survives in a letter to Ethel Mannin, and there Yeats says that he only half understands it himself. There remains the dialectical structure of symbolism, the separation of reality into an apocalyptic and a demonic world where all images in each world are identified by metaphor. This symbolism is quite clear in Yeats's poetry, but *A Vision* is not an adequate guide to it. We proceed to deal with the three main aspects of Yeats's symbolism, the historical cycle, the individual cycle, and the apocalyptic imagery, using *A Vision*, for the reasons just given, in a progressively more fragmentary way.

II

There are two great rhythmical movements in all living beings: a movement towards unity and a movement towards individuality. These are opposed and contrasting movements, and are symbolised in Yeats by a double gyre, a movement in one direction which, as it grows more pervasive, develops the counteracting movement within itself, so that the apex of the next gyre appears in the middle of the base of the preceding one and moves back through it. The simplest way to represent the entire double-gyre rotation is by a circle. Because of its traditional association with the moon, this circle has twenty-eight phases, and the twenty-eight-phase cycle exists, Yeats says, in every completed movement, whether it takes a moment or thousands of years to complete itself. But, of course, it is in the larger rhythms of history that the detail is easiest to see. Yeats sees history as forming a series of cycles, each lasting about two thousand years, with each cycle going through twenty-eight parallel phases. The conception is similar in many ways to that of Spengler's *Decline of the West*, and Yeats often remarks on the similarity of his views to Spengler's.

In Spengler, who is most rewarding when he is read as a Romantic and symbolic poet, each historical cycle or 'culture' exhibits the rhythms of growth, maturation and decline characteristic of an organism, though Spengler also uses the metaphor of the four seasons. There were, for instance, a Classical and a Western cycle, each having a 'spring' of feudal economy and heroic aristocracy, a Renaissance 'summer' of city-states, an 'autumn' in Periclean Athens and the eighteenth century, when the cultural possibilities of the cycle were exhausted, and a 'winter', ushered in by Alexander and Napoleon respectively, when a 'culture' changes to a technological 'civilisation' of huge cities, dictatorships and annihilation wars. In between comes a Near Eastern or 'Magian' culture, with its spring at the birth of Christ and its later stages in the period of Mohammedanism, the religion of the crescent moon. In each cycle the period of highest development is the period of greatest individuality in both art and political life, and both the early and the late stages are marked by a strong sense of communal or mass-consciousness.

In Yeats this communal consciousness is part of the drive toward unity. It is the primitive mentality in which all historical cycles begin, and the decadent mentality in which they end, hence it is the 'primary' rhythm of existence. Over against it is an 'antithetical' development of individuality, which reaches its greatest height in the hero. In primitive society the communal consciousness is so strong that there hardly seems to be any real individuality, as we know it, at all. Those who show signs of individual consciousness often have simply a different kind of unity, with animals or with the fairies and other spirits of the invisible world, like the inspired fools who haunt romantic literature (Phase 2). The types from Phase 2 to about Phase 6 are intellectually simple and self-contained: Phase 6 is the phase of Walt Whitman, who never quite distinguished individual from communal well-being. Individuality begins in the unhappy and tormented souls who are aware of a double pull within them around Phase 8. As we cross the quadrant of Phase 8 we begin to move into the antithetical area, beginning with intense and withdrawn figures like Parnell (Phase 10) or Nietzsche (Phase 12). Individuality then advances to heroic proportions, and we have 'sensualists' so complete that they represent a kind of antithesis to sanctity (Phase 13), artists of tempestuous passion, women of fully ripened physical beauty, and heroes of arrogant pride like the heroes of Shakespeare's tragedies.

At the point of highest development represented by Phase 15 the counter-movement back to communal consciousness begins. Artists become less embodiments of passion and more intellectualised (Phase 21), or technicians (Phase 23); heroes come to think of themselves as servants of impersonal force, like Napoleon (Phase 20), or the money-obsessed characters in Balzac; women come to be guardians of a generally accepted morality like Queen Victoria (Phase 24). The 'personality', which is the fully developed individuality, becomes the 'character', a subjective conception implying that something objective to it is greater. Yeats speaks of the antithetical types as subjective, too, but their subjectivity creates its own world, whereas primary subjectivity first separates itself from the objective world, then is increasingly drawn to it as a unity destined to absorb all subjects. These two aspects of subjectivity are symbolised in Yeats by two expressions of the eye: the stare, which sees nothing but expresses an inner consciousness, and the glance, the subject looking *at* a reality set over against it. At later primary stages personality becomes more fragmented, this fragmentation being represented by the physical deformity of the hunchback (Phase 26), and the mental deformity of the fool (Phase 28). What Spengler calls the 'second religiousness' comes into society in the forms of spiritualism, theosophy, and various forms of revived occultism, seeking the same kind of kinship with the invisible world, at the other end of the social cycle, that primitive societies show in their myths and folk-tales and so-called superstitions. Yeats often recurs to the similarity between the primitive and the sophisticated conceptions of unseen beings, the legendary rumour in remote cottages and the seances in suburban parlours. The entire cycle describes a progression through the four elements of earth, water, air and fire, each quadrant having a particular relationship to each element.

The conception on which the whole of *A Vision* turns is the contrast of antithetical and primary natures, which is part of a dichotomy that runs through Yeats's writing and thinking. In an early letter he says: 'I have always considered myself a voice of what I believe to be a greater renaissance—the revolt of the soul against the intellect—now beginning in the world', and this involves a preference of the swordsman to the saint, of the aristocratic to the democratic virtues, of the reality of beauty to the reality of truth, of (to use categories from Eliot's 'Burnt Norton') the way of plenitude to the way of vacancy. The contrast is so far-reaching that it may be simplest to set all its aspects out at once in a table, though many of them will not be intelligible until farther on in this essay.

ANTITHETICAL	PRIMARY
individuality	unity
Leda and Swan	Virgin and Dove
Oedipus	Christ
son kills father	son appeases father
incest with mother	redemption of mother and bride
drive toward nature	drive toward God
tragic	comic
master-morality	servant-morality
aristocratic	democratic
discord	concord
quality	quantity

freedom	necessity
fiction	truth
evil	good
art	science
ecstasy	wisdom
kindred	mechanism
particularity	abstraction
lunar	solar
natural	reasonable
war	peace
personality	character
Michael Robartes	Owen Aherne
Oisin	St. Patrick
(Eros)	(Agape)
(Chinese Yang)	(Chinese Yin)
(Nietzsche's Apollo)	(Nietzsche's Dionysus)
(Blake's Orc, 'Devils', Rintrah, 'Science of Wrath')	(Blake's Urizen, 'Angels', Pala-mabron, 'Science of Pity')

Many of these categories come from page 52 of *A Vision*, that of quality and quantity from page 130. The Apollonian and Dionysiac categories seem curiously placed, but Yeats thinks of Apollo as a creative force and of Dionysus as a transcendent one.

The drive to individuality is a drive toward nature, Yeats says, and has for its goal a complete physical self-fulfilment or 'Unity of Being', which may be attained in the phases close to Phase 15, the phase of the full moon. Phase 15 itself realises this so completely that it cannot be achieved in human life at all. We thus arrive at the difficult conception of a creature which is superhuman because it is completely natural. We are not told much about these Phase 15 beings, beyond a mysterious passage in 'The Phases of the Moon', but, of course, a perfect human harmony could also be symbolised by perfect sexual intercourse, and we are told in that delightful poem 'Solomon and the Witch' that a union of this kind would restore man to the unfallen world. Yeats strongly hints that Christ was a superhuman incarnation, a unique entry of Phase 15 into human life, though an explicit statement on this point would doubtless have annoyed his instructors. He often refers, for instance, to an alleged belief that Christ was the only man exactly six feet high. Why so arbitrary a measure as the foot should have been in the mind of the Trinity from all eternity is not clear, but the meaning is that Christ had the perfect 'Unity of Being' which, Yeats tells us, Dante compares to a perfectly proportioned human body.

The opposite drive toward an objective unity is a drive toward 'God', and has as its goal an absorption in God (Phase 1) which is similarly a superhuman phase of pure 'plasticity'. Hence the real direction of the attempt in the primary phases to subordinate oneself to objective powers is revealed in the religious leader (Phase 25) and most clearly of all in the saint (Phase 27). As far as this twenty-eight-phase cycle of being is concerned, 'God' for Yeats appears to be a character like the button-moulder in *Peer Gynt*, pounding everything to dust with the pestle of the moon, a cosmic spider or vampire who swallows the Many in the One. In short, God occupies the place of Death, which makes Yeats's remark that he tends to write coldly of God something of an understatement.

We have spoken so far of a general social cycle from primitivism to decadence, but there are two more specific ones in Yeats, which correspond to the Classical and Western cycles in Spengler. Draw a circle on a page and mark its four cardinal points 1, 8, 15 and 22. These phases on Yeats's historical calendar (or at least the most important of several he uses) are a thousand years apart. Phase 1 is 2000 B.C.; Phase 8 is 1000 B.C.; Phase 15 is the time of Christ; Phase 22 is A.D. 1000; Phase 1 is therefore our own time as well as 2000 B.C., and Phase 8 is also a thousand years from now. Classical civilisation extends from Phase 8 to 22, 1000 B.C. to A.D. 1000, and Christian civilisation, which is our own, from A.D. 1000 to 3000, Phases 22 to 8. We are half-way through the latter now, at the same point Classical civilisation reached in the time of Christ. Phases 8 and 22 are represented by Troy and Byzantium, one an Asiatic city destroyed by Europeans and the other a European city captured by Asiatics, yet so close together that Byzantium, when it became a centre of Roman power, was thought of as a new Troy. Each civilisation is the opposite or complement of its predecessor. Classical civilisation was essentially antithetical, tragic, heroic and strongly individualised; Christian civilisation is therefore essentially primary, democratic, altruistic and based on a subject-object attitude to reality. Byzantium was the main source of early Irish culture, and its place in Yeats's thought gives a special significance to his allusions to people roughly contemporary with its golden age, such as Charlemagne and Harun Al-Rashid.

Half-way through, a civilisation generates the beginning of its counteracting movement, hence Christ, the presiding genius of the civilisation that began a millennium later, appears in the middle of the Classical cycle. 'The Incarnation', says Yeats, 'invoked modern science

and modern efficiency, and individualised emotion.' Thus a religious
movement cuts the cycle of civilisations at right-angles, and Christianity as a religion extends from the time of Christ to about our own
day. It follows that a similar Messianic figure announcing Classical
civilisation must have appeared around 2000 B.C., and that another,
announcing a second antithetical civilisation of the future, is to appear
somewhere around our own time. Yeats speaks of an antithetical influx
setting in 'a considerable time before' (p. 208) the close of its predecessor,
perhaps to get it more exactly into his own time. In 2000 B.C., in the
middle of a pre-Classical culture associated vaguely by Yeats with
'Babylonian starlight', the annunciation of the Greek culture pattern
was made, in what way we do not know, but surviving in two myths.
One is the myth of Leda and the swan, the divine bird impregnating
the human woman, the fulfilment of their union being, eventually, the
fall of Troy, which began Greek history, properly speaking. The other
is the myth of Oedipus, whose parricide and mother-incest set the
tragic and heroic tone of an antithetical culture. The complementary
myths appear with the birth of Christ, the myth of the dove and the
Virgin and the myth of the son appeasing his father's wrath and redeem-
ing his mother and bride. Our own day is the period of the annunciation of a new Oedipus and Leda mythology, heralding the tragic and
warlike age of the future and ushering in a religion contrasting with
Christianity. The Messiah of our day is an Antichrist, that is, an antithetical Christ, the terrible reborn Babe of Blake's 'Mental Traveller'.
As Christ's mother was a virgin, so the new Messiah's mother, in 'The
Adoration of the Magi', is a harlot and a devotee of the Black Mass,
resembling the Virgin only in being rejected by the society of her time.
In *The Herne's Egg* the new Messiah is to be born in Ireland, the Judea of
the West, the offspring of a heron and his fanatical priestess. What this
Messiah has to announce, of course, is the future age when 'another
Troy shall rise and set'.

In Spengler each culture has a 'prime symbol' expressing its inner
essence, which is a Doric column for the Classical, a cavern for the
Magian, a garden for the Chinese, and so on. For some reason he gives
no primary symbol for Western culture, saying only that it is charac-
terised by a drive into the infinite. Yeats, learning from Pound that
Frobenius found two major symbols in Africa, a cavern and an altar
with sixteen roads leading from it, suggests that Spengler took his
Magian cavern from Frobenius and should have provided us with the
altar for the Western symbol. In Yeats the middle 'Magian' cycle is

replaced by the conception of a religious cycle cutting the historical one midway, but Yeats resembles Spengler in associating Christ, who was born in a manger and rose from a tomb, with the cavern. Hence 'At or near the central point of our civilisation must come *antithetical* revelation, the turbulent child of the Altar'. Yeats, however, does not use the altar as a symbol for our own time in his poetry, though the cavern appears as an image of the passage from death to rebirth (Phase 1, more or less) in 'The Hour Before Dawn'. The chief images he does use are those of birds and animals. The bird is often the swan, for obvious reasons, but with a whole parliament of fowls in addition. If we take three representative poems on this theme, 'The Second Coming', 'Demon and Beast', and 'On a Picture of a Black Centaur by Edmund Dulac', we find a gyring falcon in the first, a gyring gull and a green-headed duck in the second, and 'horrible green birds' in the third, accompanying the age in which the 'demon' (not daimon, which is a quite different conception) of late phases gives place to the 'beast' of early ones, the 'rough beast' of 'The Second Coming' who modulates into the centaurs of the Dulac poem.

Everybody belongs fundamentally to one of the twenty-six human phases or types, but, of course, a man of any phase can be born at any time in history. If a social cycle has reached, say, Phase 22 (more or less the Victorian period in European culture), those who belong to phases near 22 will be typical of their time, and those of early phases (George Borrow and Carlyle in Phase 7, for example) have a more difficult adjustment to make. But a man may also be typical or atypical of his own phase, and Yeats begins many of his descriptions, very confusingly, by dealing with the 'out of phase' variant of the type. Yeats further tells us that in practice he cannot point to historical examples of several of the phases, partly because many of the more primary ones do not produce types who make any impression on history.

For one reason or another, what Yeats calls in 'The Gift of Harun Al-Rashid'

> Those terrible implacable straight lines
> Drawn through the wandering vegetative dream (*C.P.*, 517)

turn out in practice to be nearly as accommodating as Baconian ciphers in Shakespeare. For instance, Yeats tells us that each millennium of the two-thousand-year cycle can be considered as a complete twenty-eight-phase wheel in itself, so that we are also near the Phase 1 end of the first millennium of our Christian civilisation, which adds to its chaos. This millennium reached its antithetical height of Phase 15 at the Quattrocento, when 'men attained to personality in great numbers', and when Europe was infused by the spirit of the recently fallen Byzantium. This curtailed millennial version of the rhythm of Western culture, which incidentally is much closer to Spengler, lies behind most of Yeats's references to Michelangelo and to one of his seminal books, Castiglione's *Courtier* (see, for example, 'The People'). In the Renaissance there was also a kind of minor annunciation of the opposite kind of civilisation, and so Yeats has reasons (he tells us in a passage in *On the Boiler* inexplicably omitted from the recent volume *Explorations*) both to 'adore' and to 'detest' the Renaissance.

Again, there are larger rhythms in history, obtained by adding a solar and zodiacal cycle to the lunar one. One of these is the 'Great Year', traditionally formed by the precession of the equinoxes, and which lasts for twenty-six thousand years, a 'year' of twelve 'months' of two thousand odd years each. One of these Great Years ended and began with Christ, who rose from the dead at the 'full moon in March' which marks that point. Caesar was assassinated at another full moon in March a few decades earlier. Yeats points out how contemporaries of Christ, such as Virgil in the Fourth Eclogue and Horace in the *Carmen Saeculare*, felt a peculiar cyclical significance about that time which Christianity itself, anxious as it was to get away from cyclical theories, ignored. The birth of Christ took place at a (primary) conjunction of Mars and Venus, and our new Messiah will be born at the opposite conjunction of Jupiter and Saturn, when the 'mummy wheat' of the buried Classical civilisation will start to sprout.

The emotional focus of *A Vision* is also that of Yeats's life, the sense that his own time is a time of a trembling of the veil of the temple, eventually defined as a myth of a new religious dispensation announcing a new God to replace Christ and accompanied by the traditional signs of the end of the world. Yeats traces his sense of an imminent Armageddon back to such early poems as 'The Hosting of the Sidhe' and 'The Valley of the Black Pig'. A note to the former poem tells us that the sidhe or fairy folk of Ireland dance in gyres or whirlwinds which are called the dance of the daughters of Herodias: the last section of 'Nineteen Hundred and Nineteen' applies this imagery to Yeats's own time. Although our own time is Phase 15 of the Christian era, it can be read in different ways on Yeats's various clocks, and Yeats tends to think of it primarily as a passing through Phase 1, when a great age has finally reached the crescent of the 'fool' and hears the irrational cry ('the scream of Juno's peacock') of a new birth.

Yeats's treatment of the theme of contemporary annunciation exhibits a complete emotional range, from the most raucous nonsense to the most serene wisdom. We may divide his personal reactions to it into a cycle of six phases. First comes the phase of the deplorable if harmless rabble-rouser of On the Boiler, shouting for a 'just war', hailing Fascism as the force that will restore all the traditional heroic dignities to society, and prophesying a new 'science' compounded of spiritualism and selective breeding. Some of Yeats's instructors appear to have been incapable of distinguishing a lunar vision from a lunatic one, and this phase in Yeats seems to be part of the backwash from revising A Vision around 1937. In an early letter Yeats says: 'Every influence has a shadow, as it were, an unbalanced—the unbalanced is the Kabalistic definition of evil—duplicate of itself.' Fortunately this phase is not allowed to spoil much of his poetry, though it is creeping around the fringes of 'Under Ben Bulben'.

The second phase is that of the traditionalist who stresses the importance of convention and manners, 'where all's accustomed, ceremonious', and sees the preservation of this as preliminary to developing a new aristocracy. Yeats's cabinet of great Irishmen, Swift, Burke, Berkeley and others, are called upon to endorse this attitude, which is also heard in a simpler form in the contented reveries emanating from Coole Park and Stockholm on the values of hereditary privilege. The third phase is that of the neo-pagan, the poet who celebrates a rebirth of physical energy and sexual desire, who insists on the sacredness of bodily functions, who helps Crazy Jane to refute the Bishop on the primacy of the life of the soul, and who asks the unanswerable question:

> If soul may look and body touch,
> Which is the more blest? (C.P., 344)

The fourth phase is that of the teacher, the author of the Samhain essays who stands out against a 'primary' mob, assuming the role, in his own literary context, of

> A great man in his pride
> Confronting murderous men. (C.P., 264)

This is the critic who patiently points out to his Irish audience that no true patriotism can be built on the stock response and no true religion on the consecration of it; that the morality of art must always be liberal, and that the sectarian instinct, 'a pretended hatred of vice and a real hatred of intellect', is always part of the mob, whether it expresses itself in politics, religion or art. The fifth phase is the prophet, the troubled visionary of 'The Second Coming' and elsewhere, who sees and records but does not try to rationalise the horror and violence of his own time, who can understand the ferocity of 'The weasel's twist, the weasel's tooth' without confusing it with heroism. Finally, there is the phase of the sage, the poet of 'Lapis Lazuli' who can speak of the 'gaiety that leaps up before danger or difficulty', and who under-stands that even horror and violence can inspire a kind of exuberance. We notice that all these phases which are directly connected with literature are very precious attributes of Yeats, but that for the others the best we can do is to apply to Yeats what Yeats himself says of Shelley: 'Great as Shelley is, those theories about the coming changes of the world, which he has built up with so much elaborate passion, hurry him from life continually.'

Or, as Yeats also says, 'All art is the disengaging of a soul from place and history'. It has doubtless occurred to more than one reader of *A Vision* that Yeats might more easily have seen his cycle, not as the archetypal forms of human life, but of human imagination: in other words as a perfect circle of literary or mythical types, which is how Blake saw the pilgrims of Chaucer. Many of Yeats's examples are writers who, like Whitman at Phase 6, have made their lives conform to literary patterns, or who, like Shakespeare at Phase 20, are described by the kind of poetry they produced and not personally. The primitives of phases 2 to 7 are much easier to understand as archetypes of pastoral or Romantic conventions in literature; Dostoievsky's Idiot is the only example given of Phase 8; and Nietzsche's Zarathustra fits better into the 'Forerunner' position of Phase 12 than Nietzsche himself. Phase 15 would then become intelligible as the phase of the poet's ideal or male Muse: the Eros of Dante and Chaucer, the 'Ille' of 'Ego Dominus Tuus'; the beautiful youth of Shakespeare's sonnets, and the like. The high antithetical phases would be much more clearly represented by characters in Shakespeare or Irish legend, and the high primary ones by characters in Balzac and Browning, than they are by Galsworthy or Lamarck or 'a certain actress'.

Such a rearrangement would bring out the real relation of the *Vision* cycle of types to Yeats's own characters. The fool and the blind man who remain on the stage at the end of *On Baile's Strand* symbolise the disappearance of the Cuchulain cycle (which is symbolically the

Christian cycle, too, as Cuchulain was contemporary with Christ), the blind man representing the dark moonless night of Phase 1. The happy natural fool of *The Hour-Glass* is also a fool of Phase 28, with a Creative Mind from the 'Player on Pan's Pipes' of Phase 2. In *Resurrection* a blind man and a lame man, the two together making up the physical deformity of the 'hunchback', appear beside a saint, and in *The Player Queen* the opposition of Decima and the Queen she supplants is a burlesque illustration of the opposition of Phases 13 and 27, antithetical and primary perfection. The Queen in any case is a much better example of what Yeats appears to mean by sanctity than the historical examples he gives, which are Socrates and Pascal.

III

In the cycle of 'The Mental Traveller' Blake symbolises the subjective and objective aspects of life as male and female. All human beings including women are symbolically male, part of the reborn 'Boy', and nature, or the physical environment that is temporarily transformed into human shape by a culture, is what is symbolically female. Male and female cycles rotate in opposite directions, one growing older as the other grows younger. *A Vision* refers briefly to this symbolism (pp. 213 and 262), but *A Vision* says little about the objective aspect of civilisation. The conception of the individual is much more complicated. Here, as in Blake, there are subjective and objective factors, but there are two of each, making four 'Faculties' in all. An individual may be thought of as acting man (Will) or as seeing, knowing or thinking man (Creative Mind). In so far as he thinks or knows or sees, man operates on a known or seen world, a set of *données* or given facts and truths and events that make up what Yeats calls the Body of Fate. In so far as he acts, he acts in the light of a certain vision of action, which Yeats calls the Mask, and which includes both what he wants to make of himself and what he wants to make of the world around him. In 'antithetical' phases action is motivated by an 'image' springing from the self which complements the Will: in 'primary' phases, where man is more apt to say, with Hic in 'Ego Dominus Tuus', 'I would find myself and not an image', it is motivated by a desire to act on the world as a separated or impersonal thing, and eventually by a desire to be absorbed in that world. Each man is defined by the phase of his Will, and his Mask comes from the phase directly opposite, fourteen phases away. The Body of Fate is similarly opposite the Creative Mind, and Will and Creative Mind are related by the fact that, like male and female principles in Blake, they rotate in opposite directions. The details are too complicated to go into here, but a man of Phase 23 is actually made up of a Will of Phase 23, a Mask of Phase 9, a Creative Mind of Phase 7, and a Body of Fate of Phase 21.

In the Platonic tradition the relation of Creative Mind and Will is differently conceived. There is a superior intelligible world and an inferior physical world. In the latter the body perceives and acts on the image; in the former the soul perceives the form or idea, not as an object, but as something ultimately identical with itself. The soul and the world of forms are imprisoned in the physical world and struggle to break out of it. For Yeats, too, there is another way of looking at the four Faculties we have just dealt with. If we think of man as actor and creator, we see his life as an interplay of action and thought; if we think of him as a creature, we see his life as a physical contact with objects out of which a higher kind of identity is trying to emerge. In this perspective the four 'Faculties' become four 'Principles'. Will and Mask now become two lower Principles, Husk and Passionate Body, the physical subject and the physical object. Creative Mind and Body of Fate become Spirit and Celestial Body, the soul and the world of forms. This introduces a dialectical element into the cycle, a movement out of it into a world of changeless being.

From the beginning Yeats's poetic world comprised a state of experience and a state of innocence, the latter being associated with the Irish fairy world, a 'land of heart's desire' where there was an eternal youth of dancing and revelry. In *The Celtic Twilight* this world is once described as the Paradise still buried under the fallen world, but its associations are usually more specific. Yeats quotes legends indicating that the seasons of this world are the reverse of ours, like the southern hemisphere, and, in the *Autobiographies*, a remark of Madame Blavatsky that we live in a dumbbell-shaped cosmos, with an antipodal world at our North Pole. This conception is most readily visualised as an hour-glass, the emblem of time and the basis of Yeats's 'double gyre' diagrams, and in the play that is explicitly called *The Hour-Glass* we are told that 'There are two living countries, the one visible and the other invisible; and when it is winter with us it is summer in that country'. The fairy world has occasionally, according to legend and folk tale, caught up human beings, who found, when they returned to their own world, that time moves much faster here than there, and that a few days in fairyland had been many years of human life. As Yeats began to try to fit together what he knew of Irish legend with what he read in

Swedenborg or learned at seances, he also began to think of his fairy world as complementary to our own in time as well as climate, and as moving from age to youth. He often refers to Swedenborg as saying that the angels move towards their youth in time, as we move towards age.

Yeats's doctrine of reincarnation eventually annexed this world and transformed it into the world that we enter at death and leave again at birth, which is also a rebirth. It lost most of its cheerfulness in this process and acquired many of the characteristics of a penal régime. Book III of *A Vision*, called 'The Soul in Judgement', is supposed to tell us what his instructors knew about the antipodal world, but Yeats speaks of this section with some disappointment as more fragmentary than he hoped it would be. It uses a good deal of material from the earlier essay 'Swedenborg, Mediums, and the Desolate Places'. The discarnate soul is pulled in the ideal direction of Spirit and Celestial Body, and away from Husk and Passionate Body, by a series of spiritual or imaginative repetitions of the major emotional crises of its earthly life, which tend eventually to exhaust them, as the confessional techniques of psychology are supposed to do with neuroses. Yeats calls this the 'dreaming back', the most important of several stages of the return to rebirth. A violent crime may be re-enacted for centuries in the same spot, a fact which accounts for many types of ghost story; brutal masters and submissive slaves may exchange roles in a tenebrous saturnalia. Yeats suggests that our dreams, though they use our own experiences and desires as material, are actually part of the psychic life of the dead moving backwards to rebirth through us. The more fully a life has been lived, the less expiation is needed and the more successful the next life. Another life is, in fact, part of the whole 'dreaming back' operation, so that every life is a movement from birth to death and simultaneously part of a purgatorial movement from death to rebirth. When a Spirit is completely purified and ready for what in Christianity would be heaven, it may seek rebirth as an act of deliberate choice, like the Bodhisattva in Buddhism.

In the Eastern religions the cycle of life, death and rebirth is regarded as an enslavement, from which all genuine spiritual effort tries to liberate itself by reducing the physical world to unreality. The attitude of the Christian saint, even without a belief in reincarnation, is similar. Such a course is, according to some moods of Yeats, opposed to that of the poet and artist, whose function it is to show the reality incarnate in the appearance of the physical world and in the physical emotional life of man. The poet accepts the plenitude of the phenomenal world, and in the cycle of Faculties the most strongly 'antithetical' types, heroes and beautiful women who are driven by the passions of a titanic ego, are the poet's natural subjects. Long before *A Vision* Yeats had written: 'If it be true that God is a circle whose centre is everywhere, the saint goes to the centre, the poet and artist to the ring where everything comes round again.' Hence his emotional preference of the 'antithetical' to the 'primary', of the way of the poet to the way of the saint, leads to a preference for cyclical and rebirth symbolism in contrast to the kind of symbolism that separates reality into an apocalyptic and a demonic world.

The conflict of the abstract vision of the saint and the concrete vision of the poet, one seeking deliverance from the wheel of life and the other ready to accept the return of it, is the theme of many of Yeats's best-known poems. The setting of such poems is some modification of the top of Dante's mountain of purgatory, a winding stair in a tower leading upwards to a point at which one may contemplate both an eternal world above and a cyclical world below. In 'A Dialogue of Self and Soul' the Soul summons to an upward climb into the dark; the Self, preoccupied with the dying-god symbol of the Japanese ceremonial sword wrapped in embroidered silk with flowers of 'heart's purple', looks downward into rebirth and maintains 'I am content to live it all again'. In 'Vacillation', where there is a similar dialogue between Soul and Heart, the opening image is the tree of Attis which stands between eternity and rebirth, and the final contrast is between the saint whose body remains uncorrupted and the poet who deliberately seeks the cycle of corruption in generation symbolised by Samson's riddle of the lion and the honeycomb. In 'Among School Children' there is a similar antithesis between the nun and the mother, the former symbolising the direct ascent to eternity and the latter the cycle of generation. Here the tree, appearing at the end instead of at the beginning, seems a resolving or reconciling image rather than one of 'vacillation', but the contrast remains in the poem's argument.

However much imaginative sympathy we may have with these poems as poems, they indicate a deficiency in *A Vision* as an expression of some of Yeats's more profound insights. Yeats speaks of Emerson and Whitman as 'writers who have begun to seem superficial precisely because they lack the Vision of Evil', but his own lack of a sense of evil borders on the frivolous. Visions of horror and violence certainly haunt his poetry, but in *A Vision* and elsewhere in his later essays, even in much of the poetry itself, they are all rationalised and explained away as part of the necessary blood-bath accompanying the birth of his new and repulsive Messiah. The absence of any sense of a demonic world, a world of evil and tyranny and meanness and torment, such as human desire utterly repudiates and bends every effort to get away from, is connected with, and is perhaps the cause of, the absence in *A Vision* of the kind of dialectical imagery that appears in, say, 'The Two Trees', which in Blake would be the tree of life and the tree of mystery. Occasionally in earlier prose writings we get glimpses of a whole dimension of symbolism that seems to have got strangled in *A Vision*. Yeats says in an early essay: 'To lunar influence belong all thoughts and emotions that were created by the community, by the common people, by nobody knows who, and to the sun all that came from the high disciplined or individual kingly mind.' This imagery is repeated in 'A Dialogue of Self and Soul', but in *A Vision* the sun is 'primary', and has been absorbed into the lunar cycle: the solar and zodiacal symbolism in *A Vision*, already glanced at, only extends the lunar cycle, and adds nothing new in kind.

What we miss in *A Vision*, and in Yeats's speculative prose generally, is the kind of construct that would correspond to such a poem as 'Sailing to Byzantium'. This poem presents an eternal world which contains all the concrete imagery and physical reality associated elsewhere with the cycle of rebirth, which is not a mere plunge into nothingness and darkness by an infatuated soul, and yet is clear of the suggestion that nothing really lasts except what Blake calls the 'same dull round'. Such a poem is apocalyptic, a vision of plenitude which is still not bound to time. *The Shadowy Waters*, also, differs from the later poems of the 'Vacillation' group in that the chief characters go on to finish their quest and the subordinate characters (the sailors) return to the world. The goal of the quest is also described in apocalyptic terms:

> Where the world ends
> The mind is made unchanging, for it finds
> Miracle, ecstasy, the impossible hope,
> The flagstone under all, the fire of fires,
> The roots of the world. (*C.P.*, 477)

For a theoretical construct to match this apocalyptic imagery we have to set aside the main body of *A Vision*, with its conception of unity and individuality as opposed and impossible ideals which only super-human beings can reach, and look for another construct in which they are at the same point, and that point accessible to human life.

There are two apocalyptic symbols in *A Vision*: one is the 'Record'

(p. 193) or consolidated form of all the images of 'ultimate reality', associated by Yeats, I think correctly, with Blake's Golgonooza. The other and more important one is the 'Thirteenth Cone', which is not really a cone but a sphere, and which 'is that cycle which may deliver us from the twelve cycles of time and space'. We are further told, in what ought to be one of the key passages of *A Vision*, that this thirteenth cone confronts every cycle of life, large or small, as 'the reflection or messenger of the final deliverance', and at the very end of the book it is said to exist in every man and to be what is called by man his freedom. There are also 'teaching spirits' of this thirteenth cone who direct and inspire those who are in the cycle, and Yeats calls the thirteenth cone his substitute for God. He speaks of it as 'like some great dancer', recalling the great last line of 'Among School Children' which unites being and becoming, imagination and image. (pp. 210, 240)

The temporary mixture of four Faculties that constitutes what is ordinarily thought of as an individual is not final human reality. A poet discovers this, for example, when he realises that the images that great poetry uses are traditional, archetypal, conventional images, and that the emotions he employs to set these images forth are traditional and conventional emotions, representing states of being greater than himself. Thus the poet finds himself drawn out of his Husk into his Spirit, and thereby enters into much larger conceptions of what subject and object are. He is drawn up into a world in which subject and object become the human imagination and the human image, each being archetypes that recur in every individual man and poem. These great traditional states of being which the poet enters into and expresses are akin to the 'giant forms' of Blake's prophecies, Orc, Tharmas, Los and the rest, and, more generally, to the 'gods' of beauty and nature and war who inform so much of literature. Yeats sometimes calls them 'moods', and speaks of them as divine beings whose dreams form our own waking lives. Thus in *The Shadowy Waters* the central characters discover that

> We have fallen in the dreams the Ever-living
> Breathe on the burnished mirror of the world. (*C.P.*, 478)

In *A Vision* the poetic imagination begins in the self of the individual, but moves in the direction of identifying with a greater self called the 'daimon', and the process of purgation between lives has for its eventual goal a similar identification.

Apart from the contrast of self and soul, there is also an abstract vision associated, not with sanctity, but with art itself. This is the vision linked with the name of Pythagoras, whose mathematical genius 'planned' the art of exquisite proportion embodied in Greek sculpture and architecture. The role of art in imposing mathematical proportion on reality is connected by Yeats also with the geometrical diagrams of his own *Vision*, which he compares to the forms of Brancusi sculpture. Here we see how art, no less than sanctity, moves in the direction of a greater identity. In the poem 'To Dorothy Wellesley' it is not the soul that climbs the stair towards darkness, but the poetic power, which ascends in search of identity with the greater forms and figures of existence represented by the 'Proud Furies'. Such identity is no loss of individuality; it is merely a loss of what we might call the ego. In Yeats's terms, it loses character and gains personality. The saint attains a powerful personality by forgetting about his ego; but the poet, too, as Yeats says, 'must die every day he lives, be reborn, as it is said in the Burial Service, an incorruptible self'. For the poet, Yeats also says, 'is never the bundle of accident and incoherence that sits down to breakfast: he has been reborn as an idea'.

'I think', says Yeats, 'that much of the confusion of modern philosophy . . . comes from our renouncing the ancient hierarchy of beings from man up to the One.' The process of entering into a life greater than our ordinary one, which every poet knows, is a process of entering into this hierarchy, and of beginning to ascend the stair of life. The Thirteenth Cone, therefore, is a symbol of the way in which man emancipates himself by becoming part of Man, through a series of greater human forms. Here we move toward an existence in which Phases 1 and 15, unity and individuality, are the same point. It is therefore impossible that the 'One' could be anything but Man, or something identical or identifiable with man. Yeats refers occasionally to the 'One' as a sleeping giant like Blake's Albion or Joyce's Finnegan ('The Mountain Tomb', 'The Old Stone Cross', etc.), but he is even nearer the centre of his own intuitions when he speaks of man as having created death, when he says that there is nothing but life and that nothing exists but a stream of souls, and that man has, out of his own mind, made up the whole story of life and death and still can

> Dream, and so create
> Translunar Paradise. (*C.P.*, 223)

The Thirteenth Cone, then, represents the dialectical element in symbolism, where man is directly confronted by the greater form of himself which challenges him to identify himself with it. This confrontation is the real form of the double gyre. 'The repose of man is the choice of the Daimon, and the repose of the Daimon the choice of man . . . I might have seen this, as it all follows from the words written by the beggar in *The Hour-Glass* upon the walls of Babylon.' He might also have seen that this conception of the double gyre reduces his twenty-eight-phase historical cycle to something largely useless as a commentary on his own poetry, except for the poems deliberately based on it.

Yeats often speaks of entering into these personal archetypes, daimons or moods as a process of literal or symbolic death. 'Wisdom is the property of the dead', he says, and his fascination with the remark in *Axël*, 'As for living, our servants will do that for us', is connected with the same conception. Yeats's own interpretation of the *Axël* passage is indicated in 'The Tables of the Law': 'certain others, and in always increasing numbers, were elected, not to live, but to reveal that hidden substance of God which is colour and music and softness and a sweet odour; and . . . these have no father but the Holy Spirit'. Two of his poems describe the direct passage across from ordinary life to archetype, 'News for the Delphic Oracle' and 'Byzantium'. The latter poem is mainly about images, which are, as always in Yeats, generated in water and borne across water by dolphins into the simplifying and purgatorial world of fire. The former poem applies the same movement to human souls, and makes it clear that nothing of the physical or concrete world is lost, or even sublimated, by the kind of redemption here described.

These two poems, then, deal with the consolidation of imaginations and images, the true subjects and the true objects, into a timeless unity. But, of course, the image is a product of the imagination: in the imaginative world the relation of subject and object is that of creator and creature. In this perspective the whole cycle of nature, of life and death and rebirth which man has dreamed, becomes a single gigantic image, and the process of redemption is to be finally understood as an identification with Man and a detachment from the cyclical image he has created. This ultimate insight in Yeats is the one expressed in his many references (one of which forms the last sentence of *A Vision*) to a passage in the *Odyssey* where Heracles, seen by Odysseus in hell, is said to be present in hell only in his shade, the real Heracles, the man in contrast to the image, being at the banquet of the immortal gods. Here we come to the heart of what Yeats had to say as a poet. The vision of Heracles the man, eternally free from Heracles the shadowy image bound to an endless cycle, is nearer to being a 'key' to Yeats's thought and imagination than anything else in *A Vision*. To use the phraseology of *Per Amica Silentia Lunae*, it is an insight he had acquired, not by eavesdropping on the babble of the *anima mundi*, but from his own fully conscious *anima hominis*, the repository of a deeper wisdom than the ghostly house of rumour ever knew.

III

'The Green Helmet' and 'Responsibilities'

T. R. HENN

*

I

THE poems written between 1908 and 1914 show a strange, powerful and relatively sudden growth in Yeats's technique. We must make the reservation of 'relatively', for as early as 1904 certain lyrics in *In the Seven Woods* give promise of the new style. There are several aspects of his rejection of much that he had written: 'My very remorse helped to spoil my early poetry, giving it an element of sentimentality through my refusal to permit it any share of an intellect which I considered impure' (*Auto.*, 188). Spenser, Shelley, Morris, who had been dominant influences, are now rejected, though never wholly forgotten; there is a progression from pre-Raphaelite colour and sensation. The self-criticism is deliberate, but the 'new style', which is clearly marked in *Responsibilities*, seems to be the result of many complicated factors. What he himself called 'Choice' and 'Chance' began from about 1909 to work fiercely upon his life, though not with that seminal violence that was marked by the 1916 Rising. Both volumes draw upon this experience in poems that are closely related to contemporary events. Yeats listed some of these in a Note:

> The first was the Parnell controversy. There were reasons to justify a man's joining either party, but there were none to justify, on one side or on the other, lying accusations forgetful of past service, a frenzy of detraction. And another was the dispute over *The Playboy*. There may have been reasons for opposing as for supporting that violent, laughing thing, though I can see the one side only, but there cannot have been any for the lies, for the unscrupulous rhetoric spread against it in Ireland, and from Ireland to America.[1]

[1] See, e.g., Lady Gregory's account in *Our Irish Theatre*, pp. 112–31; U. M. Ellis Fermor, *The Irish Dramatic Movement*, p. 48 *et seq.*

The third prepared for the Corporation's refusal of a building for Sir Hugh Lane's famous collection of pictures. (*C.P.*, 529)

To these three events we may add others. The hopes of the late 'nineties for the resurrection of Irish poetry and mythology, and the dream—perhaps too facile—of the high destinies of the Irish National Theatre, had been succeeded by the nine years of fruitful and exhausting drudgery at the Abbey:

> My curse on plays
> That have to be set up in fifty ways,
> On the day's war with every knave and dolt,
> Theatre business, management of men. (*C.P.*, 104)

Maud Gonne had married MacBride in 1905: she had separated from him, and it was said that she had been hissed at the Abbey by her husband's partisans.[2] She had become a Roman Catholic; hence the lines in 'King and No King':

> And I that have not your faith, how shall I know
> That in the blinding light beyond the grave
> We'll find so good a thing as that we have lost? (*C.P.*, 102–3)

The love story equated with Helen's seemed to have ended in a doubly 'barren passion' as Maud Gonne became steadily more concerned with politics:

> Why should I blame her that she filled my days
> With misery, or that she would of late
> Have taught to ignorant men most violent ways,
> Or hurled the little streets upon the great,
> Had they but courage equal to desire? (*C.P.*, 101)

Agrarian troubles, that had risen and fallen like tides during the past century, were swelling again, and gave rise to the poem 'Upon A House Shaken by the Land Agitation'; the House is Coole Park. The prophecy which it embodies was to be exactly fulfilled, when the stones of the house were carted to build cottages on a Galway housing estate, and make 'mean roof trees . . . the sturdier for its fall'. Synge died in 1909, and I do not think the effect of that event, or of Synge's gifts to Yeats in inspiration and example, has yet been properly estimated. In the same year Lady Gregory had come close to death; this is reflected

---

[2] A. Norman Jeffares, *W. B. Yeats, Man and Poet* (1949) pp. 140–1: see also 'Against Unworthy Praise'.

in 'A Friend's Illness'. And he had embarked, about 1910, upon a
liaison with an unmarried woman which lasted for some years.[3]

It is also clear that Yeats felt that his popularity, even his planned
career as a poet, had ended. So many things seemed to have converged
in discouragement: the rejection of Synge, and of the plans for Lutyens's
Gallery; Lane's gift of the French pictures gone astray; Lane's failure
to secure the well-deserved appointment as Director of the Municipal
Gallery ('An Appointment'); perhaps even his own talked-of Chair,
that 'wicked temptation', at Trinity College. His uncle, George Pollexfen, to whom he was devoted, died in 1910. Maud Gonne seemed lost
except as a memory, though he stayed with her and her daughter
Iseult in Normandy in 1908 and again in 1912. The Parnell affair,
O'Leary's death, and the newspaper attacks on himself and his friends,
had once more shown the fickleness of the Dublin mob: 'The Irish
always seem to me like a pack of hounds dragging down some noble
stag' (*Auto.*, 483, quoting Goethe). There are many lines to witness all
these events:

> I had this thought a while ago,
> 'My darling cannot understand
> What I have done, or what would do
> In this blind bitter land' . . . (*C.P.*, 100–1)

or

> And how what her dreaming gave
> Earned slander, ingratitude,
> From self-same dolt and knave . . . (*C.P.*, 104)

and the line that was to be quoted against him later in the Senate:

> The seeming needs of my fool-driven land. (*C.P.*, 109)

The sense of the pressure of events to be moulded into verse is confirmed
by the 1908 Diary. One instance will serve:

> To-day the thought came to me that [Maud Gonne] . . . never
> really understands my plans or notions or ideas. Then came the
> thought—what matter?—how much of the best that I have done
> and still do is but the attempt to explain myself to her? If she
> understood I should lack a reason for writing and one can never
> have too many reasons for doing what is so laborious.[4]

Against this we may quote the last two stanzas of the poem:

[3] Jeffares, p. 175, and see 'The Dolls', *infra*.
[4] 22 January 1909 (*cit.* Jeffares, p. 141).

That every year I have cried, 'At length
My darling understands it all,
Because I have come into my strength,
And words obey my call';

That had she done so who can say
What would have shaken from the sieve?
I might have thrown poor words away
And been content to live. (*C.P.*, 101)

The brightness of his heroic mythology was linked to Maud Gonne,
and it had failed him:

And while we're in our laughing, weeping fit,
Hurl helmets, crowns, and swords into the pit. (*C.P.*, 102)

The statement is repeated in 'A Coat'. Now he is to 'walk naked', and
this becomes a key word. With the discarding of the 'embroideries'
there goes also an abandonment of the luxuriant nostalgic mood.
Between *The Green Helmet* and *The Wild Swans at Coole* imagery from
nature, and the vague symbolism of sun, moon, stars, seems to decrease.
There are few traces of esotericism deriving from the Golden Dawn.
Such of the Celtic myth as is retained is not, I think, used successfully.
Two symbols become dominants, Maud Gonne and Helen for *The
Green Helmet*, the beggar for *Responsibilities*. As early as the Quaritch
Edition of Blake he had discussed the archetypal symbolism of Lear
on the Heath; in old age he was to return again to it.[5]

II

But it would be a mistake to imagine that the period between 1908 and
1914 showed any slackening of Yeats's energy. The Abbey still took
much of his time. He was also reading extensively, and as haphazardly,
perhaps, as he usually did, although he was much troubled with sick-
ness and weakness of the eyes. To detail his reading at this period would
be too long a task, but we may indicate some of his new interests.
Austin Clarke was, I think, the first to suggest a general emotional
rediscovery of major English poetry about 1912.[6] In that year he had
been introduced to Ezra Pound, who had undertaken something of
Yeats's poetic education. He had met Tagore, and afterwards contributed the introduction to *Gitanjali*. It seems likely that he was rereading

[5] In, e.g., 'An Acre of Grass'.
[6] 'W. B. Yeats', *Dublin Magazine*, April/June 1939, p. 8.

Ben Jonson, and certain that he was reading Dante and More. Above all there is the discovery, through Sir Herbert Grierson, of Donne . . . 'I find that at last I can understand Donne. Your notes[7] tell me exactly what I want to know. Poems that I could not understand or could but vaguely understand are now clear, and I notice that the more precise and learned the thought the greater the beauty, the passion. The intricacy and subtlety of his imagination are the length and depth of the furrow made by his passion. His pedantry and the obscenity, the rock and loam of his Eden but make us the more certain that one who is but a man like us has seen God.'[8] Yeats had, of course, been conscious of his over-richness far earlier than this:

> I cannot probably be quite just to any poetry that speaks to me with the sweet insinuating feminine voice of the dwellers in that country of shadows and hollow images. I have dwelt there too long not to dread all that comes out of it.[9]

We can trace in the new style, at least in part, a strange amalgam of these new experiences, reading, friendships, defeats, and his consciousness of a quickening of the political events of the Ireland of 1912–14. These included the labour troubles headed by Larkin and abetted by Maud Gonne; Redmond's Home Rule Bill, the formation of the Irish Volunteers, the arming of Ulster and the threat of a civil war. Romantic Ireland was, for the moment, dead and gone. We see instead a complex of tensions; the poet confronted with the pettiness and meanness of the practical world, the conflict between the aristocratic idea of service and the suspicion and ingratitude with which it is received. This predicament is dramatised in a tragic pose which finds relief in double-edged irony. In technique, the trisyllabic feet, the longer metres, are abandoned in the main for the more rapid octosyllabics (that seem to owe something to Swift). There are exercises in a Jonsonian compression of the epigram. Checks and hypermetrical syllables are slowly becoming integrated into something that can approach speech-rhythms. There is a use of homely, even brutal idiom, that I connect with Synge's demand for a poetry that should have its 'strong roots among the clay and the worms', and that reflects the *King Lear* antinomies of clothes and nakedness, king and beggar.

[7] To the 1912 Edition of Donne's Poems.
[8] Grierson, Preface to Menon, *The Development of William Butler Yeats*, p. xii. *v.* also *Letters*, 570.
[9] W.B.Y. to 'A.E.' (? April 1904), *Letters*, 434.

All this was noted by Ezra Pound in his review of *Responsibilities*. 'There is a new robustness; there is the tooth of satire which is, in Mr. Yeats's case, too good a tooth to keep hidden . . . There are a lot of fools to be killed and Mr. Yeats is an excellent slaughterman, when he will but turn from ladies with excessive chevelure appearing in pearl-pale nuances.'[10]

It is also of interest that the revisions of the poems in *The Green Helmet* and *Responsibilities* are slight compared to those of the earlier volumes. We may draw certain deductions. The events that gave rise to the poems were certainly more imminent, his own concern deeper and more violent. There is less of the conscious artefact in them, fewer memories of the singing schools of the 'nineties in which he had studied. There are exceptions: 'His Dream' belongs to the earlier kind, the poetry of dream-symbolism. Saul has given the raw material (Saul, 82), but I would also suggest a reference to the *Morte d'Arthur* (e.g. Bk. xviii, Ch. 20). The whole vision seems typical of Shelley, and of that river-and-boat symbolism which had interested him so much and of which he had found so many examples.[11] 'The Grey Rock' is to some extent an architected poem, and won the prize offered by *Poetry*.[12] 'The Two Kings' was originally printed as the third poem of *Responsibilities*, and is now set out at the end of *Collected Poems*. It is a long blank-verse poem, giving the story of King Eochaid's encounter and fight with the miraculous stag, followed by the story from 'The Wooing of Etain' in *The Book of the Dun Cow*. Stylistically it seems to belong to an earlier period of Yeats's technique; the blank verse owes something to both Tennyson and Morris.

The dedicatory poem to *Responsibilities*, 'Pardon, old fathers . . .' has been much praised, and I think too highly. In it Yeats depicts himself as 'propp'd by ancestry' and rehearses these quasi-historical image-figures with an epic sonority. This assumption into history is reflected in various forms in later poems. There is some difficulty over his statements. 'Free of the ten and four' was, as he admits in a note (*C.P.*, 529), written under a misapprehension. The lines relating to the

---

[10] cit. Häusermann, *W. B. Yeats' Criticism of Ezra Pound*. The 'pearl-pale nuances' is presumably a reference to:
> 'You need but lift a pearl-pale hand,
> And bind up your long hair and sigh;
> And all men's hearts must burn and beat . . .'
>   *'He Gives his Beloved certain Rhymes'*
[11] e.g., 'The Philosophy of Shelley's Poetry': *Ideas of Good and Evil*.
[12] It was for £50; of this he gave £40 to Ezra Pound (Hone, 273).

Battle of the Boyne were altered when Yeats realised that the Butler in question had fought for, and not against, King James (Hone, 2). The 'Dublin merchant' is Jervis Yeats, and the claim that the blood transmitted

> has not passed through any huckster's loin

seems excessive. John Yeats, a clergyman, was a contemporary and friend of Robert Emmet's. The 'silent and fierce old man' is William Pollexfen, who is also the 'skipper' of l.13. The lines on the Boyne suggest to me Morris's famous

> As clearly as they saw thy townsmen meet
> Those who in vineyards of Poictou withstood
> The glittering horror of the steel-topped wood.[13]

It is Yeats's evocation of the virtues and the wisdom of his ancestors, his attempted alignment with an aristocracy of notability, action, scholarship, that we may find unpleasantly *arriviste*.[14] The 'barren passion' is, of course, for Maud Gonne; and it is a little overdramatic to call the virtues 'wasteful'. But in some sense the poem sets the tone for much of what follows: to relieve his sense of bitterness and defeat, to justify his friends, and to nurse the love story that was to continue for so long. This characteristic tone can best be seen in the group 'To a Wealthy Man . . .', 'To a Friend Whose Work Has Come to Nothing', 'An Appointment', 'Paudeen', 'To A Shade'. Some discussion of the first of these may suggest his technique in this kind.

Yeats opens with colloquial vigour and directness. The poem moves in a triple structure, which the typography in *Collected Poems* does not quite bring out. The object of the attack is one William Martin Murphy, who is also glanced at in 'September 1913' and 'To A Shade'. Paudeen and Biddy are generic names for Irish beggars, or rather the people of 'the little streets', and Swift would have approved them. There is speed, drive, energy in the concise strongly rhymed octosyllabics, closely articulated by the verbs. Each word is fully charged:

> . . . That things it were a pride to give
> Are what the blind and ignorant town
> Imagines best to make it thrive . . .

---

[13] *Life and Death of Jason*, XVII, ll.22-24.

[14] *v.* the attempts in, e.g., 'The Tower', 'September 1913', 'Blood and the Moon', 'Meditations in Time of Civil War'.

Blind and *ignorant* are linked phonetically to *town* and from both epithets *town* seems to derive a Swiftian contemptuous flavour; *imagines* has an echo of both, its weight of contempt striding on the ambiguity of *best*; the best the town's imagination can do, and how it can best thrive: which itself gathers up, ironically, *blind*[15] and *ignorant*, for the *thriving* is wholly material. Then Yeats changes from the low to the high style, invoking history and the historical alignments already foreshadowed in the introduction to *Responsibilities*. Coole Park is Urbino, the first of many such comparisons. Contempt, pride, magnanimity, are welded into the verse by alliteration, and by the hypermetrical foot which emphasises the contempt of *th' onion-sellers*, huckstering peasants:

> What *cared D*uke Ercole, that bid
> His *mummc*rs to the *m*arket-place,—

(We may think of Yeats's own propaganda for the popular theatre, and perhaps an overtone-echo of Bacon's contemptuous usage.)[16]

> —What th' onion-sellers thought or did
> So that his *P*lautus[17] set the *p*ace
> For the Italian comedies?

These set out the proud aristocratic virtues of the *Dedication*. Then the rhythm slows, becomes quieter; we arc now invited to consider the implications of this laminated view of recurrent history. Cosimo de' Medici is Hugh Lane, Michelozzo is Lutyens, the San Marco Library is the projected Gallery over the Liffey. For this enterprise might have set a kind of seal on Ireland's Renaissance, while its new 'grammar-school of courtesies' was taking shape in the drawing-room of Coole. The great names are invoked, in the traditional manner of the rhetoricians, to certify ironic contrasts and values. We move on, in the classic triple structure of the poem, to the exhortation, with the often-used image from Blake of the eagle's eye and the sun.

It is rhetoric with a new fierce note, of power kept in check by volition. It is not the rhetoric of persuasion, for its aristocratic allusiveness could have persuaded nobody, certainly not those of 'this blind bitter land'. It is rather Yeats's own purgation of his anger, the hero

---

[15] c.f. 'Blind and leader of the blind
Drinking the foul ditch where they lie.' (*C.P.*, 207)
[16] *v.*, e.g., *Novum Organum*, I.39.
[17] *v.* Castiglione's *The Courtier*, No. 203. Duke Ercole had produced five Plautine comedies for the wedding festivities of his son.

H.G.–D

finding his Renaissance—perhaps Swiftian—mask in an arrogance of defeat, an assumption of pride and race, and in power over words. Of this same kind is 'To a Friend Whose Work Has Come to Nothing'; she is Lady Gregory. It is a small poem, its rhythm strong and compressed, dramatic in its sudden opening:

> Now all the truth is out,
> Be secret and take defeat
> From any brazen throat . . .

Again it is the expression of an ideal of aristocracy, this proud and tragic reticence in the face of vulgar abuse. And indeed there was reason:

> While Lady Gregory has brought herself to death's door with over-work, to give us, while neglecting no other duty, enough plays, translated or original, to keep the Theatre alive, our base half-men of letters, or rather half-journalists, that coterie of patriots who have never been bought because no one ever thought them worth a price, have been whispering everywhere that she takes advantage of her position as director to put her own plays upon the stage. When I think, too, of Synge dying at this moment of their bitterness and ignorance, as I believe, I wonder if I have been right to shape my style to sweetness and serenity . . . (*Auto.*, 482)

The impetus carries strongly over the rhymes, so that they go unnoticed, even that of *out-throat*. There are in it the seeds of much of the later poetry; we may think of 'Upon a Dying Lady', Mabel Beardsley:

> . . . She knows herself a woman,
> No red and white of a face,
> Or rank, raised from a common
> Unreckonable race. (*C.P.*, 179)

Yeats returns continually to the thought that we must aim at achieving 'Of all things not impossible the most difficult'. The fine and mysterious 'Amid a place of stone'[18] has its own monumental stillness in contrast to the 'brazen throat', shameless and strident, of the journalists. But the stone—the monument or the churchyard—is also of Aran or the Burren Hills near Lady Gregory's home, and these were linked in his mind to the loneliness of genius, as in his tribute to Synge.[19]

The fourth poem is 'Paudeen': the image of 'our old Paudeen in his

---

[18] He uses this of Synge and of the Aran Islands.

[19] *v.* 'Preface to the First Edition of John M. Synge's *Poems and Translations*', and the prefixed quotation from Proclus (*E. & I.*, 306).

shop' suggests less the city shopkeeper than the 'gombeen man' of some little county town, part usurer, public-house owner, dealer in cattle and all sorts of petty merchandise, proverbial for avarice and meanness.[20] The *fumbling* wits, the *obscure* spite, suggest one, perhaps two, deliberate ambiguities. The poem follows a structure that is often used by Yeats: the personal statement, the reflection on that experience, generally in another setting, and the moment of vision in which the tensions set up are unified or reconciled by a new perception in terms of an image. 'To a Shade' has the same pattern; it is addressed to Parnell, and the current example of the victim-hero, also slandered and rejected, is Hugh Lane. But because of the significance attached to Parnell, both in poems and in prose,[21] we may sketch the events which moved Yeats so deeply and so long after their occurrence.

Parnell was an Anglo-Irish landowner who had thrown himself with great energy into the Home Rule Movement: therefore he is linked with Hugh Lane when Yeats praises Lady Gregory:

> A man
> Of your own passionate serving kind.

He was believed to hold opinions of a more revolutionary character than those current leaders who believed in a constitutional progression towards federal Home Rule, and he attempted by systematic obstruction in the House of Commons to ensure the passing of the Home Rule Bill, hoping that the English Government would go to any lengths to get rid of the Irish Members. A prosecution of him and his party by Gladstone broke down: whereupon the Government brought in a Bill to suspend *Habeas Corpus* in Ireland. Parnell, Davitt and others were imprisoned, but released shortly afterwards. Conciliation seemed possible, but was wrecked by a series of 'incidents', culminating in the Phoenix Park murders, when Lord Frederick Cavendish and another official were shot while walking there. Parnell and Davitt were accused, falsely, of connivance at the murder. Suspicion of the Irish Members was widespread, and is echoed in Kipling's bitter poem, 'Cleared'.

Parnell was then involved in a divorce suit, having eloped with Kitty O'Shea. The ensuing controversy, exacerbated by Catholic views on divorce, split the Home Rule Party and dissipated its energies. Parnell

[20] There is a good sketch of such a one in Somerville and Ross's story 'The Finger of Mrs. Knox' (*The Irish R.M. and his Experiences*).

[21] e.g. 'Ireland After Parnell'; *Auto.*, 197–250: also 'Parnell's Funeral' a complicated and violent alignment of politics, mythology and history (*C.P.*, 319).

himself was violently attacked on grounds of immorality. He died a year after the divorce suit, in 1891. The controversy continued while the body was being brought back to Glasnevin Cemetery for burial. In the presence of a huge crowd (Yeats was not present) a star was seen to fall when the coffin was lowered into the grave (Hone, 89, 90). This gave material for the highly complex alignments of politics, myth and history in 'Parnell's Funeral' as well as for the verse

> The Bishops and the Party
> That tragic story made,
> A husband that had sold his wife
> And after that betrayed . . . (C.P., 356)

Thus Parnell, Lady Gregory, Synge and Lane converge as types of the leaders rejected out of stupidity, malice, suspicion, specious morality, ingratitude for service. In 'To A Shade' Yeats mocks the behaviour of the Irish, their proverbial casualness ('I wonder if the builder has been paid?') and doubles the irony by pretending to mock the heroic dead. Yeats believed that the great poets and sculptors were given to the people 'so that instinct might find its lamp'; that boys and girls should be guided, by looking on such work, to make their sexual choice aright. Hence the rejected pictures

> . . . Had given their children's children loftier thought,
> Sweeter emotion, working in their veins
> Like gentle blood . . .

The 'Glasnevin coverlet' is the ground of the great cemetery outside Dublin, where O'Connell—the 'Great Comedian' of 'Parnell's Funeral' —is also buried; the contemptuous or homely *coverlet* suggests, perhaps, the flimsy value of the unpaid-for monument. It is worth remembering that a similar Elizabethan image was to be used later in 'Reprisals':

> Then close your ears with dust and lie
> Among the other cheated dead.[22]

The group of 'Beggar' poems in *Responsibilities* require explanation of a somewhat different kind. We can begin with two assertions. In Yeats's hierarchy the beggar is the third of the triad—'Workman, noble and saint'—and, together with the tinker-figure (Mannion), stands for strength, virility, freedom and 'earthly wisdom' ('The Seven Sages' is relevant). Again, as we have seen, one of the key words in this poetry

[22] *The Variorum Edition*, Allt and Alspach, (1957), p. 791; not yet published in *C.P.*

is 'naked'; the stripping off the lendings of Celtic mythology, and of his own dramatically perceived and even masochistic abandonment of the hope of popularity or fame or love. Yet the beggars seem to become mere mouthpieces for the fables; they have nothing of the individuality or richness that Synge has presented in his tramps and tinkers, and which Yeats, for all his proclaimed intentions, never succeeded in understanding in the marrow-bone.

'The Three Beggars' begins and ends with the solitary heron fishing in a stream; the mysterious *lebeen-lone* is a phonetic rendering of *líbín leamhan*, small fish or minnows. We know that the heron (for 'crane' is merely *Hibernicé* for it) appealed powerfully to Yeats's imagination. In fairy lore it is linked to human transformations. Crazy Jane's Bishop has a 'heron's hunch upon his back'.[23] He associated such birds with subjective, and therefore lonely, men.[24] The white heron occurs as a symbol in *Calvary*, as dissociated from Christ, even in opposition to Him; perhaps as I have suggested elsewhere,[25] as the killer of the ἰχθύς, the Fish. From the persistence of its appearance in art it seems to be archetypal: he could have seen the heron fishing in a mosaic dome at Ravenna, in Mantegna's *Agony in the Garden*, in Chinese paintings. We know that he was excited by the appearance of a heron in flight. The image of the Fisherman, which I believe to be founded upon the personality of Synge, becomes a considerable poem later. The lines:

> *And maybe I shall take a trout*
> *If but I do not seem to care*

present a phenomenon familiar to all fishermen (the deliberate rejection, in loneliness, of overt concentration upon the act), which is of some possible application to his own private life as well as to his poetry.[26] The structure, with its use of counterpointed verses in italics, had been already used in 'The Happy Townland' in 1904.

I see no more in this poem than a rather thin morality, in which Yeats draws some sardonic amusement from King Guaire's experiments with human nature. They are studies in human stupidity. 'These controversies, political, literary and artistic, have showed that neither religion or politics can of itself create minds with enough receptivity

---

[23] This is the origin of Dylan Thomas's 'heron-priested shore' ('Poem in October').
[24] *v. P. & C.*, 459.
[25] *The Lonely Tower*, p. 129.
[26] This is supported by *'the old crane of Gort'*.

to become wise, or just and generous enough to make a nation.'[27] It is possible that some allusion is intended to the contemporary literary scene (we remember 'To a Poet, who would have me Praise certain Bad Poets' . . .) and 'A Coat'.

'The Three Hermits' continues the doctrine of indifference, but this time indifference to the religious views and fears of the second and third hermits with their doctrines of transmigration and fatalism—'We're but given what we have earned.' Yeats, the singer and *unnoticed*, appears to be the first hermit, who has rejected holiness. The verse, of no great subtlety, is savagely counterpointed in Synge's manner:

> While he'd rummaged rags and hair,
> Caught and cracked his flea, the third,
> Giddy with his hundredth year,
> Sang unnoticed like a bird.

The theme of isolation and withdrawal (which is in part autobiographical)[28] is emphasised in 'Beggar to Beggar Cried'; the phrase 'make my soul' is familiar peasant idiom. The last and best stanza contains an image which is worth noting:

> 'And there I'll grow respected at my ease,[29]
> And hear amid the garden's nightly peace,'
> *Beggar to beggar cried, being frenzy-struck,*
> 'The wind-blown clamour of the barnacle-geese.'

The barnacle goose, mysterious in its birth,[30] is the symbol of subjective man, of the wildness of the spirit, contrasted with the peace of the gander, the clamour of public controversy, but suggests, too, the mysterious Wild Hunt (*Myth.*, 114), linked to the hound-like baying of the skeins of geese at night 'Running to Paradise', with its strange and exciting rhythms and assonances, checked by the accented *is* in the refrain, suggests a further amalgamation of images, between the Beggar and the Fool. For it seems to be related to the passage concerning the Amadán, the fool of Faery, in *The Celtic Twilight*; whom the boy who was cutting bushes in a wood saw 'coming at him':

[27] *cit. Variorum*, p. 818.
[28] See, e.g., J. Unterecker, *A Reader's Guide to W. B. Yeats*, (1959), pp. 122–3: and 'The Dolls', infra.
[29] Compare 'What Then' (*C.P.*, 347).
[30] For this (and for much that is relevant to Yeats's perception of bird cries), E. A. Armstrong, *The Folk-Lore of Birds* (1958).

'He had a big vessel in his arms, and it was shining, so that the boy could see nothing else; but he put it behind his back and then came running, and the boy said he looked wild and wide, like the side of the hill.' (*Myth.*, 114)

The most obscure poem is 'The Hour Before Dawn' which appears to be the poet's defence of the waking life against that of the man who has succeeded in enjoying to the full the two sensualities of drink and sleep. Some glosses are necessary. Cruachan or Croghan was the capital of Queen Maeve's kingdom: the (eight or) nine sons of Maeve are mentioned in the familiar source-book, Rhys's *Celtic Heathendom*.[31] Goban is Goibnui, formerly the smith of the gods, afterwards an architect and builder. I myself believe that a drawing by Jack Yeats for a Cuala Press Broadside[32] supplied a visual image. It is called *Two Tinkers*. The elder, dark and sinister, crouches among the stones at the side of a cairn upon some mountain-top. Beside him stands a much younger man, bare-headed, drinking in the light and wind: both suggested by the cloud formations of a fresh spring day.

There is a further possible source:

Two examples [of the work of Yen Hui] are in the British Museum. In one, a large picture, three hermits sit together in a recess in the mountains. The other shows us Li T'ieh-Kuai, the Taoist wizard of the hills, breathing out his spiritual essence towards the sacred mount of the immortals. He is represented as a beggar with ragged garments . . . one hand grasps a crutch, the other props his chin, and his eyes look out from the picture under his black matted hair with the smile of a magician.[33]

It was Yeats's habit to accept these multiplex appearances of an image in history, mythology, dreams or physical experience to certify or confirm its validity; and it does not matter that dramatically contrived realignments were made in order that the correspondences might be the closer. The theme of the Seven Sleepers of Ephesus had intrigued Yeats and Donne. The debate that follows is between weariness, 'the longing for the tomb', and judgement; set against the intermittent sensual awakenings to the life of the world, and the desire for the south or fertile wind of spring:

[31] pp. 367-8.
[32] No. 2, Sixth Year. July 1913.
[33] Laurence Binyon, *Painting in the Far East* (1908), p. 148. I am indebted for this reference to Dr. F. A. C. Wilson. We may compare the use of the carving in 'Lapis Lazuli'.

> . . . 'My sleep were now nine centuries
> But for those mornings when I find
> The lapwing at their foolish cries
> And the sheep bleating at the wind
> As when I also played the fool.'

But the beggar rejects the sleeper's life. The place on the mountain-top is one of sensual enchantment, though of the most vulgar—beer and sleep. Yet the enchantment is also of women. If, as I believe, the poem is again ambivalent, the link with Maeve is given both by Cruachan, and by the scene that I think Jack Yeats had in mind, which is the cairn known as Queen Maeve's Grave on the summit of Knocknarea at Sligo. Maeve as well as Helen stands for Maud Gonne. A passage from 'The Autumn of the Body' seems relevant:

> Man has wooed and won the world, and has fallen weary, and not, I think, for a time, but with a weariness that will not end until the last autumn, when the stars shall be blown away like withered leaves. (*E. & I.*, 192–3)

I find myself puzzled over the poems 'The Magi' and 'The Dolls'. So far as my knowledge goes, all critics have taken at its face value Yeats's own note to the second poem, which it is as well to quote:

> The fable for this poem came into my head while I was giving some lectures in Dublin. I had noticed once again how all thought among us is frozen into 'something other than human life'. After I had made the poem, I looked up one day into the blue of the sky, and suddenly imagined, as if lost in the blue of the sky, stiff figures in procession. I remembered that they were the habitual image suggested by blue sky, and looking for a second fable called them 'The Magi' . . . complementary forms of those enraged dolls. (*C.P.*, 531)

There seem to me various difficulties. The two poems are utterly different in style, and, I believe, in the emotion behind each. 'The Magi' seems to be imaginatively in the same class as 'The Cold Heaven', and looks forward to 'The Second Coming'. 'The Dolls' is a different sort of poem, and suggests some hidden meaning.

There would appear to be a certain mystery, too, about the dates of composition. 'The Dolls' is given in Ellmann's earlier work as written 'late in 1912',[34] but in his second volume the date is 20 September 1913.[35] That is also the date which he gives for 'The Magi', and for

[34] *Yeats, The Man and the Masks*, p. 211.
[35] *The Identity of Yeats*, p. 289.

'Running to Paradise'. Now on general grounds it is most unlikely that one of Yeats's fastidious habits in composition wrote two such utterly different poems on the same day as 'The Dolls' and 'The Magi': 'The Dolls (if we are to trust his Note) being the earlier. That three poems were of the same date seems to me hard to believe.

I have already [36] suggested the possible relevance to 'The Magi' of a passage in Yeats's Preface to W. T. Horton's *Book of Images* (1898):

> I closed my eyes a moment ago, and a company of people in blue robes swept by me in a blinding light, and had gone before I had done more than see little roses embroidered on the hems of their robes . . . and recognized one of the company by his square black curling beard. I have often seen him.

I have, however, grown less certain of this, but I still suspect a pictorial source. Further, the accepted connection between the two poems rests on the rather tenuous link of the cradle, the birth, and the 'intrusion' of the child. Nor do I find MacNeice's exposition of the theme of 'The Dolls' as Being and Becoming a convincing one. I prefer to see a possible connection with the passage that Jeffares quotes from Synge's *The Aran Islands:*

> This old man talks usually in a mournful tone about his ill-health, and his death, which he feels to be approaching, yet he has occasional touches of humour . . . Today a grotesque twopenny doll was lying on the floor near the old woman. He picked it up . . . 'Is it you is after bringing that thing into the world,' he said, 'woman of the house?'[37]

I put forward an alternative solution, though tentatively, that the Note in *Collected Poems* has some intention to mislead. I myself think that 'The Dolls' has a parabolic significance, which we need not labour here:[38] and that the linking with 'The Magi' was to direct the 'uninitiated' from autobiographical interpretation.

Let us consider each poem on its merits.

'The Magi' is clearly related to 'The Second Coming', to *The Resurrection*, and to Yeats's scheme of history. Calvary has brought to the world the 'Galilean turbulence'—there may be a reminiscence of Swinburne[39]—and a second coming, as of the 'rough beast', is to be expected

---

[36] *The Lonely Tower*, p. 45.
[37] *Aran Islands*, p. 37: Jeffares, p. 178.
[38] See Ellmann, *The Man and the Masks*, p. 211 n.
[39] e.g. 'Hymn to Proserpine'.

at the end of some historical cycle. The Magi are not quite the wise men of the nativity story, but are extended, symbolic figures[40] who have grown old in their search. There is a suggestion of the characters of 'Lapis Lazuli'. They are warlike as well as old and wise; in their silver helms they suggest faintly the hovering flight of angels in a Blake or Doré illustration. This perception is intuitive, visionary, and perpetual.

The key word of the poem, twice repeated, is *unsatisfied*. It is possible to interpret this as an antonym of the liturgical term 'oblation and *satisfaction* for the sins of the whole world'. They are unsatisfied by the crucifixion for several reasons; perhaps because of the uncertainty surrounding His resurrection (we may remember *The Brook Kerith*), and because of the historical consequences of the coming of Christianity that broke the continuity and rationality of the classical world:

> Odour of blood when Christ was slain
> Made all Platonic tolerance vain
> And vain all Doric discipline. (*C.P.*, 240)

In this reading the Magi see the Birth and Crucifixion as an insufficient fulfilment of the prophecy in their historical meaning and outcome. Yeats is continually probing beyond the boundaries of orthodox Christianity, as in the persona of Ribh[41] the hermit. The old heretical definition of the Trinity, Father, Mother, Son, is closer to his thought. Neither the dogma, nor the historical outcome, of the Christian events can satisfy wisdom. There is 'the abstract Greek absurdity' of the Trinity, as well as the crowning irrationality:

> What if there is always something that lies outside knowledge, outside order? What if at the moment when knowledge and order seem complete that something appears? (*C.Pl.*, 591)

So the multiple meanings of the word *bestial*: brutal, stalking but inevitable as the *slouches* of the Rough Beast in 'The Second Coming'. We recognise in it the traditional stable scene, the element of violence that Yeats perceived in the coming of Christianity, ('I am come not to bring peace but a sword'), and a Swiftian revulsion at the body. It is at this point that we have one link with 'The Dolls'.

Yeats seems to have been shocked or even revolted by the physical aspects of a baby's life; or perhaps by the physical processes of the human birth. We may quote from *The Resurrection*:

[40] Ellmann, *op. cit.*, p. 68; he considers them 'as men of reason and perhaps all reasoning men'.
[41] See, generally, *Supernatural Songs*.

The Hebrew. It was always foretold that he would be born of a woman.

The Greek. To say that a god can be born of a woman, carried in her womb, fed upon her breast, washed as children are washed, is the most terrible blasphemy. (*C.Pl.*, 584)

—from 'The Mother of God':

> What is this flesh I purchased with my pains,
> This fallen star my milk sustains . . . (*C.P.*, 282)

—from 'A Prayer for My Son:

> You have lacked articulate speech
> To tell Your simplest want, and known,
> Wailing upon a woman's knee,
> All of that worst ignominy
> Of flesh and bone. (*C.P.*, 239)

The Dolls are disturbed by the entry of the human baby, the 'noisy and filthy thing', into their calm world of the artefact, the world perhaps of the Statues (we may think of the poem of that title). There may be some resemblance in the stiff painted clothes of each. They, too, represent an older and more rational order of peace, stability, that is suddenly and violently broken by the human child. The oldest doll, perhaps like Zeus or Jahveh, is being replaced by a new order.

But this does not explain the doll-maker's wife and her words (with a tenderness of rhythm that Yeats was to use as a refrain in 'The Three Bushes'). It does not seem to me unlikely that Yeats's metaphysical imagination formed, at this point, a wholly characteristic synthesis.

III

'The Cold Heaven', another difficult and I think considerable poem, seems to have affinities with 'The Magi'. It has the clarity and vehemence of a visionary moment: made credible and vivid by the epithet *rook-delighting*. The stark visual impression of the black rooks, in the wild aerobatics[42] in which (on just such a day in spring) they sometimes revel, might echo the 'rooky wood' of *Macbeth*. The lightness and faintly blue quality of the air are given by the fire-ice antithesis, which adds a further meaning of unity in conflict, as in some metaphysical imagery. Such a vision of unity is to be given expression later in 'Stream

---

[42] Rooks and green plover are among the few birds which seem to do this, in a kind of ecstasy.

and Sun at Glendalough', though here irrelevancies have impaired its
purity.[43] In this ecstatic state the whole being is driven wild: the word
has peculiar overtones, in Anglo-Irish, of intensity, exaltation, strength
born of excitement, and irresponsibility in mundane things. Emotions
connected with past love return in their first intensity: in that moment
of acceptance and humility the poet is conscious of illumination. This
is of the same image-kind as in the Glendalough poem, for it is based
on the arrows of illumination—*Riddled with light*—used of any com-
munication between heaven and man, but characteristically of the
Annunciation:

> What woman hugs her infant there?
> Another star has shot an ear. (*C.P.*, 387)

and:

> What motion of the sun or stream
> Or eyelid shot the gleam
> *That pierced my body through?* (*C.P.*, 289)

What follows is more difficult. The last three and a half lines break
the sense, and we must look for some metaphysical connection. In this
state of spiritual illumination the spirit is liberated from the body.
Bishop Berkeley had given orders that his body should lie undisturbed
so that his soul should have time to disengage itself from the 'confusion
of the death-bed'. The ghost, liberated and purified by its ecstatic
experience, may go naked—the key word—on the road, like a beggar
or tramp. Perhaps this is its way of purgation, dreaming backward
through its past life, re-enacting its sins, till it recovers 'radical innocence'. Heaven, which the ghost would now recognise, is *cold*, both in
the purity of ice and fire (those Elizabethan antinomies) which initiates
the vision, and in its injustice. But the imagination turns back, for the
poet has taken the blame for his past 'out of all sense and reason'. He
has loaded himself with remorse without any justification; the meditation on death is no more than that, because he has transcended, in the
moment of vision, all contact with earth's reality.

IV

The transition from *Responsibilities* to the 'great period', which is
usually considered to cover the decade 1919–29, is marked by a new
series of events that 'rush upon' the poet 'like waves'. They appear now

---

[43] Some stupid thing that I had done
Made my attention stray. (*C.P.*, 288)

as more physically violent, more cosmic, less narrowly personal in their effects upon his life than those which we have been so far considering. The outbreak of the 'great war beyond the sea' ('Shepherd and Goatherd') is overshadowed by Hugh Lane's death on the *Lusitania*, and by the imminence of the North-South conflict that hardens into Sinn Fein's preparations for the 1916 Rising, and the preceding mutiny at the Curragh Camp which had seemed likely to support it. Then followed the Rising itself, 'that crazy fight' ('The O'Rahilly'), which was afterwards to crystalise into a central myth. The death of Robert Gregory gives material for the three elegies. Yeats's rejection by Iseult Gonne (now the poetic image of her mother), his marriage to Miss Hyde-Lees; the purchase of the Tower; these are all important. But he could hardly have foreseen, when he bought the Tower at Ballylee, how the chances of war and civil war would serve to set it up into such a multiplex and powerful emblem.

The destruction of the Great Houses, those ironic burnings which he half-believed were his responsibility, and which were to destroy, within a few years, the civilisation which he valued so greatly, is carried through into the even more brutal and senseless war between Free Stater and Republican. All these mirror, though faintly, the larger war, the falling apart of Europe with its ancient battlements. Yeats himself emerges into politics as a Senator of the new State, the 'sixty year old smiling public man'. All these help to make the poetic statement more profound and significant. There is now a total commitment of the poetic personality, for the concern with dramatic work is both less urgent and more closely fused with the poems; the problem, which he solved in several ways, was 'to keep his intensity'.

IV

'The Wild Swans at Coole'

GRAHAM MARTIN

*

He remains an artist by determination, even though he returns down-cast and defeated from the great quest of poetry . . . we are certain that somehow, somewhere, there has been disaster. He is empty now. He has the apparatus of enchantment, but no potency in his soul. He is forced to fall back upon the artistic honesty which has never forsaken him . . . it is an insufficient reserve.[1]

Middleton Murry's review of *The Wild Swans at Coole* must rank as one of the strangest misjudgements in the history of modern criticism. In 1919, far from being 'empty now', Yeats was on the threshold of his greatest achievements. And even if *Wild Swans* contains few hints of this, in comparison with any previous collection of lyrics, it must surely have seemed newly rich and various. Admittedly, some poems express exhaustion or defeat, and one or two others complain of the sacrifices which the artist had had to demand of the man, but Murry's sweeping diagnosis rests on more than these poems. He assumes that the volume as a whole, represented in these poems, faithfully expresses Yeats's state of mind in or about 1919; and this assumption, in a more sophisticated form, has persisted. It has become usual, that is, to examine each Yeats collection as made up of poems chosen and ordered to express specific themes; as having, therefore, quasi-artistic identity and meaning. Yet, granting that Yeats planned each volume with great deliberation, what does this really amount to? How far can authorial rearrangement of relatively short poems written over a number of years really affect the primary chronological relationship between them? The answer will vary with the collection, but the question needs always to be asked. And in the case of *Wild Swans* it quickly becomes evident that the poems Murry reviewed are much too various to

---

[1] J. M. Murry, *Countries of the Mind* (1922).

express anything simple or definite about Yeats in 1918–19—without, at least, certain preliminaries.

There were, in fact, two *Wild Swans* volumes: a Cuala edition of twenty-nine poems and the play *At the Hawk's Well*, published on 17 November 1917; and a Macmillan edition of forty-six poems, published on 11 March 1919—this now appears, dated 1919, in *Collected Poems*—and in both volumes Yeats took trouble about the selection and order of the poems.[2] The omission from both of 'Easter 1916', written in September 1916, is well known.[3] Other Rising poems of the next year were also delayed,[4] not appearing in book form till 1921 in *Michael Robartes and the Dancer*. Some personal poems written before 1917 only appeared in the 1919 volume, while others written during 1918–19 were delayed till 1921. Similarly, as to order, the poems of the Cuala edition are in unchronological sequence, and the Macmillan additions were disposed in two groups, before and after a central block taken over from the earlier volume. While poems in the second group were all written about 1918–19, the first mixes together poems from 1918, poems from 1917 but not then published, and poems published in 1917 but written before it. Here is precisely the sort of evidence from which Hugh Kenner concluded that Yeats's book-making was no casual affair; and pursuing this approach, John Unterecker's commentary on the Macmillan volume assumes that the order of the poems expresses a *meaningful* design—'Death, Life, and the Patterns of Life and Death. Yeats's Masks are Survivor, Defeated Lover, and Scholar.'[5]

But against this, one must first set the implications of the compositional history. The forty-six poems of the Macmillan volume were written over seven years from January 1912 to January–February 1919. Two peaks of creative output in 1915 and 1918 each account for about half the total, the other half being spread fairly evenly over the remaining five years. Not only is this the longest span covered by a single collection, it comes from the period when Yeats's poetry was undergoing its most radical developments. At one end there are about twelve poems from 1912 to 1914, stylistically similar to their contemporaries in *Responsibilities*; and at the other, eight poems from

[2] Allan Wade, *A Bibliography of the Writings of W. B. Yeats* (2nd ed., 1958), pp. 122, 127.

[3] For dates of composition, see Richard Ellmann, *The Identity of Yeats* (1954), pp. 289–90, and Saul, 101–16.

[4] So was the political play *The Dreaming of the Bones*. See *Letters*, 626.

[5] Hugh Kenner, 'The Sacred Book of the Arts', *Sewanee Review*, LXIV, (1956) 574–90; John Unterecker, *A Reader's Guide to W. B. Yeats* (1959), p. 131.

1918 to 1919 closely resembling the bulk of *Michael Robartes and the Dancer*, whose contents were all but completed by the time the Macmillan volume appeared. Any argument for the unity of the 1919 volume must take these points into account. The Cuala volume, on the other hand, is, by the same reasoning, relatively homogeneous. Of its twenty-nine poems, only one[6] was not certainly written between January 1912 and October 1916; and the majority (twenty) fall between May 1914 and October 1916, a period which also includes the composition of *At the Hawk's Well*. Between the earliest and latest poems ('Upon a Dying Lady' and the title-poem) there is certainly marked development, but the volume as a whole shows a more uniform idiom than that of its successor. Its unity, correspondingly, is easier to establish. And to be more concrete about 'style'—though both volumes include several Yeatsian 'kinds', this is very strikingly the case in the Macmillan collection. There are (1) the dense symbolic mode of the title-poem, or of 'The Double Vision of Michael Robartes'; (2) the formal-occasional mode (not yet, as it will be, integrated with the symbolic) of the Beardsley, Pollexfen and Gregory elegies; (3) (*pace* John Unterecker on Yeats's Masks) the relatively *un*-dramatised personal lyrics (contrast with the series to Maud Gonne, a later group like 'A Man Young and Old'); (4) the two pastoral ballads; and (5) the discursive-didactic sports, 'Ego Dominus Tuus' and 'The Phases of the Moon'. No other collection is so varied. Whatever unifying design may be claimed for the volume has to be set against a strong impression of experiment and development both within a given 'kind'—from 'Upon a Dying Lady' (1912–14) to 'In Memory of Major Robert Gregory' (1918); and from one 'kind' to another—from the simpler to the more complex personal poems, from 'On Woman' (1914) through 'The Wild Swans at Coole' (1916) to 'The Phases of the Moon', (1919). What matters, in fact, is not that many of these poems have themes in common, but the quality of 'realisation' for a given 'kind' or date. And this varies so widely that only by violent abstraction can one find evidence for a meaningful design.

Finally, there is the complex biographical fact that between the 'making' of the two volumes Yeats married and began work on what became *A Vision*. As one would expect of a poet so autobiographical and so deeply immersed (as by this time Yeats was), in the poetic

[6] 'The Balloon of the Mind.' Published September 1917, but it versifies an image from *Reveries Over Childhood and Youth*, completed during 1914. See *Auto.*, 41.

expression of 'abstract ideas',[7] the 1919 volume directly reflects both events. But there is also an indirect reflection equally responsible for differences between the Cuala and Macmillan poems. It arises from the connection between Yeats's marriage and the genesis of *A Vision*, which was so close as to have constituted a sort of marriage between two different parts of Yeats's mind. To explain this, a brief recapitulation of some familiar facts is necessary.

There is, first, the personal story of Yeats's relationship during the *Wild Swans* period with Maud and Iseult Gonne, which terminated in his marriage to Georgie Hyde-Lees. Despite Maud's withdrawal in 1909 from the 'spiritual marriage' she had agreed to after her estrangement from her husband,[8] Yeats kept up a close friendship with her during 1910–16, and also became sentimentally attached to Iseult. After Major MacBride's death in the Rising, Yeats again proposed to Maud, and was again rejected. In 1916–17 he proposed twice to Iseult, the second time within a few weeks of his acceptance in October 1917 by the future Mrs. Yeats,[9] whom he had known since 1914. Poems reflect all three situations. The largest group, dating from about 1915, celebrate the 'phoenix', and the lover's faithfulness to her; a smaller group, mainly from 1916 to 1917, register the poet's interest in Iseult; another group from 1918 (many not appearing till *Michael Robartes . . .*, however) reflect his marriage. Ageing is a theme common to many of these poems (Yeats was 50 in June 1915), but in each group the stress is very different. In most poems to Maud the fact of age means a loyalty sustained, a hard victory over time and change; in those to Iseult it means lost vitality, shrinking horizons, the pain of accepting these;[10] and this mood dominates the 1917 volume. But in the third group the ageing theme has been transformed. Age is now evidence of maturity and settlement, of an affirmed continuity between past and present. In the 1919 volume this new note complicates, and even contradicts, the prevailing spirit of its predecessor.

[7] In September 1914 Yeats wrote: 'What you say is true about abstract ideas. They are one's curse and one has sometimes to work for months before they are eliminated, or till the map has become a country. Yet, in some curious way, they are connected with poetry or rather with passion, one half its life and yet its enemy.' *Letters*, 588.

[8] Virginia Moore, *The Unicorn, William Butler Yeats's Search For Reality* (1954), pp. 197–202.

[9] Joseph Hone, *W. B. Yeats 1865–1939* (2nd ed., 1962), pp. 303–5; Richard Ellmann, *The Man and the Masks* (1949), p. 222; *Letters*, 632–3.

[10] See especially 'Owen Aherne and His Dancers', written October 1917, not published till June 1924 (as 'The Lover Speaks' and 'The Heart Replies').

Secondly, and this is less easy to summarise, there is the 'philosophical' situation over the same period. It begins in 1912 with Yeats's psychic researches, and serious reading in More, Glanvil and Swedenborg,[11] studies directly reflected in the denouement of the new *Hour Glass* (published 1913), in 'Swedenborg, Mediums and Desolate Places', and 'Witches and Wizards in Irish Folk Lore' (1913–14),[12] and in the early drafts of *Per Amica Silentia Lunae* (early 1914). Richard Ellmann links the latter, especially its evasive attitude towards the reality of the spirit-world, with Yeats's ambiguous exchanges with Leo Africanus, the spirit who accosted him through séances.[13] The debate of 'Ego Dominus Tuus' reflects this, and more generally, throughout these years, Yeats's tenacious search for spiritual certainty and failure to find it. Two Cuala poems from 1914 possibly register the theme in their disparagement of wisdom, and 'Lines Written in Dejection' (?October 1915) records a mood of spiritual exhaustion. There is also *At the Hawk's Well*, written during the winter of 1915–16, and an integral part of the Cuala volume.[14] Its closing lyrics (which ought, incidentally, to be more prominent in accounts of Yeats's writing in this decade) summarise its theme:

> Come to me, human faces,
> Familiar memories;
> I have found hateful eyes
> Among the desolate places,
> Unfaltering, unmoistened eyes.

> . . . O lamentable shadows,
> Obscurity of strife!
> I choose a pleasant life
> Among indolent meadows;
> Wisdom must live a bitter life. (*C.Pl.*, 219)

[11] Ellmann, *Masks*, pp. 197–200; Moore, p. 218, gives 1911–16 for the period of spiritualist investigation.

[12] Yeats's feeling about these essays may be judged from his comment in a letter to Lady Gregory, dated 20 January 1919, in whose *Visions and Beliefs in the West of Ireland* (1920) they appeared: 'I have 3 books coming out: (1) *Two Plays For Dancers* (Cuala), (2) *Cutting of Agate* (with new essays), (3) *Swans at Coole*, and the Stage Society are to do *Player Queen* and I am hoping that *Visions and Beliefs* will come to crown all.' Cited Hone, p. 316.

[13] Ellmann, *Masks*, pp. 201–3; but Moore, p. 218, disagrees.

[14] The Cuala volume prints the poems in a continuous series, and makes no typographical distinction between poems and play. The Macmillan volume begins a new poem on a new page.

'Come to me, *human* faces . . . *Wisdom* must live a bitter life'—the Cuala volume ends on this note of the frustration and disappointment of the searching visionary, whether Cuchulain or the Old Man.[15] Here is the 'philosophical' counterpart to the 'personal' note struck in the Maud-Iseult groups of poems. Yeats was later to describe *Per Amica Silentia Lunae* as '. . . part of a *religious system* more or less logically worked out',[16] so that it is worth noting that though begun in 1914 it was not completed till 1917, a year after *At the Hawk's Well*, and several months after the latest of the Cuala poems. The Cuala volume thus expresses a definite stage in Yeats's difficult progress towards the certainties of *A Vision*.

As a successor to *Per Amica*, Yeats planned an extension of More's concept of the after-life, but the automatic handwriting of November–December 1917 gave birth to the more ambitious *Discoveries of Michael Robartes*, which in its turn grew into *A Vision*,[17] sub-titled in its 1925 edition as *An Explanation of Life*. The 1919 volume includes several poems written during *A Vision*'s seminal period, sharing its symbolism, which take the place of *At the Hawk's Well* in the Cuala volume. The collection ends, therefore, not in lamenting the 'obscurity of strife' from which only 'idiots' fail to turn away, but in poems recording visionary knowledge—'The Phases of the Moon' and 'The Double Vision of Michael Robartes'. Just as the 'marriage' poems (direct and indirect) alter the 'personal' emphasis of the 1917 volume, so the new *Vision* group reverse its 'philosophical' spirit, speaking of achievement instead of laborious effort or defeat. Thus, in both volumes, personal experience and intellectual searchings make similar contribution, and the close relationship that this suggests is confirmed in the auto-biographical 'The Gift of Harun Al-Rashid',[18] whose philosophical lover finds that his new esoteric wisdom actually derives from his marriage:

[15] Helen H. Vendler in *Yeats's VISION and the Later Plays* (1963), pp. 203–16, thinks the play affirms Cuchulain's heroism. F. A. C. Wilson in *Yeats's Iconography* (1960), pp. 27–72, thinks it a 'profoundly disillusioned and pessimistic play' (33). Birjit Bjersby in *The Cuchulain Legend* (1950), pp. 40, 93, also argues that both protagonists are cheated. Both conclusions seem too emphatic; the Musicians express the concluding balance of feeling, but Cuchulain's affirmative cry—'He comes! Cuchulain, son of Sualtim, comes!' should be remembered.

[16] *Letters*, 627.

[17] Ellmann, *Masks*, pp. 224–5; Hone, p. 309; *Letters*, 644 and n.

[18] Dated 1923, but Yeats was thinking of a narrative poem early in 1918, i.e. during or just after the genesis of *A Vision*. See Hone, p. 308.

All, all those gyres and cubes and midnight things
Are but a new expression of her body . . .
A woman's beauty is a storm-tossed banner;
Under it wisdom stands, and I alone—
Of all Arabia's lovers I alone—
Nor dazzled by the embroidery, nor lost
In the confusion of its night-dark folds,
Can hear the armed man speak. (*C.P.*, 519)

The inner reconciliation which this implies accounts for the less explicit differences between Cuala and Macmillan poems: the alterations of tone, the robuster, more complex approaches to common themes. The 1919 volume therefore consists of poems drawn from two distinctly different phases in Yeats's development. It is not a unity but a mixture, and Yeats's final arrangement represents an authorial scheme which overrides the real character of the poems.[19] The more detailed discussion that follows is accordingly divided into two sections: one on the poems of the Cuala volume and a second on the new poems added for the Macmillan edition.

Taken chronologically, the Cuala poems roughly follow the curve of the poet's biographical experience. 'On Woman', 'The Dawn', 'The Fisherman' of 1914, 'Her Praise', 'The People', 'His Phoenix' of January 1915 display the rhythmic vigour, inner buoyancy, and (occasionally) the satiric verve of the *Responsibilities* poems. But with 'The Collar Bone of a Hare' (July 1915), 'Lines Written in Dejection', and 'Broken Dreams' (both of October), failure or loss begin to dominate a tone which persists, though with qualifications, through 1916 in 'Men Improve with the Years' (July) and 'The Wild Swans at Coole'. ('A Song' in 1915 and 'The Living Beauty' in July 1917, published in the Macmillan volume, belong to this phase.) In the characters of resolute Cuchulain and defeated Old Man, *At the Hawk's Well* (winter 1915–16) juxtaposes the earlier and later states of feeling in an unresolved tension.[20] 'Ego Dominus Tuus' (October–December

[19] e.g. Unterecker, p. 135, speaks of 'The Collar Bone of a Hare' (July 1915) and the adjacent 'Under the Round Tower' (March 1918) as having 'precisely parallel' themes, without noting the later poem's greater strength and maturity. The difference between them well represents the order of difference between the Cuala volume and the Macmillan additions.

[20] Yeats completed *Reveries Over Childhood and Youth* in December 1914. Ellmann (*Masks*, p. 219) links its closing sentences—'all life weighed in the scales of my own life seems to me a preparation for something that never happens.' (*Auto.*, 106)—with the conclusion of the first draft of *At the Hawk's*

1915)[21] combines a Cuchulain-like tone of heroic dedication with inner questionings (even uncertainties) about the chosen goal, a complexity briefly anticipated in 'The Fisherman', and directly related to the play's concern with the painful costliness of any sustained dedication, whether Cuchulain's for heroic achievement or the Old Man's for immortal life. The chronological movement from poem to play is foreshadowed in 'On Woman' and 'The Dawn', which prefer the life of the body and the feelings to that of the 'pedantry' of intellect. Thus, the earlier poems recount directly or simply experiences generalised or more deeply probed in the meditative-didactic works, whose analysis is then assimilated into the more complex personal poems of 1916. In rearranging this sequence for the Cuala volume Yeats makes explicit its faint pattern of meaning, beginning with the more generalised personal poems of 1916–17, returning to the earlier poems to explore their 'conclusions' in detail, and ending with 'philosophic' 'Dominus' and the play from the middle of the period of composition.

With the title-poem, discussion naturally turns on the meaning of the symbolic swans,[22] but this, finally, can only be decided by their

---

Well: 'Accursed the life of man—between passion and emptiness what he longs for never comes. All his days are a preparation for what never comes.' Wilson (*Iconography*, p. 60) thinks these lines summarise the poet's sexual and mystical disappointments of this period. The play was probably begun in autumn 1915. On 26 September, Yeats wrote: 'I have been wrapped up in a new play' (*Letters*, 601). This could only have been *At the Hawk's Well*, which was dictated to Pound 'early in 1916' (Ellmann, *Masks*, p. 215), and in rehearsal shortly after 5 March 1916 (*Letters*, 607). The change of mood recorded in the lyrics falls, therefore, between *Reveries* and the first work on the play.

[21] Ellmann, *Identity*, p. 290, dates 5 October; *Per Amica* gives December (*Myth.*, 324); Saul, 112, gives October and December for the respective dates of the first and second MSS.

[22] Both Vendler (pp. 171, 178) and Wilson (pp. 195, 198) link the poem with a note to *Calvary* (1920–1): '. . . such lonely birds as the heron, hawk, eagle and swan, are the natural symbols of subjectivity, especially when floating upon the wind alone or alighting upon some pool or river.' (*Four Plays for Dancers* (1921), 136). But—of the various post-*Vision* possibilities—what does 'subjectivity' mean? Wilson's answer to this leads him to the view that the poem is 'primarily concerned with reincarnation'. Vendler, supported by an early draft of *Calvary*, links it closely with the play's theme of 'the creative imagination'. A chronologically more appropriate passage occurs in a letter of 5 March 1916: '[Art] . . . often uses the outer world as a symbolism to express subjective moods . . . it seems to me that the song of the bird itself is perhaps subjective, an expression of feeling alone . . .' (*Letters*, 607).

relationship to the poem as a whole, which at least offers one a reasonably secure line of interpretation. The poem's speaker (the 'I' is, as usual, dramatic, not biographical) calls the swans 'lovers', upon whom 'passion or conquest *attend*' (the verb is as important as the nouns), and describes them as explosively vigorous, at one with the physical universe of water and air. To the speaker, the swans are also his youth, and the annual counting rite amounts to a familiar kind of magic which keeps him in illusory contact with it. When the swans lift from the lake they establish their independence of this personal meaning and two recognitions then follow: (1) that he must soon lose his present slight hold over 'passion or conquest'; but that (2) the swans will still delight other men, will nest and build in other lakes. In following their imaginary flight into a future which excludes him the speaker thus begins to transcend his own nostalgia and despair. The action of the poem[23] embodies his discovery that far from commanding the swans he is commanded by them and must resign himself to the situation they represent (for him): physical-emotional life as an order of transcendence. All the subsequent poems may be seen as exploring aspects of this condition, or trying to escape from it, attempts which the concluding play summarily dismisses in its final lyrics. Hearing the question: 'Who but an idiot would praise / Dry stones in a well?'—one remembers the 'brimming water among the stones' with the semi-divine swans floating upon it, careless of their solitary worshipper.

'Men Improve with the Years' introduces one alternative to the tyranny of swans: art. Instead of thoughts of 'passion or conquest', 'this lady's beauty' invites the calm appraisal one gives to a portrait; and the speaker, no longer in his 'burning youth', sees himself as a statue, an artist's creation, 'among the streams' but not of them. (Contrast the different stress in 'Enchanted to a stone / To *trouble* the living stream', from 'Easter 1916', written a few weeks later.) Explicitly ambivalent, the speaker both laments his lost youth and gives his present condition, power and dignity. But there is also an obscurity in the suggestion that 'dreams', and not simply old age, have brought him to this. What are these exhausting dreams about? Are they the idealising fantasies of the artist? But a marble triton is a strange image for being 'worn out'. Are they about youthful conquests which middle age cannot repeat? Or youthful failures which middle age would like to

---

[23] This 'progressive' structure is not in the text of first publication (*The Little Review*, June 1917), where the 'transcendent' stanza occurs in the middle, not at the end. (Numbering by the later text, the earlier runs 12534.)

make up for? Either of these leaves the connection with the artist unexplored. But though the poem's experience is not wholly in focus, its inner tension contains the seed of several later poems.

The next two poems introduce simpler, more unqualifiedly bitter laments. 'The Collar Bone of a Hare' contrasts a dreamt-of eternity of youthful love (as if men were swans) with the human reality of moral inhibition ('churches'), and death; and 'Lines Written in Dejection' speaks of a loss of imaginative or visionary energy.[24] 'Vision' is another alternative to the sway of nature, but the terms which here formulate it are unexpected: wavering bodies, leopards, angry tears, centaurs (cf. tritons, and 'A Thought from Propertius'), hills, sun and moon. 'Physical beauty, strong feeling, natural energies'—here is at least one level of meaning, whose implications link up with the poem's neighbours in the Cuala context. 'Lines' is the fourth of the volume's opening quartet of 'dejection' poems (i.e. post mid-1915), to be followed by 'The Dawn', which makes the transition to the affirmative energy of its successors, 'On Woman' and 'The Fisherman'. These, in their turn, separately initiate the two themes (love and poetry) which are interlinked in the succeeding lyrics to Maud Gonne. Thus (in Cuchulain-like mood) 'On Woman' welcomes reincarnation because the lover will

> . . . find what once I had
> And know what once I have known,
> Until I am driven mad,
> Sleep driven from my bed,
> By tenderness and care,
> Pity, an aching head,
> Gnashing of teeth, despair;
> And all because of some one
> Perverse creature of chance,
> And live like Solomon
> That Sheba led a dance. (*C.P.*, 165-6)

Whatever 'pedantry' may say, this is the substance of Solomon's

---

[24] See Ellmann, *Masks*, pp. 194-5; and Moore, p. 247. Thomas Parkinson argues plausibly that the subject is Yeats's disappointment with the failure of the Abbey Theatre's heroic phase, but nevertheless concludes that '. . . it is privately elliptic, obscure, allegorical in the most infuriating and abstract manner and altogether fails to communicate its proper meaning. The words, in fact, mean less than the aura of mystic import would lay claim to meaning.' ('The Sun and the Moon in Yeats's Early Poetry', *Modern Philology*, L (1952), 54.) The *Wild Swans* context helps to dissipate this vagueness.

wisdom.[25] So also 'The Dawn' rejects 'pedantic Babylon's' approach to
moon, sun and stars, preferring an ignorance that only wants to enjoy
their beauty. But 'The Dawn's' tone is very unlike that of 'On Woman'.
Instead of the latter's buoyantly assertive

> May God be praised for woman
> That gives up all her mind,
> A man may find in no man
> A friendship of her kind (C.P., 164)

the opening lines of 'The Dawn' stray and linger as if any decision were
too like 'pedantry' to be tolerable:

> I would be ignorant as the dawn
> That has looked down
> On that old queen measuring a town
> With the pin of a brooch, (C.P., 164)

Subtle interlinkings of rhyme and metre overlay the firm rejection of
the withered astronomers, which prepares for the poems that follow,
with a languid, even exhausted tone reminiscent of the 'dejection'
mood of 'Lines'. But why, by introducing the shift in feeling between
'Lines' and 'On Woman', did Yeats make a transitional poem necessary?
As in several cases, the more explicit *At the Hawk's Well* gives the clue.
The Musicians open the play and prefigure the juxtaposition of Cuchulain and the Old Man with a formal dialectic of attitudes represented in
the couplet:

> The heart would be always awake
> The heart would turn to its rest. (C.Pl., 209)

In the opening 'dejection' poems, however protestingly, the heart is
turning to its rest, whereas in the succession of poems from 'On Woman'
forwards the 'blind stupefied heart' is very much awake. In both phases
its experience remains the source of reality, but the attitude towards this
changes, and 'The Dawn' is the first poem to find pleasure in a condition
sadly or bitterly contemplated by its predecessors, yet to voice this in
terms ('I would be . . .') appropriately unemphatic. That the volume
opens with 'dejection' rather than 'Cuchulain' poems underlines, of
course, where the balance of feeling will finally lie.

Two short poems touch on the themes of the Maud series—in 'The

---

[25] See Wilson, pp. 276–83, for comments on the Solomon-Sheba symbolism,
and note that 'The Gift of Harun Al-Rashid' finally overcomes the opposition
between wisdom and love.

Hawk' the conflict between the claims of friendship and the distracting fantasies of the 'yellow-eyed hawk of the mind';[26] and in 'Memory', the past's power over immediate present experience. The poems that follow, though they incidentally commemorate and reaffirm a past love, are equally concerned to analyse it for its meaning. Incidents are recalled, but they are also questioned. It is as if the poet is exploring his experience for those qualities which can survive nature's threat of ageing and decay. The beloved in 'Her Praise' is not remembered in the fashionable literary world, with its lack of memory and sustaining purpose, but in a timeless landscape of wind and thorn, by beggars for whom her kindness has become a legend. In 'The People' she is a 'phoenix' (i.e. of, yet beyond nature), with the 'purity of a natural force', with semi-political authority over both the poet's mind and the lover's heart. 'His Phoenix' and 'A Thought from Propertius' advance her deification on traditional lines of literary and classical myth. 'Broken Dreams' is more complex. Reversing the idealising movement of its predecessors, it introduces the actual ageing woman ('There is grey in your hair . . .'), and the immediate presence of the poet as an ageing lover. The repeated 'Vague memories, nothing but memories' suggests first that memory is inadequate to the task of recalling her perfect beauty, but then that this matters less than the imperfect actuality of the 'hands (that) were not beautiful. . . . Leave unchanged / The hands that I have kissed, / For old sake's sake.' And the last lines

> All day in the one chair
> From dream to dream and rhyme to rhyme I have ranged
> In rambling talk with an image of air:
> Vague memories, nothing but memories (C.P., 174)

replace the ideal figure of the stubbornly passionate poet with an actual man groping vaguely into his vanished past. 'Broken Dreams' thus insists that it *is* art, less real than experience, yet also a way to rescue experience from the vague idealisations of memory. It is both 'rambling talk with an image of air' and a formal structure commemorating an actual experience—the experience of recalling his vanished love. The

---

[26] Unterecker, p. 40, notes the regular connection between Cuchulain, a Yeats Mask, and the hawk symbolism, but not the changes of attitude which went with it. In *On Baile's Strand*, Cuchulain and the hawk are at one; in *At the Hawk's Well*, they are antagonists, if not enemies; while in 'Meditations in Time of Civil War', the hawk symbolises the forces that threaten to destroy the poet.

poem is as much about itself as about love, and demonstrates in practice the general idea proposed in 'Men Improve with the Years'.

'The Balloon of the Mind' and 'To a Squirrel' introduce the final group—the first returning the poet from the world of 'mind' to that of sense; the second reminding him that death is as much a part of nature as love. Two elegies follow. 'In Memory of Alfred Pollexfen' laments not only the relative, but more generally that 'a *man* should die', and the poet becomes spokesman for the commonest human defence against impermanence, the ties of place and family. (cf. *At the Hawk's Well*, 'I choose a pleasant life . . .') 'Upon a Dying Lady' confronts death not so much as everyman's natural end, but as an immediate threat to be lived with, a general condition made explicit by fatal illness. There is an implicit parallel here with the love poems, both in the combination of analytic intent and commemorated incident; and in the values which the poet discovers. As the lover needs loyalty and courage to sustain his passion, so Mabel Beardsley faces death with stoical gaiety, with a passionate defiance encouraged by art rather than religion (a position formally approved in poem 3). Finally, 'Ego Dominus Tuus' sets the artist-visionary's dedication against the unsatisfactory transitoriness of life, which the 'common dream' of happiness disguises, but, to those intent on 'reality', cannot hide. Yet here again the 'vision of reality' affirmed by art is strangely formulated.[27] Despite the atmosphere of Faustian conjuration, of ascetic withdrawal from life's ordinariness, *Ille* looks for the complete self-fulfilment which 'modern hope' denies. His model, 'The chief imagination of Christendom, / Dante Alighieri, *so utterly found himself* . . .', and the result was less the Beatific Vision than lasting cultural power over successive generations. Moreover, the secret will reveal itself, not in study or cloister, but on 'wet sands by the edge of the stream'; and since the wisest writers 'Own nothing but their blind, stupefied hearts', *Ille*'s goal seems a truth not very different from Solomon's. *Ille*'s passionate self-dedication is also a more extended example of the poet's scornful dismissal of the real world in 'The Fisherman', or 'His Phoenix', or the lover-poet's search for the ideal elements in his beloved. 'Ego Dominus Tuus' thus generalises the implications of

[27] Yeats used the phrase in a letter of September 1914: '. . . the poet seeks truth, not abstract truth, but a kind of vision of reality which satisfies the whole being. It will not be true for one thing unless it satisfies his desires, his most profound desires. Henry More . . . argues . . . that all our deep desires must be satisfied and that we should reject a philosophy that does not satisfy them. I think the poet reveals truth by revealing those desires' (*Letters*, 588).

these earlier poems. Estranged from, yet affirming man's life in nature, the artist-visionary seeks a reality as 'spiritual' as the lover's loyalty to a spiritualised mistress, which remains the source of value, the only lasting alternative to the superficialities of the 'common dream'. In the play there is a similar juxtaposition of the 'pleasant life' envisaged in the closing lyric with the wasted patience of the Old Man, and Cuchulain's heroically vain commitment to a doomed life. But where the poem endorses *Ille*'s aspiration, the play regards both of its questing 'idiots' from the point of view of the choric Musicians. In the end, neither vision, nor art, nor heroic achievement are worth the sacrifice they entail. This, at least, is the question that we are left with at the end of the Cuala volume.[28]

★   ★   ★

The Macmillan additions include a quartet of consecutive lyrics based on Yeats's relationship with Iseult Gonne, three written before his marriage and one after, which conveniently illustrate the most immediate difference between the Cuala and Macmillan poems: tone. Consider the rhythmic contrast between

> My dear, my dear, I know
> More than another
> What makes your heart beat so;
> Not even your own mother
> Can know it as I know, ('To a Young Girl' (1913–15))
> (*C.P.*, 157–8)

and

> Dear fellow-artist, why so free
> With every sort of company,
> With every Jack and Jill?
> Choose your companions from the best;
> Who draws a bucket with the rest
> Soon topples down the hill. ('To a Young Beauty' (1918))
> (*C.P.*, 157)

Equally striking is the more explicit contrast of attitude between the melancholy refrain 'O who could have foretold / That the heart grows old?' ('A Song', 1915), the resigned conclusion that 'The living beauty is for younger men' ('The Living Beauty', ?July 1917), and the last verse of 'To a Young Beauty':

[28] cf. 'We artists ... are, as seen from life, an artifice, an emphasis, an uncompleted arc perhaps. Those whom it is our business to cherish and celebrate are complete arcs ... We are compelled to think and express and not to do' (*Auto.*, 475). But Yeats was to find this role more difficult to live than to define.

> . . . I know what wages beauty gives,
> How hard a life her servant lives,
> Yet praise the winters gone: (*C.P.*, 157)

Once the painful reminder of his lost youth, Iseult is now the poet's fellow artist,[29] a transformation which, with the hard-earned detachment of 'I know what wages beauty gives', or the crisply-buoyant 'praise', shows how Yeats has transcended the earlier opposition between man and artist. How does this reconciliation show, then, in the two main groups of new Macmillan poems? For the poems connected with *A Vision*, the answer is straightforward. Where, in the Cuala volume, 'Ego Dominus Tuus' merely searched for art's 'vision of reality', the new poems expound its nature. In 'Dominus', *Ille*'s quest entailed withdrawal from the 'common dream', but in the Macmillan volume, the immediately following 'A Prayer on Going into My House' states that whatever the poet dreams 'is a *norm*'. 'The Phases of the Moon' then recounts the dream's content; an animal fable in 'The Cat and the Moon' uses its central dogma; short dramatic lyrics develop some of its detail; and 'The Double Vision of Michael Robartes' rounds the group off by expressing the poet-visionary's gratitude for his new long-sought knowledge. These poems fulfil what, in the 1917 volume, *At the Hawk's Well* had half negated: the heroic aspiration of 'Ego Dominus Tuus'. But what does this fulfilment mean?[30] Despite its 'spiritual' penumbra, 'Dominus' is more concerned with the artist's psychology than the vision he discovers; and correspondingly, whatever further metaphysical claims the new *Vision* poems make, the peculiar nature of the artist's experience is still their centre. In 'A Prayer', the poet takes possession of the tower both as 'passionate' man, and as dreamer, or image-maker. In 'Phases', writing from within the tower, he dramatises his artist's identity (suggested in the references to Shelley and Milton) in the structure of the poem: the *personae* who recount his scheme supposing he will not understand it turn out to be puppets, a mere device of exposition, who vanish with the light the poet extinguishes when he has completed the poem. The key to the scheme is Phase 15, towards and away from which all other phases move.

[29] For a related change, but at a deeper level, contrast the balanced and paternal 'Michael Robartes and the Dancer' (1918) with 'Owen Aherne and His Dancers' (1917), which is full of unworked feeling.

[30] The following account is much indebted to Mrs. Vendler's discussion of *A Vision*, the only commentary which succeeds in avoiding tautologous dilution of Yeats's own terminology.

> . . . body and soul
> Estranged amid the strangeness of themselves,
> Caught up in contemplation, the mind's eye
> Fixed upon images that once were thought;
> For separate, perfect, and immovable
> Images can break the solitude
> Of lovely, satisfied, indifferent eyes. (C.P., 186)

All other types of human experience are seen in relation to this, the condition of creative trance, of estrangement from everything but 'images (in) the mind's eye', under the full moon. In 'The Cat and the Moon' the creature's 'animal blood' is both 'troubled' and controlled by the moon's 'pure cold light'—the other-world of the imaginative intellect, permanent even in its changes. In the 'Double Vision' the image which signalises the artist-visionary's release from the long tension of self-discovery is the dancing child, symbol of art's reconciliation of body and mind.[31] It is for this image that the speaker gives thanks. Where the Cuala volume voiced the artist's awareness of self-division these poems show his self-acceptance. The peculiar self-discipline his nature enforces, once protested against or painfully endured, has now been systematised as a general human condition represented in the lunar wheel, with its fated strugglings towards a brief balance and fulfilment. As 'A Prayer' promised, the artist's condition has been made (however sketchily) a 'norm' for all human endeavour.

The remaining new poems show the same situation in less explicit ways. Like 'Phases', and in contrast with the Cuala poems, several use *dramatis personae*. 'Under the Round Tower' re-expresses the theme of its fellow from the Cuala volume, 'The Collar Bone of a Hare', but with a new self-awareness conveyed in comic-dramatic terms. 'Tom O'Roughley', another dramatic ballad, is a more successful because less didactic handling of the pastoral contrast of nature and society in a poem like 'The Fisherman'. With its refrain, 'Or so did Tom O'Roughley say', Yeats disengages himself from Tom's opinions, and concentrates on the innocent joyfulness which is their real justification. Similarly, 'Shepherd and Goatherd' compares favourably with the earlier elegies, partly because of its dramatic character.[32] In the Beardsley

[31] See Frank Kermode, *Romantic Image* (1957), p. 59. The Dancer is one example of the Image which the artist constantly pursues.

[32] Yeats quotes the Goatherd's song in a note to *The Dreaming of the Bones* as an example of the 'dreaming back', an idea which he first describes in the Swedenborg essay of 1913, where the soul's visions are said to be '. . . earth-

poem, for example, Yeats is either too prominent or not prominent enough. Formally concerned with the character of a dying friend, he is also trying to define values which will steady his own courage in the face of the 'great enemy'. And the after-life he imagines for his subject suffers from this too-personal character (especially since he dismisses the one which, as a Roman Catholic, she might be supposed to imagine for herself.) In 'Shepherd and Goatherd' the consoling religious idea is not less eccentric, but the poem's dramatic formalism prevents its assuming a too-prominent position. The effect of the interchanges between the two singers is to concentrate all the attention on the dead man, and the bereaved living. The Shepherd asks his companion about his other-worldly knowledge because

> . . . it may be that your thoughts have plucked
> Some medicable herb to make our grief
> Less bitter. (C.P., 162)

And after both elegies have been sung, the Shepherd suggests they should be written out because

> To know the mountain and the valley have grieved
> May be a quiet thought to wife and mother,
> And children when they spring up shoulder-high. (C.P., 163)

No account of *Wild Swans* would be complete without some mention of its greatest poem, perhaps Yeats's first indisputably great poem, 'In Memory of Major Robert Gregory', but here the emphasis must fall upon its relationship to the other poems in the volume. If 'Phases' deals with the artist's special nature, the elegy shows him in his social role, affirming what he shares with all men, and, more completely than any other poem, reconciling the artist with the man. Thus, unlike the pastoral elegy, Gregory's death is not only (and perhaps even not primarily) a matter for grief, and its formal structure contributes something further than dramatic detachment or an appropriate decorum.

> Soldier, scholar, horseman, he,
> As 'twere all life's epitome.
> What made us dream that he could comb grey hair? (C.P., 151)

---

resembling life . . . the creation of the image-making power of the mind, plucked naked from the body, and mainly of the images in the memory' (*Explorations* (1962), p. 35). This interesting link with the mind's imaginative powers recurs in 'The Bounty of Sweden' (*Auto.*, 541). For the Platonic and Shelleyan sources, see F. A. C. Wilson, *W. B. Yeats and Tradition* (1958), pp. 200–5.

The death is here seen as a heroic apotheosis of the human activities that make life valuable. Yeats is, in effect, answering a question asked of the heroic Cuchulain in the play—'What were his life soon done? / Would he lose by that or win?'—and left unanswered by its refusal to decide finally between sensible survival and fatally resolute dedication to the ideal. In the elegy the hero's death is a victory—since to have survived would have been to 'comb grey hair'. Yet for this answer to be given the poet must survive—'damp faggots', to Gregory's 'single flare'—and in the context of the whole volume this image is full of interest, since it shows Yeats transcending and clarifying the obscure tension at the heart of a poem like the neighbouring 'Men Improve with the Years'. Torn in 1916 between nostalgia for his 'burning youth' and a dignified but ambiguous survival 'among the streams', in 1918 he objectifies the 'flare' in another man's completed life, accepting for himself the 'damp faggots' (which both burn *and* are watery) of a mundane continuity. The content of this 'dampness', moreover, is realised within the poem. The poet-survivor has a long memory, is tenacious of his many friendships, well immersed in the emotions of living—marriage, quarrels, setting up house, domestic routines. (In the words of the Musician, he has 'married and stays / By an old hearth'.) And just as Gregory-the-artist had, alive,

> . . . counselled us
> In all lovely intricacies of a house . . .
> All work in metal or in wood,
> In moulded plaster or in carven stone . . .

so the domesticated survivor commemorates him, not just as a friend, but as an artist. It will be recalled that 'Broken Dreams' was so constructed as to end in a reminder to the reader that a poem is what he has been reading, and 'In Memory . . .' has the same self-reflexive structure. On the one hand, the title gives its real business, but in the last verse we hear of a supposedly original intention to recall 'All those that manhood tried, or childhood loved / Or boyish intellect approved', i.e. of a general autobiographical scheme overcome in this most deliberate of poems by an allegedly spontaneous uprush of feeling; and a skilful use of detail (wind, shaking shutter,) returns us to the actual situation from which the poem began. This structural movement (a subtler version of the self-dramatisation conveyed in 'Phases') dramatises the poem's speaker as an artist, without losing the directness of his personal voice. It is then in the actual form of the elegy that the man and the artist meet.

Finally, 'In Memory' offers no other after-life than that provided in the memory of survivors like the poet and friend. What in 'Shepherd and Goatherd' exists as esoteric theory, 'In Memory' converts into exoteric poetic structure, one of art's 'monuments of unageing intellect'. And a brief contrast with the immediately preceding title-poem indicates how this corresponds to Yeats's firmer and deeper grasp of his attitude towards death. 'The Wild Swans' attempts an exploratory movement away from the ageing individual life towards other future lives, thus ensuring the permanence of 'passion or conquest', experiences which age is forcing the speaker to give up. 'In Memory' stands this situation on its head. The speaker survives the death of his friends, but by commemorating them in the artificial stability of his poem gives them a defined, and human, rather than merely swan-like eternity. The wistful nostalgias, the submerged yearnings of 'The Wild Swans' give way to a fully articulated meditation. 'In Memory' realises in detail the continuity which the earlier poem grasps at through symbols which, if not vague, remain hard to interpret with any certainty. The two poems confront one with, in Yeats's own words, the difference between 'the cry of the heart against necessity' and the 'knowledge and insight' which have come to terms with it.[33] It is as good a way as any to put the difference between the original Cuala volume and the poems that were added to it for the enlarged Macmillan publication.

[33] '. . . it is not the poetry of insight and knowledge, but of longing and complaint—the cry of the heart against necessity. I hope some day to alter that and write poetry of insight and knowledge.' (*Letters*, 63).

V

'Michael Robartes and the Dancer'

DONALD DAVIE

★

Michael Robartes and the Dancer is less intricately interrelated, and less powerfully made to serve a concealed unity, than some of Yeats's other collections. Indeed, a casual glance over these fifteen poems might see them as quite heterogeneous, their assembly merely fortuitous. In particular the collection might seem to fall between two stools, between on the one hand the extremely private life of man and wife in love and on the other hand the public life of politics and armed insurrection.

A second reading, however, reveals that all but two or three of the poems have one concern in common—the matter of woman's role in society. It is generally accepted that Professor Jeffares is right to identify the Queen of Sheba in the second poem of the collection 'Solomon and the Witch' with Yeats's wife; and it seems clear that Mrs. Yeats is likewise the woman in 'Under Saturn', 'Towards Break of Day', and 'An Image from a Past Life', as also, of course, in the tailpiece to the volume, where she is named. In 'A Prayer for My Daughter' the woman is Anne Butler Yeats, born 26 February 1919, though the poem makes mordant reference also to another woman, Maud Gonne. If George Brandon Saul[1] is right about the unsatisfactory poem, 'The Leaders of the Crowd', when he reads it as directed against the Dublin Bohemian circles frequented by Constance Gore-Booth Markievicz, then this poem joins 'On a Political Prisoner' (about Constance Markievicz in Holloway Gaol) and 'Easter 1916', where Constance Markievicz is remembered along with Pearse, MacDonagh, and Mac-Bride. And whereas the speaker in the title-poem need not be identified, as Professor Ellmann suggests, with Iseult Gonne, there is in any case no doubt that in this poem the question how a woman best fulfils herself is discussed more explicitly than in any other. Each of these poems gains greatly from being read in the context of the others; and thus

---

[1] *Prolegomena to the Study of Yeats's Poems* (Philadelphia, 1957), p. 119.

Michael Robartes and the Dancer, no less than other collections by Yeats, illustrates Hugh Kenner's contention that 'he was an architect, not a decorator; he didn't accumulate poems, he wrote books'.[2]

How this works can be seen best with what may seem to be the most dubious case among those I have cited, 'Easter 1916'. This poem is clearer when read in the collection than it is when read in isolation,[3] because only in the collection does one see why the woman involved in the 1916 Rising is given pride of place over the male leaders who paid for their participation with their lives. And, to take another example, those who read 'The Second Coming' in the *Nation* for 6 November 1920, or in *The Dial* for that same month, missed a dimension of the poem which appears when it immediately precedes 'A Prayer for My Daughter'; 'a rocking cradle' in the third line from the end takes on poignancy, and witnesses to personal involvement, when taken along with 'this cradle-hood and coverlid' in the second line of the poem which succeeds it—the ominous prophecy made in 'The Second Coming' is uttered, we are made to realise, by a man whose newborn child gives him a stake in the tormented future he prophetically sees.

Apart from the five lines of 'A Meditation in Time of War', only three poems in the collection refuse to fit this scheme. These are the two ballads, 'Sixteen Dead Men' and 'The Rose Tree', and the poem 'Demon and Beast'. The ballads about the Rising obviously belong as corollaries to 'Easter 1916'. But 'Demon and Beast' is a more curious case, which deserves to be considered at some length.

'Demon and Beast' is an exception among the poems of *Michael Robartes and the Dancer*. But then, it would have been an exception in any of Yeats's collections, wherever it had appeared in his work, since it records a state of mind which the poet knows to be, for him, exceptional. 'The poem . . . describes how the artist is momentarily seduced by the beauty and profusion of nature into relinquishing his proper task. He is suddenly abandoned by the passions that ensured his subjectivity and his power to create; he grows objective—his mind becomes a vessel, instead of a vortex of energy, the fountain's basin instead of its abundant jet.'[4] As the terms 'subjective' and 'objective' suggest, 'Demon and Beast' can be glossed out of *A Vision* or the prolegomenon to that

[2] Hugh Kenner, 'The Sacred Book of the Arts', in *Irish Writing*, 31 (1955).
[3] For instance in the limited edition of twenty-five copies by Clement Shorter (1916); in *The New Statesman* for 23 October 1920; or in *The Dial* for November 1920.
[4] Peter Ure, 'Yeats's "Demon and Beast" ', in *Irish Writing*, 31 (1955).

symbolic system *Per Amica Silentia Lunae* (1917),[5] but I agree with
Peter Ure that 'in the poem the struggle is more broadly and more
poetically described as a war between extreme passions, the demon of
hatred and the beast of desire', both images for 'a state of intense self-
absorption and subjectivity'. That state—of intense self-absorption in
unremitting internal conflict—was not only the state which Yeats
thought natural to himself, but it was also the only state out of which,
so he maintained, a severe and worth-while art could be created. In
believing this Yeats aligned himself with the visionary painters of
nature, Blake's disciples Palmer and Calvert, not only against Wordsworth's 'heart / That watches and receives', but against Ruskin and
against his own friend Ezra Pound, and against any theory of poetry
which holds that the poet's attention to nature may sometimes be akin
to, for instance, the biologist's discipline of attentive and humble
observation. The poem is thus of capital importance in defining the
assumptions on which Yeats proceeded, and the challenging cost of
those assumptions—more important in the perspective of Yeats's *oeuvre*
as a whole than in the context of this particular collection. It is out of
place in this collection, but it would have been out of place anywhere;
and that, indeed, is just the point.[6]

With this exception, and the exception also of 'Sixteen Dead Men'
and 'The Rose Tree', all of *Michael Robartes and the Dancer* is devoted
to exhorting women above all to hate and avoid abstraction. The
emphasis is by no means new in Yeats, nor, of course, peculiar to him.
What is new is that Yeats, freed at last from his passion for Maud
Gonne with her distracting devotion to abstractions, is now able to see
woman as peculiarly responsible for escaping from 'what Blake calls
mathematic form, from every abstract thing, from all that is of the
brain only, from all that is not a fountain jetting from the entire hopes,
memories, and sensations of the body' (*E. & I.*, 292–3). It is worth
recalling this from *The Cutting of an Agate* (dated '1903–1915'), because
the stress there laid upon 'the body' explains why the female figure is
called 'the dancer'. Frank Kermode has shown[7] that this symbolic
significance investing the figure of the dancer was something that was
with Yeats from the 'nineties, when he shared it with Mallarmé. And

[5] See Cleanth Brooks, in *The Permanence of Yeats*, ed. Hall and Steinmann
(New York, 1950), pp. 80–81.
[6] For a brilliant exegesis of the poem (the last lines are particularly difficult
because so compact), see Ure, *loc. cit.*
[7] Frank Kermode, *Romantic Image* (1957).

to the extent that the dancer of the 'nineties was a female figure, with
Salome as prototype, the casting of woman in this crucial role was not
unprecedented in Yeats's writing. On the other hand, it is only at this
point that the body of the dancer is presented in all its corporeal vigour,
as much in the shamelessness which ends 'Solomon and the Witch' ('O!
Solomon! let us try again'), as in:

> While Michael Angelo's Sistine roof,
> His 'Morning' and his 'Night' disclose
> How sinew that has been pulled tight,
> Or it may be loosened in repose,
> Can rule by supernatural right
> Yet be but sinew. (*C.P.*, 198)

Though Yeats had yet to visit the Sistine Chapel, he had seen Michelangelo's 'Night' and 'Morning' in the Medici Chapel in Florence as
long ago as 1907; and yet it is only now that 'body', still opposed in
the abstract to 'mind' or 'thought' or 'spirit', takes substance in Yeats's
poetry through images taken from the great sculptor of the nude.

★   ★   ★

If at this point, however, we consult the first edition of *Michael
Robartes and the Dancer*, from the Cuala Press, we find that Yeats
apparently expected us to make much heavier weather of it. At least,
his Preface to that edition suggests as much:

> A few of these poems may be difficult to understand, perhaps more
> difficult than I know. Goethe has said that the poet needs all philo-
> sophy, but that he must keep it out of his work. After the first few
> poems I came into possession of Michael Robartes' exposition of the
> *Speculum Angelorum et Hominum* of Geraldus, and in the excitement
> of arranging and editing could no more keep out philosophy than
> could Goethe himself at certain periods of his life. I have tried to
> make understanding easy by a couple of notes, which are at any
> rate much shorter than those Dante wrote on certain of his odes
> in the *Convito*, but I may not have succeeded.

This seems to refer to a different book of poems from the one we have
been reading. Philosophical? Difficult to understand? Certainly 'Demon
and Beast' is both, and so, necessarily, are the gnomic verses called 'A
Meditation in Time of War'. But the poems to which Yeats supplies
notes are neither of these, but 'An Image from a Past Life' and 'The
Second Coming'. And as we learn to expect of Yeats's notes, these do

not 'make understanding clear', but only confound it. The notes to
'The Second Coming', for instance, speak of life as 'a double cone, the
narrow end of each cone being in the centre of the broad end of the
other'; they supply a neat diagram to illustrate this; and they explain
that within the double cone there are 'two gyres . . . two movements
which circle about a centre'. Moreover,

> the circling is always narrowing or spreading, because one move-
> ment or the other is always the stronger. In other words, the human
> soul is always moving outward into the objective world or inward
> into itself; and this movement is double because the human soul
> would not be conscious were it not suspended between contraries,
> the greater the contrast the more intense the consciousness . . .

This is familiar to any reader of *A Vision*. What is not clear is what it
has to do with the poem. We draw close to the poem only later:

> . . . This figure is true also of history, for the end of an age, which
> always receives the revelation of the character of the next age, is
> represented by the coming of one gyre to its place of greatest
> expansion and of the other to that of its greatest contraction. At the
> present moment the life gyre is sweeping outward, unlike that before
> the birth of Christ which was narrowing, and has almost reached
> its greatest expansion. The revelation which approaches will however
> take its character from the contrary movement of the interior gyre.
> All our scientific, democratic, fact-accumulating, heterogeneous
> civilisation belongs to the outward gyre and prepares not the con-
> tinuance of itself but the revelation as in a lightning flash, though in
> a flash that will not strike only in one place, and will for a time be
> constantly repeated, of the civilisation that must slowly take its place.

This does not help us to understand 'The Second Coming'; so far from
clarifying the poem before us on the page of *Michael Robartes and the
Dancer*, it replaces that poem by another which is narrower, more
hectoring and more idiosyncratic. There are lines from the poem—

> The best lack all conviction, while the worst
> Are full of passionate intensity . . .

or—

> Things fall apart; the centre cannot hold;
> Mere anarchy is loosed upon the world . . . (*C.P.*, 211)

which have seemed to speak memorably to the condition of men who
have not consulted Yeats's note, for whom 'scientific' and 'democratic'
might be hallowed words, as for the author of the note they are not.

The poem swings wide enough to embrace such readers; the different poem envisaged in the note excludes them. And the writer of the poem invites such readers. For his title, 'The Second Coming', invites into the poem all those who have had access to the Christian scheme of things as it is known far outside the circle of professing Christians. On the other hand, if we follow the implications of the note even a little way, into the theory of the Dionysian great year, we realise that 'The Second Coming' is a misnomer, even a deliberate trap, since for Yeats when he wrote the poem Christ's advent was not, as it is for Christians, the first coming of the divine into the human dimension. Behind it in time lay, for instance, that advent which he was to celebrate in 'Leda and the Swan'. Thus by his title the author of the poem invites many readers whom the writer of the note is to exclude.

And unfortunately the note to the Cuala edition was not the last gloss that Yeats was to write on his own poem. In his Introduction to *The Resurrection* (*Wheels and Butterflies*, 1934), after Yeats has told how as a boy he 'took satisfaction in certain public disasters, felt a sort of ecstasy at the contemplation of ruin', he asks himself:

> Had I begun *On Baile's Strand* or not when I began to imagine, as always at my left side just out of the range of the sight, a brazen winged beast that I associated with laughing, ecstatic destruction?
>
> (*Explorations*, 393)

And he adds in a footnote: 'Afterwards described in my poem "The Second Coming".' But, of course, it is not described in 'The Second Coming', where the beast is neither winged nor brazen:

> The Second Coming! Hardly are those words out
> When a vast image out of *Spiritus Mundi*
> Troubles my sight: somewhere in sands of the desert
> A shape with lion body and the head of a man,
> A gaze blank and pitiless as the sun,
> Is moving its slow thighs, while all about it
> Reel shadows of the indignant desert birds. (*C.P.*, 211)

It may be that we are refusing to read the poem which Yeats intended to write; but we can do no less, for the intention was never fulfilled. And if we follow the introduction to *The Resurrection* any farther, we find ourselves blurring this memorable and masterly poem into unsatisfactory Nietzschean plays of Yeats's youth, where a brazen beast is also seen in vision.[8]

[8] See Giorgio Melchiori, *The Whole Mystery of Art* (1960), pp. 35–43.

The two 'technical' terms in 'The Second Coming'—'gyre' and *'Spiritus Mundi'*—ought not to obscure the fact that the poem, as it stands in *Michael Robartes and the Dancer*, is self-explanatory. Poetically, all the meaning of the poem is in the calculated collision in the last line of the words 'slouches' and 'Bethlehem':

'Slouches towards Bethlehem to be born . . .'

What the poem says is that when the superhuman invades the human realm all that the human can say of it is that it is non-human: there can be no discriminating at such a time between subhuman and super-human, between bestial and divine. Whatever further gloss the poem may need can best be supplied by the poem which immediately follows it, 'A Prayer for My Daughter', which takes up from 'The Second Coming' not just 'cradle' but also 'ceremony', also 'innocence'. From a human point of view a time-scale of solar years can never be so affecting as a scale of decades, and those readers were surely not wrong who found the poem piercingly relevant between 1939 and 1945.

Yeats was not only the man who wrote the poems; he was also, unfortunately, the first and by no means the most intelligent of those who have attempted to explain them. This appears again with 'An Image from a Past Life', for Yeats's note to this poem does even more damage than his note to 'The Second Coming', and we resent it less only because there is less in the poem to be damaged:

. . . When I wrote 'An Image from a Past Life', I had merely begun my study of the various papers upon the subject, but I do not think I misstated Robartes' thought in permitting the woman and not the man to see the Over Shadower or Ideal Form, whichever it was.

One would like to believe that the whole business about the fictitious Michael Robartes, and his fictitious researches, is nothing more than an elaborate spoof. But although at times Yeats's tongue is undoubtedly in his cheek ('notes, which are at any rate much shorter than those Dante wrote'), at other times he writes in a grave tone which asks to be taken seriously. And if the long note is taken seriously, the poem cannot but collapse under the weight of it. In particular, one cannot help remembering how in a few years a poet was to express virtually the same perception as in Yeats's poem, without any fuss at all:

> O wha's the bride that cairries the bunch
> O' thistles blinterin' white?
> Her cuckold bridegroom little dreids
> What he sall ken this nicht.

For closer than gudeman can come
And closer to'r than hersel',
Wha didna need her maidenheid
Has wrocht his purpose fell.

O wha's been here afore me, lass,
And hoo did he get in?
—*A man that deed or was I born
This evil thing has din.*

MacDiarmid's poem suggests that 'An Image from a Past Life' might
have gone better into a folk-song or ballad-form like 'The Rose Tree',[9]
which is as fine an achievement as MacDiarmid's poem, and fine in the
same way, in having all personal manner purged away so as to seem
an anonymous product of the folk or the city street. However, although
in *The Wild Swans at Coole* Yeats had already begun casting some of his
best love poems into the form of songs (see 'Solomon to Sheba' from
that collection), his love poems in *Michael Robartes and the Dancer* are
cast in a more stilted, less satisfactory idiom.

★   ★   ★

In the Preface to the Cuala edition Yeats described himself, justly
enough, as one 'who has spent much labour upon his style'. Yet in 'The
Leaders of the Crowd', in 'Towards Break of Day', even in the title-
poem, it is possible to see an unsatisfactory strain between the sinewy
rapidity of the syntax and the vagueness of the diction. Writing to
H. J. C. Grierson in 1926, Yeats was to declare:

> The over childish or over pretty or feminine element in some good
> Wordsworth and in much poetry up to our date comes from the
> lack of natural momentum in the syntax. This movement underlies
> almost every Elizabethan and Jacobean lyric and is far more impor-
> tant than simplicity of vocabulary. If Wordsworth had found it
> he could have carried any amount of elaborate English. (*Letters*, 710)

Addressed as the letter is to Grierson, editor of Donne, the expression
'every Elizabethan and Jacobean lyric' must comprehend the poems of
Donne. And indeed the fruit of Yeats's study of Donne can be seen

[9] 'The Rose Tree' was written, according to Richard Ellmann, on 7 April
1917. It was published in the *Nation* for 6 November 1920, and in *The Dial* in
the same month.

many years before the letter was written, certainly as early as *Michael Robartes and the Dancer*:

> Was it the double of my dream
> The woman that by me lay
> Dreamed, or did we halve a dream
> Under the first cold gleam of day? (*C.P.*, 208)

'Towards Break of Day' does not live up to the promise of these, its opening lines. But the suppression of the relative pronoun, 'which' or 'that', is surely learned from Donne (though Pope could have taught it no less) and, together with the artful stringing of the words across line-breaks, it reveals what Yeats calls 'natural momentum in the syntax'. There is a similar energetic rapidity at the start of 'Michael Robartes and the Dancer':

> Opinion is not worth a rush;
> In this altar-piece the knight,
> Who grips his long spear so to push
> That dragon through the fading light,
> Loved the lady; and it's plain
> The half-dead dragon was her thought,
> That every morning rose again
> And dug its claws and shrieked and fought. (*C.P.*, 197)[10]

But here the expression 'her thought' is not weighty nor sharp enough to make its impact as the syntax whirls us past it. The rural-archaic or 'Shakespearian' flavour of 'not worth a rush' prepares us to take 'was her thought' as 'was in her thought'. We read the sixth line to mean 'It was the dragon she was thinking about', and only on a second reading do we grasp the intended meaning, 'It was her thought (or rather, her thinking) that was the dragon'. Yeats declares that with natural momentum in his syntax Wordsworth could have carried any amount of elaborate English; but here 'thought' is not so much elaborate English as slack English.

However, the rapid syntax finds appropriate diction in the splendid poem, too often overlooked, 'Under Saturn':

> Do not because this day I have grown saturnine
> Imagine that lost love, inseparable from my thought

[10] Jeffares thought the picture described was Bordone's St. George and the Dragon in the National Gallery, Dublin; but T. R. Henn suggests also Cosimo Tura's St. George and the Dragon, seen by Yeats in the Duomo at Ferrara in 1907.

Because I have no other youth, can make me pine;
For how should I forget the wisdom that you brought,
The comfort that you made? Although my wits have gone
On a fantastic ride, my horse's flanks are spurred
By childish memories of an old cross Pollexfen,
And of a Middleton, whose name you never heard,
And of a red-haired Yeats whose looks, although he died
Before my time, seem like a vivid memory.
You heard that labouring man who had served my people. He said
Upon the open road, near to the Sligo quay—
No, no, not said, but cried it out—'You have come again,
And surely after twenty years it was time to come.'
I am thinking of a child's vow sworn in vain
Never to leave that valley his fathers called their home. (*C.P.*, 202)

The reported speech, even the characteristically Irish intonation of that speech, are accommodated so effortlessly in these lines that the reader's ear supposes it to be *vers libre*. But, in fact, there is only one line, the penultimate one, which cannot be scanned as an alexandrine;[11] and I conceive that it is the ordering energy of syntax which sustains the rhythm through a measure which is notoriously too long for English breath to manage, normally.

It is not John Donne, however, who presides over 'Prayer for My Daughter', but another writer of 'Elizabethan and Jacobean lyric', Ben Jonson. In management of syntax and indeed in diction, too, Jonson, in many of his poems, is not readily distinguishable from his great contemporary. But in one genre which they both practised, the verse-epistle, Jonson can be distinguished from Donne because he is so obviously superior; and in these poems he is superior (so it has been argued) because Jonson was so much more at ease than Donne was in his relationship towards the patrons to whom verse-epistles are addressed. The poet-patron relationship had interested Yeats at least since *Responsibilities* (1914), and Ben Jonson is named in the tailpiece to that volume:

> While I, from that reed-throated whisperer
> Who comes at need, although not now as once
> A clear articulation in the air,
> But inwardly, surmise companions

[11] The elisions and/or substitutions—'mem'ries', 'lab'ring', 'you've' for 'you have', and so on—which by too scrupulous metrists are condemned as licentious in Yeats, are, in fact, decorous and proper in verse such as this which, like Donne's, is histrionic, miming impassioned speech.

Beyond the fling of the dull ass's hoof
—Ben Jonson's phrase—and find when June is come
At Kyle-na-no under that ancient roof
A sterner conscience and a friendlier home,
I can forgive even that wrong of wrongs,
Those undreamt accidents that have made me
—Seeing that Fame has perished this long while,
Being but a part of ancient ceremony—
Notorious, till all my priceless things
Are but a post the passing dogs defile. (C.P., 143)

In this passage it is not so much the line which names and quotes Jonson as it is the line about 'but a part of ancient ceremony', which looks forward by way of 'the ceremony of innocence' from 'The Second Coming', to 'A Prayer for My Daughter':

And may her bridegroom bring her to a house
Where all's accustomed, ceremonious;
For arrogance and hatred are the wares
Peddled in the thoroughfares.
How but in custom and in ceremony
Are innocence and beauty born?
Ceremony's a name for the rich horn,
And custom for the spreading laurel tree. (C.P., 214)

'Ceremony' is Yeats's word for what he values most in an aristocratic organisation of society, as he envisaged it on the model of his own relationship with Lady Gregory. It is part of what is implied in the elegy for Major Robert Gregory, the son of that noble house, when Gregory is called 'our Sidney', just as it is implied also in the many references to Urbino, and to Castiglione's record of the Renaissance court in such a city state. This was the relationship between poet and patron which Jonson celebrated in many of his verse-epistles, a relationship which he preferred to being patronised by the public at large, just as Yeats preferred it after his disappointments with the Abbey Theatre audiences, and with the Dublin city fathers who had tried to haggle about Hugh Lane's bequest of pictures.

In 'A Prayer for My Daughter' what stands out first as very like Jonson, and quite unlike Donne, is the treatment of classical myth:

Helen being chosen found life flat and dull
And later had much trouble from a fool,
While that great Queen, that rose out of the spray,
Being fatherless could have her way

Yet chose a bandy-leggèd smith for man.
It's certain that fine women eat
A crazy salad with their meat
Whereby the Horn of Plenty is undone. (*C.P.*, 212)

Classical mythology has been so much naturalised, has penetrated so far from the instructed *élite* among the folk, that classical references can be homely while still exalted. 'Being fatherless', for instance, has more to do with family life in rural Ireland than on Mount Olympus. And Jonson's classical erudition worked in just this way—towards a habituation, a *complete* translation of ancient Greece and Rome. The same neo-classicism at its Jonsonian best uses 'radical'—'radical innocence'—to link through its Latin etymology with the sustained imagery from vegetation.

But equally Jonsonian, and equally unlike Donne, is Yeats's un-embarrassed use of a literary property so hackneyed as the horn of plenty. The cornucopia, the laurel tree—no images are more hack-neyed. But that is only to say that none are more traditional. What Yeats achieves by them is just the effect that he attained in more modest compass and less surprisingly in 'The Rose Tree'. It is the effect of anonymity. And, in fact, no other effect would do, in a poem which celebrates above all the time-hallowed unwritten laws of social usage; the style, in other things besides imagery, is itself hallowed by usage—as it has to be, if style and content are not to pull apart. In thus demon-strating how on some occasions and for some purposes a hackneyed image is better than an 'original' image, in showing, too, how to move towards and rest among abstract words ('custom', 'ceremony', 'inno-cence' and 'beauty', all in the same two lines), this poem by Yeats is a standing challenge and reproach to some of the most cherished pre-judices of modern poetic theory, long incorporated into pedagogy. Just for this reason, no doubt, it is often overlooked.

In *The Death of Synge* ('Extracts from a Diary Kept in 1909'), Yeats wrote:

F- is learning Gaelic. I would sooner see her in the Gaelic movement than in any Irish movement I can think of. I fear some new absorp-tion in political opinion. Women, because the main event of their lives has been a giving themselves and giving birth, give all to an opinion as if it were some terrible stone doll. Men take up an opinion lightly and are easily false to it, and when faithful keep the habit of many interests. We still see the world, if we are of strong mind and body, with considerate eyes, but to women opinions become as their children or their sweethearts, and the greater their emotional capacity the more do they forget all other things. They grow cruel, as if in defence of lover or child, and all this is done for 'something other than human life'. At last the opinion is so much identified with their nature that it seems a part of their flesh becomes stone and passes out of life. (*Auto.*, 504)

This obviously is saying what 'A Prayer for My Daughter' was to say about Maud Gonne:

> An intellectual hatred is the worst,
> So let her think opinions are accursed.
> Have I not seen the loveliest woman born
> Out of the mouth of Plenty's horn,
> Because of her opinionated mind
> Barter that horn and every good
> By quiet natures understood
> For an old bellows full of angry wind? (*C.P.*, 213)

But it chimes also, because of the imagery of stone, with lines from 'Easter 1916':

> Too long a sacrifice
> Can make a stone of the heart. (*C.P.*, 204)

However, it is only in *Michael Robartes and the Dancer*, where Con Markievicz takes her station among so many other women, that this chime can be heard. Moreover, the assertion is made in 'Easter 1916' altogether more hesitantly and self-doubtingly than in either 'A Prayer for My Daughter' or *The Death of Synge*. For it comes only after the stone has been much discussed and much imaged in earlier lines:

> Hearts with one purpose alone
> Through summer and winter seem
> Enchanted to a stone
> To trouble the living stream.
> The horse that comes from the road,
> The rider, the birds that range
> From cloud to tumbling cloud,
> Minute by minute they change;
> A shadow of cloud on the stream
> Changes minute by minute;
> A horse-hoof slides on the brim,
> And a horse plashes within it;
> The long-legged moor-hens dive,

And hens to moor-cocks call;
Minute by minute they live:
The stone's in the midst of all. (*C.P.*, 204)

And here, although it is certainly the stream that is called 'living', and is associated with the lively and life-giving activities of sexual pairing ('hens to moor-cocks call'), yet the stone troubles the stream in a way which goes beyond the literal fact that it makes the running water eddy and popple. Moreover, the stream, with its unseizable mutability, the sliding and plashing which it induces, is clearly a much less stable and certain image to set against petrifaction than is the rooted and hidden tree which is set against it in 'A Prayer for My Daughter'. And the waterfowl which haunt the stream are no more like the linnet which haunts the tree than they are like the ducks of 'Demon and Beast' which are called 'absurd' and 'portly' and 'stupid'. They are called 'happy' also; but 'Demon and Beast' makes it plain that their happiness was bought on terms that were too easy, by a lax and passive abandonment to the course of nature. At this point, in fact, 'Easter 1916' goes past the point where exegesis can track its meaning. The imagery of stone and birds, rider and horse and stream, has a multi-valency which discursive language cannot compass—and this accrues to these images simply because of the beams which fall upon this poem out of the other poems in the same collection. Because Yeats holds and keeps faith in the discursive language, for instance by the sinewiness of his syntax, as his contemporaries Eliot and Pound do not, a moment like this when perceptions pass beyond the discursive reason is poignant in his poetry as it cannot be in theirs, and we do not dream of grudging him the right to acknowledge his defeat and to retire baffled before it, as he does in the last section of the poem.

On the other hand, up to 'Hearts with one purpose alone', the poem has been, though profound, straightforward. In a letter written to Lady Gregory on 11 May 1916, which shows Yeats already at work on the poem ('I am trying to write a poem on the men executed—"terrible beauty has been born again"' (*Letters*, 613)), Yeats reports what Maud Gonne thought of the Easter Rising: 'Her main thought seems to be "tragic dignity has returned to Ireland".' And through the first two sections of the poem this is the meaning which Yeats, too, is reading out of the event. In the refrain 'A terrible beauty is born', 'terrible' must surely point to Aristotle's definition of the tragic emotion as compounded of terror and pity; and so it strikes off against 'the casual comedy' and 'lived where motley is worn'. It is doubtless true that in the months before the Rising the Republican army was, in fact, a joke to the Dublin clubmen. But more than accurate reportage was involved for Yeats. It is a fact of literary history that the Anglo-Irish literary tradition since the seventeenth century, up to and including Synge, had scored all its most brilliant successes in comedy, even in stage-comedy; whereas Yeats, from the days of his youthful campaigning for the National Literary Society, had hoped and worked for an Irish literature that should be, on the contrary, heroic. That hope he had abandoned in 1912. The events of 1916, which proved that Irishmen were capable of a tragic gesture, seemed to show Yeats that he had abandoned hope too soon, and in the poem he seems to reproach himself for this. Yet does he, in fact, reproach himself? Certainly there is no evidence from elsewhere that the Rising made Yeats embrace with renewed enthusiasm the hopes he had entertained for Irish national culture in his youth. The truth is that the poem is an expression of self-reproach only so far as 'Hearts with one purpose alone'. At that point Yeats's reflections on the Rising move beyond Maud Gonne's, and only at that point does Yeats ask himself if the Rising makes him revise all his scheme of values. He decides that it does not; or rather, since the pity of the subject rules out any decisions being taken, he does not decide that it does. And this is perhaps the most impressive thing about the whole poem, with the impressiveness of a human utterance rather than a fashioned artifact—that the 1916 leaders are mourned most poignantly, and the sublimity of their gesture is celebrated most memorably, not when the poet is abasing himself before them, but when he implies that, all things considered, they were, not just in politic but in human terms, probably wrong.

VI

Style and World in 'The Tower'

JOHN HOLLOWAY

*

THE ostensibly modest purpose of this essay is to discuss, as it appears in *The Tower* (a representative later collection), Yeats's style. 'Modest' not only because the subject is limited in a way which precludes full discussion of the book, but also because much has been written about Yeats's style already, and one might think that another discussion must necessarily be jejune. 'Ostensibly' implied dissent from this: on two counts. The more far-reaching is that examination of style which goes to the roots of style, finds itself dealing with more than style. The expression 'style *and world*' is far from self-explanatory, but it hints at where the argument will go. The more obvious reason for employing the word 'ostensibly' is that what has been said hitherto about Yeats's later style requires not mere recapitulation, but correction and expansion: not modest tasks, but perhaps excessively ambitious ones.

T. R. Henn was one of the earlier critics to note that a major part of Yeats's achievement in his later poems was an 'achievement of style'; the expression is, in fact, one of his chapter headings in *The Lonely Tower* (the chapter deals with poems mainly from the 1930s). But clearly, 'the achievement of style is precisely this swift flashing of the images' or 'there is the certainty of control, grammar and idiom continuing to give each word its full value' leave room for later critics. Richard Ellmann's remark that when Yeats wrote *The Tower* he 'put the full weight of his heroic personality behind it' seems to me at best uninformative. Margaret Rudd speaks of 'odd phrasing' and giving concreteness to the abstract. The author of the Yeats chapter in the *Pelican Guide* refers to the poet's 'consistently public tone' and 'lofty rhythms', adding that the style of the later work is 'formal, elaborate, yet easy and humane': a paraphrase of what F. R. Leavis wrote in 1933: 'the verse . . . is idiomatic and has the run of free speech, being at the same time proud, bare and subtle'.

Altogether it seems a not very informative catalogue: especially since the belief that 'language of common speech' (the 'easy', the 'idiomatic') serves as a guiding idea for Yeats's later style is extremely misleading. That this is so will be disputed: one hopes, on the apparent authority of Yeats himself:

> My own verse has more and more adopted . . . the syntax and vocabulary of common personal speech. (to H. J. C. Grierson, *Letters*, 710)
> I believe more strongly every day that the element of strength in poetic language is common idiom. (to John Quinn, *Letters*, 462)

The quotations come pat enough; but when Yeats spoke of common idiom as the fit medium of the poet, he had distinctions in mind which are remote from 'common speech' as a current slogan indicates:

> Let us get back in everything to the spoken word . . . but . . . the idiom of those who have rejected, or of those who have never learned, the base idiom of the newspapers. (*Samhain*, 1902)

In the present context it is unnecessary to take up exactly how 'common idiom' had for him its link with the Western Irish peasantry; and their speech, its link in turn with the 'vocabulary from the time of Malory'. Yeats's general position is clear from his 'General Introduction for My Work' (1937):

> I hated and still hate . . . the literature of the point of view. I wanted . . . to get back to Homer, to those that fed at his table. I wanted to cry as all men cried, to laugh as all men laughed, . . . the Young Ireland poets . . . did not know that *the common and its befitting language is the research of a lifetime*. (*E. & I.*, 511)

How little Yeats by 'common' meant 'colloquial' can be seen in any later passage taken at random:

> Having inherited a vigorous mind
> From my old fathers, I must nourish dreams
> And leave a woman and a man behind
> As vigorous of mind, and yet it seems
> Life scarce can cast a fragrance on the wind,
> Scarce spread a glory to the morning beams,
> But the torn petals strew the garden plot;
> And there's but common greenness after that.
>   ('Meditations in Time of Civil War', iv, *C.P.*, 228–9)

Leaving aside such a phrase as 'spread a glory', which (it might be conceded) is a thought, not an idiom, remote from common speech, I

H.G.–G

find eight indisputable deviations from standard English idiom in these eight lines ('old fathers' for ancestors, 'scarce' for scarcely, 'but' for only are the most obvious); and the time has come to recognise that the staple of Yeats's later verse is not common idiom at all, but the relinquishment of one deviation from common idiom (that which strikes us, to speak very loosely, as the worn-out poetic diction of the nineteenth century, and especially the 'nineties) and its replacement by another deviation; one more original, calculated and expressive, but a deviation none the less.

Yeats's own remarks in prose offer guidance to a concept of style much more considered and articulated than merely 'common speech'. The 1926 letter to Grierson, quoted above, goes straight on to say that 'natural momentum in the *syntax*' is 'far more important than simplicity of vocabulary'. The letter to Quinn, quoted more fully, reads, 'the element of strength in poetic language is common idiom, *just as the element of strength in poetic structure is common passion*' (my italics in both cases). Looking back in 1937, Yeats underlines this once more:

> It was a long time before I made a language to my liking; I began to make it when I discovered some twenty years ago that I must seek, not as Wordsworth thought, words in common use, but a powerful and passionate syntax, and a complete coincidence between period and stanza . . . I need a passionate syntax for passionate subject-matter. (*E. & I.*, 521–2)

The idea of 'everyday speech' recedes farther and farther. In a letter to Olivia Shakespear (April 1921) Yeats writes that 'Nineteen Hundred and Nineteen' is 'not philosophical but simple and passionate' (*Letters*, 668): the echo of Milton is worth a note. So is 'I like a strong driving force' (*Letters*, 845–6). So is his comment in *A Vision* on the poems now to be discussed: 'I put *The Tower* and *The Winding Stair* into evidence to show that my poetry has gained in *self-possession and power*' (p. 8, my italics). So, again, is a particularly interesting letter which Yeats wrote to his father in March 1916, noticing the element of pattern in art as the subjective and non-imitative one, and calling it 'an intensity of pattern' (*Letters*, 607).

Power, passion, intensity, energy—the last word is recurrent in Yeats's discussions—these are the terms which weigh his own references to 'common speech' and give them a highly distinctive turn. An exact register of the language that Yeats 'made to his liking' will bring out, in fact, how the constant deviation from what he called 'common

personal speech' is always in the direction of speech in the sense of the
poet's own most personal voice and presence: of an engagement of his
own subjectivity and energy as the continuing focus of the poems and
everything in them.

That this may be traced in the thought of Yeats's later poems is not,
of course, in dispute; and to establish this no more need be quoted than
the opening lines of 'The Tower'. But those who know that poetry
lies less in thought than in language will be willing to trace the controlling attitudes of the verse down into the smaller details of language.
They will be willing to notice, for example, that when Yeats writes:

> Two men have *founded* here
> ('Meditations in Time of Civil War', ii, C.P., 227)

or

> . . . ancestral night that can . . .
> *Deliver* from the crime of death and birth
> ('A Dialogue of Self and Soul', C.P., 265)

or

> I *summon* to the winding ancient stair (*ibid.*)

he is not perpetrating an arbitrary and resultless deviation from common
idiom. In transforming these normally transitive verbs into intransitive,
and thus leaving the reader to sense their objects for himself, he is
employing a syntax which both adds speed to his verse and contributes
something to the *persona* of the author: his stance of emphatic terseness,
his demand that the reader shall submit to the demands of the verse
and recognise for himself what the writer declines to pause over. The
'strength' lies in a deviation from 'common idiom', because this is a
deviation of a particular kind and in a particular direction.

Consider another example of the same syntactical irregularity:

> What if those things the greatest of mankind
> Consider most *to magnify, or to bless,*
> But take our greatness with our bitterness?
> ('Meditations in Time of Civil War', i, C.P., 226)

Here the oracularly unidiomatic verbs are linked with another deviation
from common idiom. 'What if . . .?' is not common idiom as a
question, either in standard or Irish English. Once again, the deviation
is in the direction of the terse and passionate: for although the standard
form in 1960s English might be 'Suppose . . .' Yeats's question must
be seen as an emphatic and elided version of 'What would happen
if . . .?' or some question taking that form. It is wrong to dismiss the

point as trifling. Not only does Yeats use this form of interrogation repeatedly:

> And what if my descendants lose the flower
> Through natural declension of the soul? (*ibid.*, iv, *C.P.*, 229)
>
> . . . what if mind seem changed . . .
> And I grow half contented to be blind!
> ('All Souls' Night', *C.P.*, 258)
>
> But names are nothing. What matter who it be . . .'
> (*ibid.*, *C.P.*, 259)
>
> What matter if the ditches are impure?
> ('A Dialogue of Self and Soul', *C.P.*, 266)
>
> '*What then?*' *sang Plato's ghost* ('What Then?' *C.P.*, 347)
>
> What matter though numb nightmare ride on top . . .?
> ('The Gyres', *C.P.*, 337)

Not only is there this recurrence, but in 'Ancestral Houses' the interrogative, and the curt and authoritative form of it, sustain and indeed create the whole second half of the section. The whole closing passage is a defiant confrontation of the possibility envisaged in the question and left resolutely unresolved by the poet.

Consider, in the light of Yeats's 'made a language to my liking', the phrase 'crime of death and birth' in the passage just quoted from 'A Dialogue of Self and Soul'. A literate reader can no doubt accept the life, death = crime metaphor by half-conscious reference to the *de contemptu mundi* tradition or, more exactly, indeed, to the *Phaedo*. But Yeats does not leave him to rely on this reference. 'Death and birth' link back to 'love and war' earlier in the stanza; and the quality of both of these are already determined by the 'razor-keen' edge of Sato's sword, and its embroidery wrapping '*torn* from some court-lady's dress'. A stanza later, when Yeats claims 'a charter to commit the crime once more', it is clear by now that the poem is not merely giving meaning to its own metaphors, but doing this with a force and brevity which come from something indeed like 'making a language': a process of cumulative word-manipulation which means that the words are farther from 'common idiom' at the end of the poem than they were at the beginning.

One can by no means say that this occurs in all poetry, though it is not, of course, confined to Yeats's. Nevertheless, this aspect of his later verse contributes much to energy and creativity, not only because it helps actually to make possible Yeats's emphatic terseness, but also because it is itself an example of plastic energy: of the poet's beginning to make something which might be called a self-contained world of language within the poem. 'A Dialogue of Self and Soul' has more of this language-creation in it. This is perhaps most easily seen by working backwards from its closing image:

> When such as I cast out remorse
> So great a sweetness flows into the breast
> We must laugh and we must sing,
> We are blest by everything,
> Everything we look upon is blest. (C.P., 267)

The image is exactly that which closes 'Friends' (in *Responsibilities*, 1914); and the mood of exaltation and delight is one which Yeats recurrently felt in varying forms: reference might be made to the opening page of *Anima Hominis* ('all my thoughts have ease and joy, I am all virtue and confidence'), or to a passage in *Anima Mundi* ('everything fills me with affection, I have no longer any fears or any needs'). But in the 'Dialogue', one of Yeats's more richly esoteric poems, the force of the flowing sweetness is more explicit (and almost the opposite of its force in 'Friends'); and it acquires that force from the language-creation of the poem. Yeats is, in fact, conducting a rehearsal, in meditation during this life, of the stages of the Dreaming Back (part ii, stanzas 1–3) and the Return (the closing stanza) which are explained more fully in *A Vision*. 'In the *Return* . . . the *Spirit* . . . is compelled . . . to trace every passionate event to its cause until all are related and understood' (*A Vision*, 226). It was for a good reason that 'Trace to its cause' in the prose text became 'follow to its source' in the poem. 'Source', giving the sense of a spring of fresh water to the sweet flow, itself gains this concreteness of idea from the 'fecund *ditch*' of the immediately preceding lines:

> Or into that most fecund ditch of all,
> The folly that man does
> Or must suffer, if he woos
> A proud woman not kindred of his soul.

Other associations we might find for 'fecund ditch' are either (if present at all in a sound reading) wholly inept, or else no more than a sarcastic irrelevancy on Yeats's part. Here, 'fecund' has associations with squalor and worthlessness; and these come from the:

> if it be life to pitch
> Into the frog-spawn of a blind man's ditch

of the preceding lines. This point of reference itself takes shape from the opening lines of the whole second part:

> A living man is blind and *drinks his drop*.
> What matter if the ditches are impure?

Ditch as source of drink, ditch as home of life, may be seen branching their way through the whole poem; and it is this which gives the final transition its power; for the transition from ditch to source is no transition from an event merely back to its cause, but one from the whole life of the sensual world, back to its origin in the world of the soul. The supramundane meaning of the poem is written into the very grain of its imagery, and written there by this cumulative 'making of a language' through the poem itself.

Since I have trespassed three pages forward into *The Winding Stair* for a clear and manageable specimen of this side of Yeats's style, perhaps I may trespass a lesser distance backward into *Michael Robartes and the Dancer*, as far as 'A Prayer for My Daughter', for a simpler example, perhaps, and an even clearer one. This poem ends with an act of language-creation, of naming, which is perfectly explicit:

> Ceremony's a *name* for the rich horn,
> And custom for the spreading laurel tree. (*C.P.*, 214)

But the identity created in this act of naming works backwards at least as much as forward; and if we ask, for example, why it is a 'spreading' laurel tree, we find the answer by no means in realism, in a reference to the habit of growth of that plant; but in something entirely different. 'Spreading' already has a special sense given it by the development of the poem:

> May she become a flourishing hidden tree
> That all her thoughts may like the linnet be,
> And have *no business but dispensing round*
> *Their magnanimities* of sound.

In turn it is 'magnanimities', and 'merriment' in the lines which follow, that give the appropriate associations for 'laurel' at the end of the stanza:

> O may she live like some green laurel
> *Rooted* in one *dear perpetual* place.

Why, it may be asked, does the reader accept that 'dear' without qualm? Because the poem has already, through contrast, given to 'rooted' meanings which go beyond the tree itself:

> many a poor man that has *roved* . . .
> From a *glad kindness* cannot take his eyes.

It is 'glad kindness', in fact, which means that the reader need not recall
the cheerful unassumingness of the linnet's song (if he knows of it); and
then, when we call to mind the opening situation of the poem, where
Yeats likens the destructive forces of the future to a storm coming in
from the sea, and calls the storm a '*roof*-levelling wind' (line 5) we
can see how by the time he writes:

> Assault and battery of the wind
> Can never tear the linnet from the leaf (stanza 7)

Yeats has in effect created for himself a private language. All the important words of his sentence take their meanings from a progressive
charging which they receive from the developing poem.

It is a cumulative enrichment, quite different from the enrichment
so often to be found in Shakespeare's verse. Most characteristically,
Shakespeare's enrichment of meaning consists in eliciting a series of
ideas from a single metaphor; or in yoking of metaphors together, or
moving from one through a second and so on, in such a way that they
illuminate each other at the same time as they explore the main topic.
In Yeats's verse it is rather the realities marking out the very substance
of the poem—its opening situation, its main line of thought and meditation—which are progressively charged with richer and fuller meanings.
In respect, for example, of *King Lear*, it would not be to the gilded fly
and the vex'd sea that comparison would turn, but to the knights or
the stocks, the heath or the cliff—fixed and established realities in the
whole play. And as soon as it is recognised that this comparison would
be the appropriate one, it becomes clear that there is little real comparison to be made.

If the question is of those realities which mark out and punctuate the
landscape of Yeats's poems one by one, the next step is to take stock
of how these objects, initially, find their places in the verse; remembering always that the purpose of doing so is to explore further and comprehend better how the ultimate focus of the later poems is what Yeats
himself saw his vocabulary and syntax as *for*: self-possession and power,
passionate subjectivity. To begin with, the richness is emphatically no
richness of concrete describing. Yeats's nodal objects, if they may be so
termed, arrive starkly and as it seems arbitrarily in his poems. The
richness lies not in how they are delineated in detail, but in their

interrelation, their use. Yet in this very starkness of arrival lies the key
to their quality; the service they render to Yeats's most central intent:

> There is no obstacle
> But Gregory's wood and one bare hill.
>   ('Prayer for My Daughter', *C.P.*, 211)

> I pace upon the battlements and stare
> On the foundations of a house, or where
> Tree, like a sooty finger, starts from the earth.
>   ('The Tower', ii, *C.P.*, 219)

There is no doubt of the stark arrival, but the next lines bring out what
should perhaps be called its essential mode:

> *. . . and call*
> Images and memories
> From ruin or from ancient trees,
> For I would ask a question of them all.

This mode is nothing less than an establishing of the most characteristic
and recurrent relation between poet and what enters the world of his
poems:

> O sages standing in God's holy fire . . .
> Come from the holy fire . . .
> And be the singing-masters of my soul.
>   ('Sailing to Byzantium', *C.P.*, 217)
> It seems that I must bid the Muse go pack,
> Choose Plato and Plotinus for a friend
>   ('The Tower', i, *C.P.*, 218)
> And I myself created Hanrahan . . . (*ibid.*, ii)
> As I would question all, come all who can . . . (*ibid.*)
> It is time that I wrote my will;
> I choose upstanding men (*ibid.*, iii)
> Bid a strong ghost stand at the head
> That my Michael may sleep sound . . .
>   ('Prayer for My Son', *C.P.*, 238)
> I dream of a Ledaean body . . .
>   ('Among School Children', *C.P.*, 243)
> Horton's the first I call . . .
>   ('All Souls' Night', *C.P.*, 257)
> I summon to the winding ancient stair
>   ('A Dialogue of Self and Soul', *C.P.*, 265)

I declare this tower is my symbol
                    ('Blood and the Moon', ii, *C.P.*, 268)
I meditate upon a swallow's flight
                    ('Coole Park', 1929, *C.P.*, 273)
The gyres! the gyres! Old Rocky Face, look forth;
                    ('The Gyres', *C.P.*, 337)
I call on those that call me son,
Grandson, or great-grandson . . .
                    ('Are You Content?' *C.P.*, 370)

It must be noticed, first, that these lines are not drawn at random from the poems in which they appear. They are either the opening lines of the poems from which they come, or something not far short of that: the words from 'Among School Children', for example, mark the point at which the deeper meaning of the simple opening scene begins to be unfolded. In effect, they generate, or in one or two cases illustrate, the radical organisation of the poems where they appear. The *forming ritual* of these poems, one may say, is the solemnised calling-up of objects by the poet to people the world of his imagination. I hesitate to use the correct word, because it has become a favourite, in recent critical discussions, of writers who admit that they are uncertain of its meaning; but these ritual phrases reveal the *ontology* of what constitutes Yeats's world: the kind of reality, the status of reality, which is possessed by the objects in it. It is part of the nature of these poems that they do not offer to depict and describe things which the reader is invited to envisage as having prior, independent existence. On the contrary, the reader is invited to see them as called into being by the *fiat* of the poet, peopling a world *ab initio* as part of the creative act. This is the radical form. Yeats reverts to it again and again. Its indirect presence may be traced even in passages where the act of 'summoning' is not overt:

Around me the images of thirty years . . .
                    ('The Municipal Gallery Revisited', *C.P.*, 368)

Another example, for the implied analogy with Yeats himself seems inescapable, is the passage in 'Ancestral Houses':

Some violent bitter man, some powerful man
Called architect and artist in, that they,
Bitter and violent men, might rear in stone
The sweetness that all longed for night and day,
The gentleness none there had ever known . . . (*C.P.*, 225)

and it is in this way that all the other sections of 'Meditations in Time of Civil War' ought to be seen: if one is in doubt, for example, about the opening lines of 'My Table':

> Two heavy trestles, and a board
> Where Sato's gift, a changeless sword,
> By pen and paper lies,
> That it may moralise
> My days out of their aimlessness . . . (*C.P.*, 227)

the clue may be found in the *Letters*: 'I make my Japanese sword and its silk covering *my symbol of life* . . .' (*Letters*, 729).

Once more, it is to passion, to energy, to 'self-possession and power' that the discussion returns; for what I am arguing is that the innermost structure of poem after poem, of, in fact, the larger part of the major poems, is what ultimately gives incarnation to energised subjectivity, to passionate and powerful self-possession: and this innermost form is nothing other than the creation, by a series of as if vatic acts, of a whole world of objects ordered as their creator desires. Hence the initial starkness and simplicity; hence, as the energising and creative act proceeds, the cumulative interrelation and enrichment. One of the finest passages anywhere in *The Tower* seems to symbolise Yeats's own creativity in his later poems:

> Surely among a rich man's flowering lawns,
> Amid the rustle of his planted hills,
> Life overflows without ambitious pains;
> And rains down life until the basin spills . . . (*C.P.*, 225)

This landscape, too, is the work of a single creator; the lines in fact express in verse the same sense of what makes a work of art as Yeats had expressed twenty years before—in a note which he entitled 'First Principles':

> . . . a farce and a tragedy are alike in this, that they are a moment of intense life . . . reduced to its simplest form . . . an energy, an eddy of life purified from everything but itself.

Taken as a whole, the stanza from which those 'Ancestral Houses' lines were taken is an example, decisive in its clarity, of the 'complete coincidence between *period* and *stanza*' mentioned in a passage already quoted above (p. 90). This coincidence is not, of course, something necessary to all poetry that can move the reader. Horace is one of many who cultivated the sensitive felicity of its exact opposite. But 'period' is the key word. Yeats does not mean merely sentence. He means that unit of expression, complex not compound merely, where the thought seems to have no organisation and contour until the very instant of its completion. And 'thought' is a key, too; for just as syntax has little meaning save through the line of argument beneath it, so there is no complexity and control of syntax save what emerges from the unfolding and conclusion of that process of thinking which the syntax expresses and models. Yeats's 'intensity of pattern' is created for him by another aspect of his all-pervading energy: energy of argument.

With these points in mind, I propose now to examine 'Meditations in Time of Civil War', Section iv (C.P., 228–9), and consider in particular what 'intensity of pattern' may be seen in it from argument that creates coincidence of period and stanza; and more generally, how far the points which have emerged so far can account for what may be taken as 'style' in the verse, and how far there is something they leave unexplained.

It is easy to see in this poem the congeries of realities that, characteristically, Yeats assembles. That congeries comprises his daughter, his son, his house and its owls ('this laborious stair', 'this dark tower'), the friendly neighbour, the girl he married. Clearly (though there is here no ritual of summoning) the poem does not explore these as independent realities, but assembles them for its own sake. Clearly again, an intensifying pattern of argument runs from end to end of the poem. The first stanza argues that because one thing is so, a second must also be so in spite of something which argues to the contrary. The second stanza also has a clear logical form: if one thing happens, something else ought to follow. The third and closing stanza states an analogy which is no chance resemblance, but a systematic one (that is, the second part of it is indirectly entailed by the first).

So much for argument. In addition, there is a good deal of that progressive enrichment of ideas which was discussed earlier. The love and friendship of wife and neighbour are seen to make a 'circle', because of what is said about the owls (their lowliest counterpart under the greatest of all Circles); and the 'desolation' which the owls cry to the desolate sky is no arbitrary sentimentality, but an exact reflection of the 'torn petals' and 'common greenness' which the first stanza gave as the inevitable consequence of the flower that spread to the sun.

Yet it is both superficial and incomplete to rest in the idea of 'logic' as an adequate analysis of this 'intensity of pattern'. Part of the pattern lies in the thought-forms of the poet, but these are following relations of cause and effect as much as of logic; and in the end it becomes clear that the powers of logic at work in the poem are no more than one aspect of something more generic and comprehensive: an always-expanding network of transferring energies, of active interrelatings, among the individual realities which comprise the poem's 'world'. It is a world, in the first place, of vigorous action, of process and event, of emphatically transitive verbs.

Consider some details. It is the poet's ancestors (his 'old fathers') who impose his present nature on him; and that in turn, the birth and nature of his son and daughter. The flower of life casts its fragrance on the wind, spreads its colour before the sun; the torn petals, the common greenness, vigorously follow. If the children degenerate, it will be a 'natural declension', effect of determined causes. It shall ruin the Tower, and therefore it is that the owls shall nest in it and reach the sky with their calling. The ultimate Law of the world, which determines men's life as birds', relates the poet to his circle of friendship and affection, to wife and to neighbour; and fixes in a circle the past and a future some-times flourishing, sometimes in decline.

'The owls *shall* nest in it.' The idiom was deliberately chosen. At that point in his poem Yeats was not expressing a natural necessity so much as laying one down as a pure act of his own will. So, once more, in the last stanza. The Tower may flourish or go to ruin through the forces of nature; but it was chosen, decked and altered by decision of the poet. In fact, when Yeats is writing in this style, *three* kinds of necessity and constraining interrelation are at work between the items of his thought. First, the implications of logic (of which the only clear example in 'My Descendants' is how the circles of the owls relate to the circle of human life); second, the necessities of cause and effect; and third, the connections which the poet announces as imposed by himself. Logic, reality and *fiat* make a unity: no mere mirror of the physical cosmos, but a newly made one. Yeats's 'world' in the major later poems comprises not simply the objects which he promulgates, but also and along with them the acts of thought by which these are promulgated and manipulated. This is what follows from—or creates, depending on how one looks at it—the passionate subjectivity of the poem: an ever-present continuity in them of their vehemently feeling, thinking, willing creator.

Perhaps Yeats's version of the εὐίππου, ξένε chorus from *Oedipus at Colonus* helps especially at this point, because it shows the poet trans-forming the work of another into his own distinctive mode:

> Come praise Colonus' horses, and come praise
> The wine-dark of the wood's intricacies,
> The nightingale that deafens daylight there,
> If daylight ever visit where,
> Unvisited by tempest or by sun,
> Immortal ladies tread the ground
> Dizzy with harmonious sound,
> Semele's lad's a gay companion. (*C.Pl.*, 543-4)

If we recognise that Yeats links horses, thick wood, and singing bird all in a single act of praise; that the wood is dark *because* intricate ('If daylight ever visit . . .' explores an idea which ought in logic to preclude the idea of the previous line, but in fact does not); that the Baccantes are dizzy *because* of the harmony of the sound; that it is harmonious *because* Bacchus is a gay companion—it becomes clear at once that although Greek is a language in which necessities and implications are expressed much more readily than in English, even so nothing in Sophocles' text matches Yeats's close and nervous mesh of thought. The Greek poet merely says, starting a new sentence, that in silver Colonus the nightingale sings in the deep green woods, and 'has' wine-coloured ivy, and foliage which is windless and sunless. Then, again with a fresh start, he adds that this is where Bacchus wanders, following the Baccantes. He is describing an external and independent reality. Yeats is creating one that comes into existence through a synthesis within the poem.

The word 'synthesis', which can barely escape being used at this point, is an invitation to make comparison with something I introduce hesitantly, because it may seem that in attempting to elucidate Yeats by the *Critique of Pure Reason* I am less adding to than airing knowledge. But I have been genuinely helped, in thinking about the synthesis of realities which I find in many of Yeats's later poems, by Kant's discussion of the fundamental patterns which in his view cannot but run through the 'world' of external realities which we know in sense-perception. The discussion comes in the second and third parts of the section of the Critique entitled *Analogies of Experience*. The problem with regard to Yeats is: with what reason, and for what reasons, one can say that poems such as 'The Tower', 'Nineteen Hundred and Nineteen', 'All Souls' Night' and many others produce the poetic effect of being, by the totality of what is in them, not a mere reflection of some external reality, but an independent reality with a nature of its own. This undoubtedly bears a resemblance to Kant's problem: which is, what differences there are or must be between a multiplicity of sensations that mean nothing—they are merely themselves— and a multiplicity of sensations that demand assembly into a 'world': an order, that is, of independently existing objects.

In the Second *Analogy*, Kant argues that one characteristic which must necessarily run through the multiplicity of our perceptions, if these are perceptions of a world of independent objects, is that they should not be related to each other merely by relations of before and after, which might as well run one way as the other:

> A world of images becomes a world of realities if there is a rule which makes inevitable one particular pattern of connection in the complexity of particulars.

Perhaps it has been something like this which the present discussion traced in the network of necessities linking not only Yeats's objects but (both among themselves, and to and fro with those objects) the acts of thought that organise those objects. In the Third Analogy, however, Kant argues that if experience is genuinely experience of a world of objects it must display a further characteristic. It is not easy to express this clearly, but perhaps it may be put by saying that the relations of necessary connection discussed in the second *Analogy* must run comprehensively, even exhaustively, through our experience. In principle, any one perception must be capable of being causally connected with any other: experience is one, it cannot tolerate unbridgeable rifts or isolated and 'wild' perceptions at any point within itself:

> For impressions to be parts of a single *biography*, they must simply be in *communion*: must determine each other's positions by relations of before and after in time. But for them to seem impressions *of an order of objects*, they must actually make possible the perception each of the other; so that while the successiveness is attributed merely to the impressions, the objects themselves can be posited as in simultaneous existence. But this making possible is a reciprocal influence, or rather a genuine *inter-action* of objects, without which co-existence as an actually perceived relation could not occur in our experience.[1]

The Third Analogy is in effect the consequence and completion of the Second, in that it is nothing other than the Second's comprehensive application.

[1] No English edition of the *Kritik der reinen Vernunft* is available to me at the time of writing this essay; and in translating from the German the two passages quoted, I have taken the opportunity to express Kant's thought in rather less technical (and I hope less obscure) language than is normal.

This discussion has by now assembled ideas of a number of different kinds of interrelation which may be traced through the 'world' of the poems. In examining Yeats's creation of language, it was concerned with the work of metaphor, which meant the delineation of links between objects through the analogy of *partial resemblance*. This is a sense of 'analogy' quite different from Kant's: for the interrelations of which Kant wrote were those of *cause and effect*, branching out in the end into a reciprocal system. In addition to these two kinds of link, it has become clear that links of *logic*, holding, of course, between statements not objects, are of some importance in the tissue of the later verse; and so are those which, as acts of the poet's *will*, or movements of his intense and effortful thinking, link objects together—or him, or his thinking, to them.

If these varied ideas are brought to bear upon a long and ambitious piece like, say, Section ii of 'The Tower' (*C.P.*, 219–22), they begin, I think, to unfold its radical structure, its fundamental mode of organisation. Using the ambiguous word 'figure' to mean either a person or a physical object, one can say that all the figures of this piece are called into being by creative *fiat* of the poet (see p. 97 above). None is described or explored for its own sake and as an external reality: they are there to subserve a total order which is within the poem. Yeats calls into being the *dramatis personae* of his piece, 'for I would ask a question of them all'. Even by now an act of the poet's will has placed him within the world of his figures; and the involvement is sustained throughout by irruptions of the poet's own thinking—of which the most eye-catching is perhaps:

> Hanrahan rose up in frenzy there
> And followed up those baying creatures towards—
> O *towards I have forgotten what*—enough!

But the figures in the piece are all the time being drawn together systematically by interrelations the emphatic activity, the vehement movement of which cannot be missed. The song 'conferred a glory' on the peasant girl, made the farmers jostle, drove the drunkards mad; the great bog drowned one of them, the moon crazed them all. Yeats drove Hanrahan 'through the dawn', the 'ancient ruffian' bewitched the cards into hounds that pursued the hare, Mrs. French's serving man ran and clipped the farmer's ears, the men-at-arms clambered iron-shod up the stairs of the Tower, their great wooden dice 'beat upon the board'. It is a world of emphatic action and interaction; it genuinely seems to be made one by the to-and-fro of its network of causality.

But also by a network of analogy in the other sense: those partial resemblances which the poet creates—for that is the word—as he builds up a non-realistic and mythical landscape. Yeats himself paces to and fro as the evening sunlight fails: like Hanrahan, who ran 'drunk or sober' through the dawn; and the drunkards who, wanting to see the girl, ran through the moonlight—'O may the moon and sunlight seem / One inextricable beam', Yeats immediately adds. Homer telling the tale of Helen (stanza 5); the blind song-writer; Hanrahan the 'old lecher with a love on every wind' (he lost Mary Lavelle, in Yeats's prose tale,[2] through staying too long at the cards); and by the end of the section Yeats himself learning the answer to his riddle—'beauty's blind rambling celebrant' in stanza 10 is in fact the song-writer, but could be any or all of those four. Link by resemblance shades back into link by cause ('Helen has all living hearts betrayed' leaves her as more than any simple archetype); and sometimes into plain geographical proximity. Mrs. French lived beyond the rocky ridge, the peasant beauty somewhere upon it, Hanrahan 'somewhere in the neighbouring cottages', the Tower itself stands close enough for 'these rocks' to be near the door.

The details have no special importance. But taken together what they justify is nothing less than the use of the term 'world'. Yeats is making a unity, not a mere aggregation, by enmeshing all his figures in a network of resemblance, cause and effect, logic—

> Rose from the table and declared it right
> To test their fancy by their sight

and his own thinking effort (an effort, needless to say, of logic as well):

> Strange, but the man who made the song was blind;
> Yet, now I have considered it, I find
> That nothing strange; the tragedy began
> With Homer that was a blind man,
> And Helen has all living hearts betrayed.
> O may the moon and sunlight seem
> One inextricable beam,
> For if I triumph I must make men mad.

The thinking, passions and will of the poet are united in the synthesis of the world he creates:

[2] For the prose version see *Myth.*, 217–18.

> . . . intellect no longer knows
> *Is* from the *Ought*, or *Knower* from the *Known*—
> That is to say, ascends to Heaven . . . (*C.P.*, 266)

In Yeats's 'General Introduction' the first section is entitled 'The First Principle'; and the opening sentence runs 'A poet writes always of his personal life . . . he never speaks directly as to someone at the breakfast table, there is always a phantasmagoria'. (*E. & I.*, 509)

In this essay, 'style and world' have been names for exactly that: for the phantasmagoria which Yeats creates as expression of his passionate subjectivity; his energy, self-possession and power. There are doubtless those who find such writing uncongenial, and accept only poetry which explores the physical creation, for example, as against that constituting in the first place a creation in itself. This essay does not attempt to win them over. As far as Yeats is concerned, they may be left to time; or he to others. Defence of this poet against sweeping charges of that kind seems to me both otiose and impudent.

VII

On 'The Winding Stair'

DENIS DONOGHUE

*

I

My text is *The Winding Stair, and Other Poems* (1933), the book which includes *The Winding Stair*, *Words for Music Perhaps*, and *A Woman Young and Old*.

In one of his loftiest moments in *A Vision* Yeats says:

The ultimate reality, because neither one nor many, concord nor discord, is symbolised as a phaseless sphere, but as all things fall into a series of antinomies in human experience it becomes, the moment it is thought of, what I shall presently describe as the thirteenth cone. (*A Vision*, 193)

And in 'Vacillation':

> A brand, or flaming breath,
> Comes to destroy
> All those antinomies
> Of day and night; (*C.P.*, 282)

Between extremities Yeats runs his course. In *The Winding Stair* one extreme is the poem 'Chosen' in which the Zodiac is changed, under learned auspices, into a sphere; another is the 'frog-spawn of a blind man's ditch', in 'A Dialogue of Self and Soul'. Sometimes the poet yearns for the brand or flaming breath; often the resultant simplicity, 'the fire that makes all simple', is too severe, too remote to satisfy his blood-sodden heart. Hence *The Winding Stair*, a book misleadingly titled, is a storm of antinomies, the cry of their occasions.

The book begins with the memorial poem to Eva Gore-Booth and Con Markiewicz, the first of many Mutabilitie-Cantos in which we see the storm and hear the cry. The mood is caught from such poems as 'Nineteen Hundred and Nineteen' and 'Meditations in Time of Civil

War', and Yeats offers to resolve it, as Robert Gregory did, in a con-
flagration of self-begotten splendour: 'Bid me strike a match and blow.'
Later, in such poems as 'Spilt Milk' and 'The Nineteenth Century and
After', it will be too late for arson. Sometimes the fact of mutability is
given with a show of urbanity ('the toil has left its mark'), but more
often the tone is unyielding ('a raving autumn shears / Blossom from
the summer wreath'; 'that high horse riderless'; 'by that inhuman bitter
glory wrecked'; 'Time's filthy load'). From an earlier poem, 'Man is
in love and loves what vanishes, / What more is there to say?' There
is, in fact, a great deal more to say, and Yeats will say most of it in
The Winding Stair, but he will begin with 'what vanishes'. Hence the
first two poems are all mutabilitie; great dead houses, a beautiful
woman now 'withered old and skeleton-gaunt', life declined into
politics, the assassination of Kevin O'Higgins.

And hence the question which storms and cries through the entire
book: in a world of mutability, what remains, what is possible, where
does Value reside?

The answer, but not the whole story, is: in the imagination of Man.
In the memorial poem Yeats offers his own imagination as the appropriate reply to Time, the only enemy of the innocent and the beautiful:

> Arise and bid me strike a match
> And strike another till time catch (*C.P.*, 264)

—so the work can finish in that flare. And in the second poem 'Death'
the great man who

> Casts derision upon
> Supersession of breath (*C.P.*, 264)

knows death to the bone, and in that sense 'Man has created death'.
Reality and the Imagination, to use Wallace Stevens's terms and a little
of his idiom, are equal and inseparable. This is a consolation, in its way,
but the antinomies persist, and Yeats recites an elaborate version of
them in the next poem, the crucial 'Dialogue of Self and Soul'.

The Self is man committed to his mortality, assenting to time, place,
history, the earth, 'this and that and t'other thing', death and birth,
grateful for all liaisons, but ready, in extremity, to live—to go on—
without them. Soul is man on the high road, climbing the winding
stair, aspiring to a condition in which the antinomies of day and night
are transcended. Blake said, 'The cistern contains, the fountain over-
flows', and the Soul aspires to a Heaven which features, among its
pleasures, an irrefutable unity of mind:

> For intellect no longer knows
> *Is* from the *Ought*, or *Knower* from the *Known*—
> That is to say, ascends to Heaven; (*C.P.*, 266)

a formulation already given in *A Vision*, incidentally, as a description of
the relation between Will, Mask, Creative Mind, and Body of Fate
(*A Vision*, 73). The speech of Soul, in the 'Dialogue', has freed itself
from the hysterical intensity of its earlier version in 'All Souls' Night',
the last poem in *The Tower*, indicating that the condition of being
'wound in mind's wandering / As mummies in the mummy-cloth are
wound' was not final. And for the rest of the poem Yeats gives his
casting vote to the Self; the voice claims all the victories for 'Life', the
low road, the crime of death and birth, the ignominy of flesh and bone,
accepted without remorse. And Blake is still there:

> When such as I cast out remorse
> So great a sweetness flows into the breast
> We must laugh and we must sing,
> We are blest by everything,
> Everything we look upon is blest (*C.P.*, 267)

—a condition later designated, quite simply, as the 'happiness' of
'Vacillation'.

The 'Dialogue' is not, indeed, an outstanding example of free
democratic speech; the casting vote is delivered before the poor Soul
has well begun. Yeats has moved away from the allegiances of *The
Tower*, and he is anxious to speak up on behalf of the new cause; now,
at least, whatever one may say about the other occasions in the book
on which the dispute is carried out more rigorously. But the argument
of Self and Soul is the structural figure of the entire book; the text
annotated with footnotes like 'Veronica's Napkin', where the Heavenly
Circuit, Berenice's Hair, and other emblems of Soul are 'answered' by
Self, 'a pattern on a napkin dipped in blood'. Self will occasionally be
called the Heart, as in the seventh section of 'Vacillation', but the voice
is the same, and when the Soul invokes once again the fire that makes
all simple, the Heart answers: 'What theme had Homer but original
sin?'

The dispute of Self and Soul takes many forms in *The Winding Stair*;
including very simple ones, like—from 'Her Vision in the Wood'—
'Why should they think that are for ever young?' or the enforced
choice between perfection of the life or of the work; emblems of day,
set off against those of night; and so on. In 'Byzantium' the fury and the

mire of human veins are scorned by the moonlit dome; the complexities of mire or blood, by the golden bird 'in glory of changeless
metal'; the fury of blood-begotten spirits, by the 'flames begotten of
flame'. (But the allegiance of 'Byzantium' is a difficult story.) The
claims of Soul are advanced by many terms and symbols; some are
easy, like the miraculous oil of 'Oil and Blood', darkness, night, Heaven,
Moon, salvation, hermit, Plato, water as the generated soul of 'Coole
Park and Ballylee, 1931', the God in whom all things remain, and even
—in parody—Crazy Jane's Bishop. Some of the devotees of Self are
also easy; Sato's ancient blade, the silken embroidery of the 'Dialogue',
earth, day, flowers, ditches, frog-spawn, blood—in several poems—
power, original sin, the Fool, milk spilt on a stone, the rattle of pebbles
on the shore, swallows, dolphins, gongs, Homer, and the body itself—
very frequently—in the Crazy Jane poems. But the crucial symbols of
the book exhibit many a sea-change and imply a much more elaborate
'argument' than the simple dispute of Self and Soul which I have
sketched; the dispute persists, but the leading terms are forced to bear
new burdens, ground is lost and won, and the dividing lines are never
as true as the leaders hope. To be specific: in the early poems of *The
Winding Stair* Yeats sets up a strict dispute between Self and Soul; as
the dispute continues, he volunteers for Self and tries to take possession
of the Soul's attributes, those values which he will reject, if they threaten
the Self, but which he would much more willingly commandeer.
What follows is an examination of the leading terms of the book;
what they are, what they suffer, what they survive.

The tower itself, for instance: one of three declared possessions in
the poem 'Symbols'; very much the place of Soul, in the 'Dialogue'—

> —and all these I set
> For emblems of the day against the tower
> Emblematical of the night . . . (*C.P.*, 266)

But in 'Blood and the Moon' it is not the lonely tower of Milton's
Platonist scholar, the contemplative man; when Yeats says, 'I declare
this tower is my symbol', the footnotes pointing to Alexandria, Babylon, and Shelley are imperious notations, but Yeats's tower is committed
now to time, event, and history; a tower in particular time and place,
broken at the top. *The Winding Stair* is a misleading title because it
conceals the mockery with which Yeats invoked it:

> In mockery I have set
> A powerful emblem up,

> And sing it rhyme upon rhyme
> In mockery of a time
> Half dead at the top. (C.P., 267)

And Yeats's Norman tower becomes his symbol now only when he
has managed, by a flick of historical fancy, to associate it with Swift,
Goldsmith, Burke, and Berkeley. Not Stevens's 'ultimate Plato'. But
the conjunction of these four men is still curious. What have they in
common, apart from genius and an Anglo-Irish inheritance? Some of
the descriptions in 'Blood and the Moon' are improbable, notably
'Goldsmith deliberately sipping at the honey-pot of his mind'—which
(even with the complication of 'deliberately') sounds more like the
Keatsian decadent featured in A Vision. In the essay on Berkeley, Yeats
brings his four horsemen together again in a prose version which
clarifies the issue:

> . . . Berkeley with his belief in perception, that abstract ideas are
> mere words, Swift with his love of perfect nature, of the Houy-
> hnhnms, his disbelief in Newton's system and every sort of machine,
> Goldsmith and his delight in the particulars of common life that
> shocked his contemporaries, Burke with his conviction that all states
> not grown slowly like a forest tree are tyrannies, found in England
> the opposite that stung their own thought into expression and made
> it lucid. (E. & I., 402)

Perception, love, delight, conviction; every possible value, in fact;
only a tower hospitable alike to all these commitments will be 'my
symbol'. And if it appears that by this conjunction Self has virtually
taken possession of Soul, well and good.

Not that the battle is over. In the third and fourth sections of this
poem—'Blood and the Moon'—the dispute continues as the antinomy
of Power and Wisdom. The scene is still the tower, built on blood-
saturated ground, and the unclouded moon has flung its shaft across
the floor; and just as in 'The Crazed Moon' 'we grope, and grope in
vain, / For children born of her pain', here we 'clamour in drunken
frenzy for the moon'. And watching the butterflies (in Dante, symbolising the souls of the dead) Yeats says:

> Is every modern nation like the tower,
> Half dead at the top? No matter what I said,
> For wisdom is the property of the dead,
> A something incompatible with life; and power,
> Like everything that has the stain of blood,

> A property of the living; but no stain
> Can come upon the visage of the moon
> When it has looked in glory from a cloud. (*C.P.*, 269)

These lines would have found a more congenial home in the poem
'Vacillation'. Wisdom is of Soul, and if a choice is inescapable, Yeats in
the spirit of the 'Dialogue' will choose Power. But—another way out—
he will try to construe Wisdom in subversive terms. In 'The Seven
Sages' he returns to Swift, Goldsmith, Burke, and Berkeley and writes
a tedious poem to assert that 'wisdom comes of beggary'; and in 'After
Long Silence' he sets up an equation which suggests that what we gain
by climbing the winding stair may not be worth the effort:

> Bodily decrepitude is wisdom; young
> We loved each other and were ignorant. (*C.P.*, 301)

After this, the 'fatherless wisdom' of 'Her Dream' seems a tenuous
boon.

Again, the self-begotten flame is one of Yeats's most persistent
symbols for the unities of Soul which he invokes; but sometimes he will
claim a corresponding blaze for the Self. In the 'Happiness' part of
'Vacillation' he takes care to place the experience, the immutable
'moment',

> My fiftieth year had come and gone,
> I sat, a solitary man,
> In a crowded London shop . . .

and then

> While on the shop and street I gazed
> My body of a sudden blazed; (*C.P.*, 283–4)

as if the body, in animation, were to certify an undissociated condition
final, beyond dispute; and Yeats recalls several times that in Dante it
was so. A similar moment occurs in 'Stream and Sun at Glendalough':

> What motion of the sun or stream
> Or eyelid shot the gleam
> That pierced my body through?
> What made me live like these that seem
> Self-born, born anew? (*C.P.*, 289)

—clearly a moment in which the antinomies of day and night, Self
and Soul, are resolved, and the only unity is the greatest, unity of being.

But even when Yeats is still bogged down in the antinomies, and—
especially in the love songs of this book—when the Soul appears as

soul and the Self as body; even then, he challenges Soul on its own ground. In 'A Last Confession' the woman promises:

> But when this soul, its body off,
> Naked to naked goes,
> He it has found shall find therein
> What none other knows,
>
> And give his own and take his own
> And rule in his own right;
> And though it loved in misery
> Close and cling so tight,
> There's not a bird of day that dare
> Extinguish that delight. (*C.P.*, 314)

Perhaps so: but in these poems generally a very small margin of possibility is held out for such soul-love; normally the soul is the luminous halo surrounding a tangible body and not otherwise verifiable. The only satisfying unity is 'All':

> 'Love is all
> Unsatisfied
> That cannot take the whole
> Body and soul';
> *And that is what Jane said.* (*C.P.*, 291–2)

The basic pattern of the book, then, is to acknowledge the antinomies of day and night, Self and Soul, only to subvert them—as far as possible; and it will be possible only rarely. If we want a motto for this, we can think of the corresponding antinomies of Time and Eternity—a common version in Yeats—and then recall Blake's vibrant aphorism, 'Eternity is in love with the productions of Time'. Yeats gloried in this assertion and took every imaginable stock in its truth. If Soul spoke through the starlit air and invoked 'the star that marks the hidden pole', the admonition was not definitive; there would be another moment in which the star is humanised with the idiom of Self, as in 'The Mother of God' Mary asks of the Christ-child,

> What is this flesh I purchased with my pains,
> This fallen star my milk sustains . . . (*C.P.*, 282)

II

But the main pressure of the book will be to resolve the antinomies of day and night. In the second stanza of 'Vacillation' such a resolution is implied in the image of the tree that is 'half all glittering flame and half all green / Abounding foliage moistened with the dew'. Joy, as in 'Michael Robartes', is the double vision:

> And he that Attis' image hangs between
> That staring fury and the blind lush leaf
> May know not what he knows, but knows not grief. (C.P., 283)

Later in the same poem the resolution is given through the ecstasy of the tragic hero, the man who, because he has conceived life as tragedy, comes 'proud, open-eyed and laughing to the tomb'; the tragic ecstasy of Lear, Hamlet, Timon, which Yeats invokes so often in the prose and verse. There is a resolution also in the answer to mutability which Yeats gives in the sixth Part of 'Vacillation', 'Let all things pass away', because this is a dignified stance in what Stevens called 'the element of antagonisms'. It is also something, another resolution, a liaison, that the body of Saint Therese 'lies undecayed in tomb'; there is the humanist version, which Yeats praises as Tradition and gives in 'Quarrel in Old Age' as 'All lives that has lived'; and there is a love to match:

> 'Uplift those eyes and throw
> Those glances unafraid:
> She would as bravely show
> Did all the fabric fade;
> No withered crone I saw
> Before the world was made.' (C.P., 297)

There is the 'stillness' of the lovers in 'Chosen', adduced in evidence of total being; as the woman says,

> I take
> That stillness for a theme
> Where his heart my heart did seem
> And both adrift on the miraculous stream
> Where—wrote a learned astrologer—
> The Zodiac is changed into a sphere. (C.P., 311)

And if all else fails, one returns to a plain sense of things, to a vision of life under Blake's auspices and attributed now to Tom the Lunatic:

> 'Whatever stands in field or flood,
> Bird, beast, fish or man,
> Mare or stallion, cock or hen,
> Stands in God's unchanging eye
> In all the vigour of its blood;
> In that faith I live or die.' (C.P., 305)

One lives with miracle, if a miracle comes; if not, one still lives. Joy is available if the attributes of Self can swell and overflow, like Blake's fountain, and fill up all the hollows left by Soul; or if Soul, in loneliness, 'descends' into the mire of humanity. Either way, the values declared in *The Winding Stair*, by majority vote if not unanimously, are those of time, place, and human limitation. A partial list would include the following: the mounting swan, 'so lovely that it sets to right / What knowledge or its lack had set awry'; the holy bird of 'Lullaby'; the innocent and the beautiful; 'the strength that gives our blood and state magnanimity of its own desire'; Tradition, 'Thoughts long knitted into a single thought, / A dance-like glory that those walls begot'; 'a woman's powerful character'; 'the book of the people'; Anne Gregory's yellow hair; the human liberty served by Swift; the actual shells from Rosses Point, 'not such as are in Newton's metaphor'; the passion of 'A Woman Young and Old'; the unchristened heart; the love sung by Mohini Chatterjee; all other loves; beauty, wherever found; mere Life, 'I am content to live it all again'; the stir through the countryside in 'The Crazed Moon', 'What manhood led the dance!'; the high breeding and 'style' of Coole Park, Lissadell, and their inhabitants; and the great dance, the dance of the human imagination, 'Men dance on deathless feet'.

Indeed, the heroes of this book—tragic heroes, most of them—are men and women who with dignity conducted a war between the mind and sky—Stevens's phrase: Blake, silently invoked throughout; Homer—

> But all is changed, that high horse riderless,
> Though mounted in that saddle Homer rode
> Where the swan drifts upon a darkening flood. (*C.P.*, 276)

Swift, 'beating on his breast in sibylline frenzy blind / Because the heart in his blood-sodden breast had dragged him down into mankind'; Goldsmith; God-appointed Berkeley; Burke; Lady Gregory, 'an aged woman and her house'; Douglas Hyde; 'that meditative man, John Synge'; Shawe-Taylor; Hugh Lane; the anonymous woman young and old; Crazy Jane; Eva Gore-Booth; Con Markiewicz; Kevin O'Higgins; Tom the Lunatic. And the imagination which Yeats praises is not that 'loose imagination' of 'An Acre of Grass' but something much closer to the 'old man's eagle mind' of the same poem:

> Grant me an old man's frenzy,
> Myself must I remake

Till I am Timon and Lear
Or that William Blake
Who beat upon the wall
Till Truth obeyed his call. (*C.P.*, 347)

What we hear in *The Winding Stair* is a man beating upon a wall.

III

In *Pages from a Diary Written in 1930* Yeats meditates upon these themes, and in one or two passages with a particular intimacy:

> I am always, in all I do, driven to a moment which is the realisation of myself as unique and free, or to a moment which is the surrender to God of all that I am. . . . Could those two impulses, one as much a part of truth as the other, be reconciled, or if one or the other could prevail, all life would cease. . . . Surely if either circuit, that which carries us into man or that which carries us into God, were reality, the generation had long since found its term.[1]

In prose-moments Yeats was prepared to concede, of Self and Soul, that one is as much a part of truth as the other, but in most of the poems he enlisted under one banner and—for the time being—served it zealously. In *The Winding Stair*, when it came to a choice between the circuit which carried him into man and that which carried him into God, he chose man; but even as he voted he felt the burden of misgiving, loss, sacrifice, waste. The longing expressed in the *Diary* points directly to two texts, the poem 'Byzantium', the play *The Resurrection*.

It is customary nowadays to read 'Byzantium' as a parable of the poetic imagination, placing it in the company of similar parables from Coleridge to Stevens; where the blood-begotten spirits are the human experiences, broken and forged by the creative imagination and refined to the 'glory of changeless metal'. And yet, read in this way, it seems a small poem enough. I should prefer to have it more literally. Indeed, the scenario for the poem is given, a few pages farther, in the first stanza of 'Vacillation':

> A brand, or flaming breath,
> Comes to destroy
> All those antinomies
> Of day and night. (*C.P.*, 282)

[1] *Pages from a Diary* (Dublin, Cuala Press, 1944), pp. 19, 21. *Explorations*, 305.

And the landscape of 'Byzantium' is very like that of the third Section of 'Blood and the Moon': the tower, the odour of blood on the ancestral stair, and the unstained shaft of moonlight upon the floor chime with the city, the fury and the mire of human veins, and the disdainful starlit or moonlit dome. And it is a trivial misdemeanour if we recall, in reading 'Byzantium', the tone of these lines:

> Odour of blood on the ancestral stair!
> And we that have shed none must gather there
> And clamour in drunken frenzy for the moon. (C.P., 269)

The first stanza is all Soul, and the rhetoric favours Yeats's second 'circuit', 'that which carries us into God' or, in alternative idiom, into the thirteenth cone. The crime of death and birth is not forgotten, but it trails out from the second circuit and barely survives the second stanza. The image which floats before the poet is identified with the superhuman:

> I hail the superhuman;
> I call it death-in-life and life-in-death. (C.P., 280)

He does so because Heraclitus—or so Yeats fancied—had already vouched for this relation: 'God and man die each other's life, live each other's death', as the Greek student of Heraclitus says in *The Resurrection*. But our emphasis must be upon God, since the speaker—all Soul— has 'a mouth that has no moisture and no breath'. And the third stanza produces a correlative eikon, the golden bird, 'more miracle than bird or handiwork' because it issues from the 'shade more than man, more image than a shade'. The golden bough which sustains the bird is nearer the second circuit than the tree half flame and half foliage of 'Vacillation'; so this is a commitment, not a resolution. The changeless metal is not that of Sato's ancient blade; it is assimilated to the metal of the moonlit dome and exhibits a corresponding scorn. But at least the 'complexities of mire and blood' are recalled. Recalled, only to be refined and simplified, the antinomies of day and night now destroyed by the brand or flaming breath, flames that no faggot feeds, because this is still the second circuit, the Way of the Soul.

Indeed, the triumph of the Soul would be complete but for the dolphin, the beast of burden totally committed to the Self, to mere 'Life'. As the dolphin carries the human soul to Paradise, the reality of the first circuit breaks in; the vatic poet looks back at the waves of this poor reality breaking upon the marbles of the dancing floor:

> Those images that yet
> Fresh images beget

—as one wave of human reality begets another, answering in their own kind the superhuman 'flames begotten of flame', and the Way of the Self, the first circuit, 'that which carries us into man', carries us into the cycle of nature, honey of generation, mire and blood and time, 'that dolphin-torn, that gong-tormented sea'.

Clearly, the antinomies of day and night, Self and Soul must be brought to the most crucial of all tests, the antinomies of God and Man. The aphorism attributed to Heraclitus links 'Byzantium' to *The Resurrection* and both to the central preoccupation of *The Winding Stair*: but Yeats did not need Heraclitus for this incitement; it was implicit in the logic of his terms. Given the antinomies already deployed, he could not have avoided bringing them to this definitive test. It is easy enough for Crazy Jane to reflect, in her Sabbath voice, that 'Men come, men go' but 'All things remain in God'; but Yeats could not answer so readily. For one thing, he had to dramatise the issue before he could face it. Hence *The Resurrection*.

In the Preface to that play Yeats is concerned with the question of the supernatural. 'What if there is always something that lies outside knowledge, outside order? . . . What if the irrational return? What if the circle begin again?' And, a few pages earlier,

> Even though we think temporal existence illusionary it cannot be capricious; it is what Plotinus called the characteristic act of the soul and must reflect the soul's coherence. All our thought seems to lead by antithesis to some new affirmation of the supernatural.[2]

In the play itself the voice of Soul is the Greek, to whom the reality is God-but-no-man; a phantom:

> No god has ever been buried; no god has ever suffered. Christ only seemed to be born, only seemed to eat, seemed to sleep, seemed to walk, seemed to die. (*C.Pl.*, 583)

Furthermore, the gods

> can be discovered by contemplation, in their faces a high keen joy like the cry of a bat, and the man who lives heroically gives them the only earthly body that they covet. He, as it were, copies their gestures and their acts. (*C.Pl.*, 587–8)

[2] *Wheels and Butterflies* (London, Macmillan, 1934), p. 107.

(The Greek's lesson is exactly the opposite of Ribh's, in the later 'Super-natural Songs': things below may indeed be copies, as the Great Smaragdine Tablet said, but Ribh has just declared,

> Natural and supernatural with the self-same ring are wed.
> As man, as beast, as an ephemeral fly begets, Godhead begets
> 　　　　　　　　　　Godhead. (*C.P.*, 328))

In the play the voice of Self is the Hebrew, to whom the reality is still Man-but-no-god: Christ 'was nothing more than a man, the best man who ever lived':

> He preached the coming of the Messiah because he thought the Messiah would take it all upon himself. Then some day when he was very tired, after a long journey perhaps, he thought that he himself was the Messiah. He thought it because of all destinies it seemed the most terrible. (*C.Pl.*, 583–4)

What a relief, then, that the second circuit can still be evaded; that the first constitutes whatever reality we are ever likely to bear.

But there is a third voice, the Syrian; the one who believes and thereafter contains within himself the great disorder which, as Stevens says in 'Connoisseur of Chaos', is itself an order. This is an approach to 'the meaning', the resolution. And the next step is the climax of the play, when the Greek, a doubting Thomas, touches the side of the 'phantom' and feels there a heart beating:

> O Athens, Alexandria, Rome, something has come to destroy you. The heart of a phantom is beating. Man has begun to die. Your words are clear at last, O Heraclitus. God and man die each other's life, live each other's death. (*C.Pl.*, 594)

And the song with which the play ends 'certifies' Christ's humanity in terms remarkably close to the idiom of Self in *The Winding Stair*:

> 　　　　Odour of blood when Christ was slain
> 　　　　Made all Platonic tolerance vain
> 　　　　And vain all Doric discipline.

The final commitment is to the cycle of nature:

> 　　　　Everything that man esteems
> 　　　　Endures a moment or a day:
> 　　　　Love's pleasure drives his love away,
> 　　　　The painter's brush consumes his dreams;
> 　　　　The herald's cry, the soldier's tread

> Exhaust his glory and his might:
> Whatever flames upon the night
> Man's own resinous heart has fed. (*C.Pl.*, 594)

'Byzantium' invoked 'flames begotten of flame'. In 'Coole Park and Ballylee, 1931' Yeats suddenly asks, 'What's water but the generated soul?' because the racing waters which dropped into a hole suggested the death of the elements—Heraclitus, again—and particularly the death of fire (the soul) in water which is therefore the generated soul. But the song at the end of *The Resurrection* moves from Heraclitus to Blake and Swift and the cry of mutability; with this difference, that the 'exhaustion' now seems purposive, no longer mere waste but a cycle of exhaustion and regeneration. (The regeneration is in the 'flame' and the actions of painter, soldier, herald, lover.) T. S. Eliot, speaking of these matters in 'Little Gidding', says, 'Between melting and freezing / The soul's sap quivers'—which is one way of putting it; and the Chorus of the Four Elements in the second part of the poem recites a Heraclitean lesson in apocalyptic terms:

> Water and fire succeed
> The town, the pasture and the weed.
> Water and fire deride
> The sacrifice that we denied.
> Water and fire shall rot
> The marred foundations we forgot . . .

—another version of the moonlight dome disdaining all that man is. So Eliot will direct his ephebe toward the refining pentecostal fire; Yeats will send him to Blake and Swift.

For several reasons. First, because Yeats himself has been to school at those masters: Swift, who 'served human liberty', the freedom and uniqueness of the first circuit: Blake, who in *Vala* spoke of divisions and antinomies and said:

> Daughter of Beulah, Sing
> His fall into Division & his Resurrection to Unity:
> His fall into the Generation of decay & death, & his
> Regeneration by the Resurrection from the dead.[3]

Second: because Blake and Swift will help Yeats—and therefore his

---

[3] *Complete Writings*, edited by Geoffrey Keynes (London, 1957), p. 264. Cf. Helen Hennessy Vendler's *Yeats's Vision and the Later Plays* (Harvard University Press, 1963).

ephebe—to know that man is in love and loves what vanishes and to know also and at the same time that 'all lives that has lived'.

IV

Yeats thought well of *The Winding Stair*. In the Introduction to *A Vision* he claims that the poetry of *The Tower* and *The Winding Stair* is a gain in 'self-possession and power', and, some pages later, glosses this claim with another, that of holding in a single thought reality and justice. When we bring these terms together—power, self-possession, reality, justice—we see that Yeats's claim amounts to nothing less than this—that in those books his doctrine of the Mask has been realised, certified. In *Hodos Chameliontos* he says:

> And as I look backward upon my own writing, I take pleasure alone in those verses where it seems to me I have found something hard and cold, some articulation of the Image which is the opposite of all that I am in my daily life. . . . (*Auto.*, 274)

And in a dozen places he speaks of the assumption of a mask in similar terms; it is conscious, creative, theatrical. Basically, the doctrine itself is merely the application of theatrical metaphors to the common idea that the human imagination is 'creative'; 'every creative act can be seen as fact', as Yeats says in *A Vision*. The only difference between Yeats's doctrine and what we may call the general Romantic theory of the creative imagination is that it takes very little stock in the idea of the art-object safe beyond time, the poem as a well-wrought urn. Instead, it aspires to the condition of drama, incorrigibly in time, and it capitalises upon the ambiguities of such terms as role, action, gesture, mask, and play. This is at once the strength and the limitation of the doctrine; when it is utterly dedicated to reality and justice, it is powerful, self-possessed, and humane, always aware of the crime of death and birth. To assume a role and accept the discipline of living it is splendid; but the temptation is merely to flaunt a pose, to strike a gesture, to cut a dash. And this is the Symbolist impasse, the poet in front of his mirror. The great poems in *The Winding Stair* seek reality and justice and let the photogenic figure take care of itself. The weaker poems are hardly concerned with justice at all and treat reality as a mere instrument in the service of a spectacularly cut dash. And sometimes even the finest poems are tainted in this way.

I have in mind, as a case in point, 'Coole Park and Ballylee, 1931', especially a moment in the second stanza:

> Upon the border of that lake's a wood
> Now all dry sticks under a wintry sun,
> And in a copse of beeches there I stood,
> For Nature's pulled her tragic buskin on
> And all the rant's a mirror of my mood: (*C.P.*, 275)

Yeats, not Nature, has pulled the tragic buskin on, and the rant is his own. One has only to recall Coleridge's 'Dejection' to see that Yeats's lines are a Romantic commonplace devoid of Coleridge's tact. Yeats is planting himself in front of a suitably grandiose backcloth; he is worried about the decor, not about reality and justice. And when he sees the mounting swan he says:

> Another emblem there! That stormy white
> But seems a concentration of the sky;

—and for the present he is more interested in self-exalting emblems than in swans. As the poem proceeds, blessedly, he returns to the particulars of reality and the images of justice.

But the poet was always liable to cast himself in 'interesting' roles; the randy old man, the Blueshirt singer, the Fascist Celt. In *The Winding Stair* he cast himself, all too often, as Swift. In the Introduction to *The Words upon the Window-Pane* he said, 'Swift haunts me; he is always just round the next corner'; when he really meant 'in the next poem'. Hence because Swift had a fanatic heart Yeats had to have one, too. And so on.

There are two or three texts which bear upon this. When we think of Yeats's reality and justice; how he served them and, in days of weariness, forgot them, turning to his mirror; we recall 'The Circus Animals' Desertion', where he speaks of certain masterful images floating before him as compensating dreams for a life gone sour: 'and soon enough this dream itself had all my thought and love'. It was the dream itself, he says, enchanted him. And then:

> Players and painted stage took all my love,
> And not those things that they were emblems of.

The man, the actor, the role, Life as a drama in place and time; Soul and Self; God-made-man; the Greek, the Hebrew, the Syrian; Heraclitus, Blake, Plotinus, Swift: in his later years Yeats was often in a mist, wondering where, in all this, truth and value might reside. And how much truth consisted in a 'great performance'.

Another text comes from *A Vision*. In the discussion of Phase 16, with instances drawn from Blake, Rabelais, Aretino, Paracelsus, and 'some beautiful women', Yeats says that people of this Phase run between extremes, now full of hate, now liberated by a symbolism that expresses 'the overflowing and bursting of the mind'. And in these men, he says, there is always

> an element of frenzy, and almost always a delight in certain glowing or shining images of concentrated force: in the smith's forge; in the heart; in the human form in its most vigorous development; in the solar disk; in some symbolical representation of the sexual organs; for the being must brag of its triumph over its own incoherence. (*A Vision*, 138–9)

The last phrase is the one we need. Yeats was never quite sure what form the triumph would take, and the 'frenzy' is a problematic force not necessarily to be identified with that for which Yeats prays in 'An Acre of Grass'. When reality seemed beyond imaginative redemption, and justice a chimera, he often turned to the mirror and saw that with an hour in the green room he could give another farewell performance. It would have to be a little broader than the last version, its effects puffed out a little, an extra dash of rant; for he must brag of his triumph over his own incoherence.

But at other, stronger times Yeats would hold in a single thought reality and justice. Notably at Algeciras, meditating upon death; when reality was acknowledged by the images, the cattle-birds, the trees, the mingled seas, the tangible shells of Rosses' level shore; and justice by a grace of tone, a propriety of cadence and measure. Or again in 'Coole Park, 1929', an example to stand for many in *The Winding Stair*.

'Coole Park, 1929' moralises a landscape—the swallows, a lime tree, a sycamore, the great house itself; then the fine things done and said and thought within its walls, 'a dance-like glory that those walls begot'. And, as in 'The Municipal Gallery Revisited' and 'In Memory of Major Robert Gregory', the 'genius of the place' is given through the people who visited or lived there; Douglas Hyde, Yeats himself, Synge, Shawe-Taylor, Hugh Lane; and the great lady herself:

> They came like swallows and like swallows went,
> And yet a woman's powerful character
> Could keep a swallow to its first intent;
> And half a dozen in formation there,
> That seemed to whirl upon a compass-point,
> Found certainty upon the dreaming air,
> The intellectual sweetness of those lines
> That cut through time or cross it withershins. (*C.P.*, 274)

The certainty found upon the dreaming air is the 'accomplishment' invoked in 'Meditations in Time of Civil War', a splendour flowing through the generations into a house, a person, a deed, a thought. And the lines cut through time not to destroy it but to mark its possibilities, like a flare. In a difficult poem called 'Stars at Tallapoosa' Wallace Stevens posits lines 'straight and swift between the stars' which have nothing at all to do with the sea-lines or the earth-lines; in fact, they are pure intellectual acts, performed by man's imagination for its own pleasure. But the lines which Yeats praises in his poem are continuous with the earth-lines and the sea-lines, they are these made articulate in speech, style, grace, accomplishment. And lest all this be lost through a breach in tact or a defect of memory—as in a broken tradition—Yeats introduces a qualified witness, of a later generation, to remember what should be remembered:

> Here, traveller, scholar, poet, take your stand
> When all those rooms and passages are gone,
> When nettles wave upon a shapeless mound
> And saplings root among the broken stone,
> And dedicate—eyes bent upon the ground,
> Back turned upon the brightness of the sun
> And all the sensuality of the shade—
> A moment's memory to that laurelled head. (C.P., 274-5)

The shade is everything included in Hopkins's 'dapple', in Whitman's 'drift', in Stevens's 'Summer', in Yeats's 'dark declivities'—it is the felt plenitude of things; and the sensuality is Yeats's 'love's play' or Eliot's 'brown hair over the mouth blown'. Whatever it is, it is in time and place. In the first stanza Yeats speaks of 'Great works constructed there in nature's spite', figuring yet again the strain between perfection of the work and perfection of the life. Even at Coole Park in a landscape which lends itself to parable this strain persists; there is still a dispute of Self and Soul. The dispute is resolved not by recourse to an idea, a Hegelian synthesis, or a categorical imperative stronger than the disputants. It is resolved by appeal to a person great enough to resolve it; Lady Gregory herself, who embodied Self and Soul in her own reality and justice. Santayana performed a similar service for Wallace Stevens: to Stevens he appeared, in those last months, 'a citizen of heaven though still of Rome', Self and Soul in poise. The question with which we began—in a world of mutability, where does Value reside?—is answered in Yeats's memorial poem; 'a woman's powerful character', rooted in place, assenting to time. All lives that has lived.

VIII

The 'Last Poems'

J. R. MULRYNE

★

I

WRITING elsewhere in this volume, Northrop Frye distinguishes what he calls the 'ultimate insight' in Yeats. In summary, this has to do with 'redemption' from the pressures of time and chance through the exercise of the poetic imagination. Redemption is secured by the poet's identifying with Man, who is also the metaphysical 'One', through the discovery of 'personal archetypes, daimons or moods', aspects of 'the greater form of himself'; 'in this perspective', Frye says, 'the whole cycle of nature, of life and death and rebirth which man has dreamed, becomes a single gigantic image', an image the imagining poet, its 'maker', has conquered. The poetic process, we might say, thrives on a conflation, or confusion, of the actual world and the world of imagination; the creation of an imaginary world becomes an act not only of artistic but of real worth; it empowers the poet and absolves from the pain of the actual. Yeats's prose confirms that at the time of writing Last Poems his view of the poet's craft and the poet's privilege was as Frye outlines it; in an essay published in 1937, two years before his death, Yeats wrote:

> A poet writes always of his personal life, in his finest work out of its tragedy; . . . [yet] even when the poet seems most himself . . . he is never the bundle of accident and incoherence that sits down to breakfast; he has been reborn as an idea, something intended, complete. . . . he is more type than man, more passion than type. He is Lear, Romeo, Oedipus, Tiresias; he has stepped out of a play, and even the woman he loves is Rosalind, Cleopatra, never The Dark Lady . . . we adore him because nature has grown intelligible, and by so doing a part of our creative power. (E. & I., 599)

The hypnotic logic of this passage offers the poetic act as a true redemption of the Self; to write poetry is to be re-born, and to be so re-born, as to conquer 'accident', 'incoherence', 'tragedy'. The syntax brooks no argument: with this version of the 'personal archetypes', artistic remaking of the poet and his beloved, as type, passion, *dramatis personae*, can render nature no longer hostile, but enabling, 'part of our creative power'. The passage is interesting as theory; more immediately important, its language and its assumptions richly anticipate those of *Last Poems*. The *dramatis personae* of the prose reappear in the verse; 'tragedy' is much considered; 'creative power', under different guises, is frequently declared. The assumptions about actual and imagined reality, and about the poet's access to 'creative power', serve as an arena within which are drawn up the encountering dispositions and commitments of *Last Poems*.

The book opens with a transforming gesture of precisely the kind the prose invisages. The territory occupied by 'The Gyres' looks familiar: the end-of-an-era turbulence explored with sensitive resource by many a Yeats poem. But called on to 'look forth' over this tragic scene are unfamiliar lineaments: the imperiously invoked 'Old Rocky Face'. The confrontation is significant; over the time-dominated events of the poem broods the oracular, timeless Rocky Face. The things of time are not ignored: the 'numb nightmare' of verse two calls up the nightmare that rides upon sleep in 'Nineteen Hundred and Nineteen'; and the following phrase, masterfully condensed, invisages the terrible paradox of the 'sensitive body' 'stained' by its own very constituents, stained in Yeatsian language by 'mire and blood', the condition of body. Yet within the imaginative economy of the poem the Rocky Face dominates; exhorted to laugh in tragic joy, to rejoice in detachment, even if aware detachment, from the time-ridden events, this figure provokes our question. He is of course deliberately an enigma; the poem's strategy demands that he arrive abruptly and unexplained before our sensibilities. With the enigma sorts a claim to oracular status; we remember the 'Rocky Voice' of 'The Man and the Echo', where the voice proceeds from a chasm associated with the Delphic Oracle; and the suggestion that the figure recalls the sage Ahasuerus in Shelley, 'master of all human knowledge', is also plausible.[1] But Rocky Face is specifically one who 'holds dear,/Lovers of horses and of women', and who awaits the return of the antithetical gyre; as Yeats himself does. I think the alteration from the 'Cavern Face' of an earlier draft[2] might have been prompted by a reading of Ben Jonson's 'My Picture Left in

[1] See T. R. Henn, *The Lonely Tower* (1950), p. 303, and *Auto.*, 171.
[2] Henn, p. 303.

Scotland'; in this beautifully deft piece of ironic self-pity a 'rockie face'
is the poet's own pictured countenance seamed by time in contradis-
tinction to his accomplished, ageless art. Yeats would have taken
pleasure in such an oblique reference,[3] and in the varied conceits the
poem suggests upon the relationship of Face with Mask and Time with
Art—the face is aged and yet preserved through art. In any case the
Rocky Face in Jonson's poem, as also evidently in 'The Gyres', is the
poet's own—or a transformation of it. Nor do we need to go so far
afield to discover its real significance; in 'Ego Dominus Tuus' Yeats
ponders the 'hollow face' of Dante:

> I think he fashioned from his opposite
> An image that might have been a stony face. (*C.P.*, 181)

In the last verse of the same poem 'Ille' (as Pound remarked: 'Willie')
indicates that he too 'seeks an image'. The Rocky Face of *Last Poems* is
Yeats's symbolic discovery of an image that parallels the 'stony face' of
Dante; for the 'antithetical' poet Will and Mask become one. The
invocation of that mantic figure stands for a declaratory claim: the
writing of poetry (and the completion of *A Vision*) liberates the poet
from the world of cyclical nature; endowed with 'creative power' he
may 'rejoice' in the midst of tragedy. 'The Gyres' declares the rewards
the prose expected; the poet is re-born as an invulnerable 'stony face'.

An opening such as this is prescriptive for much that follows; transformation of the living to the condition of sculpted image everywhere
brings its rewards in *Last Poems*. As the prose anticipated, the beloved is
also re-born invulnerable, re-made as sculpted image; 'A Bronze Head'
—Laurence Campbell's bust of Maud Gonne in the Municipal Gallery,
—undergoes its apt consideration. The poem resumes themes familiar
from earlier work. The 'withered' appearance of the face recalls Eva
Gore-Booth, 'withered old and skeleton-gaunt',[4] the victim of just such
'abstract' politics as Maud herself had engaged in. Maud's own 'image'
in 'Among School Children' had similar lineaments; its 'hollow of
cheek as though it drank the wind' bespoke its taking 'a mess of shadows
for its meat': the penalty of time's action and a misuse of talents. There
are further resemblances. Pondering on Maud in that earlier poem,
Yeats's 'heart is driven wild'; in 'A Bronze Head' he records a sympa-

[3] For a reference to Jonson in Yeats's mind at this period see *Auto.*, 480, and
p. 133 below.
[4] 'In Memory of Eva Gore-Booth and Con Markiewicz', *C.P.*, 263

thetic activity of imagination so intense as to create virtual identity of experience; until

> I had grown wild
> And wandered murmuring everywhere, 'My child, my child!'

The 'wildness' is common to both occasions. But in the earlier poem the disturbing reflection must be curtly dismissed; imagination brings together the 'living child' and the old woman, and the implied know-ledge of time's action is too painful to be tolerated long:

> enough of that,
> Better to smile on all that smile, and show
> There is a comfortable kind of old scarecrow. (*C.P.*, 243)

Now the pain is salved by the transformation of the human being to the sculpted image, the bronze head. Appropriately, the poem's gait is even-paced; the syntax is leisurely, and the connectives are the con-nectives of discussion, not of vehemence or dismay: 'Or maybe', 'But even', 'Or else'. There is leisure even to specify the actuality of the head by siting it precisely: 'at right of the entrance'. Knowledge of the sculpted image offers and asks such response; its dualities, 'human', 'superhuman', alive, dead, reconcile the contraries of his knowledge of Maud: dark, light, empty, full, human, possessed. Its imaginative redemption is final; the pain of her ageing (and by extension of Yeats's own) is salved by McTaggart's belief in the compositeness of substance, that life and death are, like other manifestations of being, mere terms in a single series—a reassurance that stands as philosophical parallel to the most extensive poetic confusion of the real and imaginary worlds, the imaginative transformation or redemption of death. A deleted stanza[5] records, if slackly and with vacillation, the 'triumph' that comes with imaginative victory. Such is the characteristic response of *Last Poems* to what had seemed the endless fascination, and the endless despair, provoked by Maud's beauty; like Michael Angelo's sculpture, the Bronze Head 'can rule by supernatural right'.[6] Yeats's knowledge of Maud shares, by the intervention of a sculpted form, the invulnerability of the presiding Rocky Face.

Many among *Last Poems* adopt the strategy of 'A Bronze Head'. Behind major poems stand specific works of art: the statue of Cuchulain in the Post Office, the pictures in the Municipal Gallery, the sculpted piece of Lapis Lazuli, the Bronze Head itself: all openly and directly

---

[5] Printed in V. Koch, *W. B. Yeats: The Tragic Phase* (1951), p. 84.
[6] See 'Michael Robartes and the Dancer', *C.P.*, 198.

acknowledged now, not present, as in earlier books, merely by implication or oblique reference. Other poems, without summoning statue or picture, equally think of body willed, transformed, to the condition of the visual arts. Persons are arrested in typical gestures: Caesar, Helen, Michael Angelo caught in moments of silent expressiveness that declare their meaning in fixity ('Long Legged Fly'); the 'beautiful lofty things', embalmed and apart like the Rocky Face, share the same condition of arrested posture: Yeats's father, Standish O'Grady, Lady Gregory, Maud. Margot Ruddock too is caught in a moment of ecstatic knowledge; in that momentary posture Yeats specifies her as a work of art: 'that girl I declare / A beautiful lofty thing,' (C.P., 349). Delacroix, Landor, Talma, Irving are presented in the immobility of cameo. Maud Gonne, 'Pallas Athene in that straight back and arrogant head', expects the sculptor's chisel. The book is peopled by a series of arrested figures, statue-like; but not inert; these are Yeats's 'personal archetypes' by imaginative knowledge of whom the poet becomes endowed with 'joy'. As will become explicit.

The Rocky Face of 'The Gyres', like the 'stony face' of Dante, implies the intervention of the sculptor's chisel. Some years ago, T. R. Henn suggested that the source of the Rocky Face might be a carving on the wall of Thoor Ballylee, Yeats's Tower; the conceit is attractive. Having climbed the winding stair to the roof of the tower, as Dante climbed the winding upward path on the mountain of Purgatory, the poet achieves apotheosis as the sculpted image. The Tower, Yeats tells us, symbolises the mind looking out upon men and events, the Cave the mind looking inward upon itself;[7] in 'The Gyres' the Rocky Face looks out—like a face on Thoor Ballylee—over the time-ridden world of cyclical change, while the voice from the cave (in a related significance, time considered as eternal recurrence[8]) bids him rejoice in achieved liberation from the pressures of mere transitoriness. Whether Yeats had that specific carved head in mind or not is of marginal importance; the defeat of the impersonal world is whether or no symbolised in Last Poems largely by reference to the sculptor's craft. The trend culminates naturally, and a whole significant aspect of Last Poems comes to focus, in 'The Statues', the poem which meditates sculpture.

The passage from On the Boiler (p. 37) which lays the groundwork for interpreting the poem stresses that Greek Statues repudiate the accidental, the time-conscious detail, which draws the attention of 'our

[7] Essays (1924), p. 107.
[8] See A Vision, 259.

democratic painters'; on the contrary the sculptors accept 'those Greek proportions which carry into plastic art the Pythagorean numbers, those faces which are divine because all there is empty and measured.' The statues discover, that is to say, the ideal laws of form, the abstract definition that stands aloof from the particular, the norm that has no counterpart in the natural world of cyclical change. As a passage from *A Vision* (p. 291) explains, 'the human norm, discovered from the measurement of ancient statues, was God's first handiwork, that "perfectly proportioned human body", which had seemed to Dante Unity of Being symbolised.' To specify in sculpture the human norm, the perfect measurements, is to regain an imaginative Eden, whence one may look forth and rejoice at cyclical accident. This is the assumption underlying 'The Statues'; and the figure transformed, as in 'A Bronze Head', is Maud. As several critics note, her beauty had in the past prompted to sculptural metaphor: 'her face, like the face of some Greek statue, showed little thought, her whole body seemed a master-work of long-labouring thought, as though a Scopas had measured and calculated, consorted with Egyptian sages, and mathematicians out of Babylon, that he might outface even Artemisia's sepulchral image with a living norm' (*Auto.*, 364–365). Maud in her living beauty had seemed a unique embodiment of the ideal laws of form. But that unearthly beauty had been threatened by the transience of life within nature. Now in 'The Statues' Yeats follows out the provisional logic of his metaphor. To transform Maud's beauty to the condition of sculpture, and to pare away altogether the natural time-dominated woman, is to gather that beauty into the appropriate imaginative idiom of *Last Poems*. 'Body' by espousal of the sculpted image becomes 'soul'. The sculptor's art is one which shares much with the poet's; in a late essay Yeats speaks of 'the sculptor toiling to set free the imprisoned image',[9] an artistic endeavour answered by the 'union of theme and thought, fact and idea, so complete that there is nothing more to do, nothing left but statue and dream' (*E. & I.*, 477). Just so in this sector of *Last Poems* Yeats offers the statues as the embodiment of the 'dream'; to write them into the poetry is symbolically to declare the discovery of their Unity of Being. Maud has become, along with the other living statues we have mentioned, one of the personal archetypes, contemplation of whom empowers the poet, the Rocky Face, to rejoice.

The significance of 'The Statues' may become clearer if we consider

[9] A conceit associated with Michael Angelo, one of the important *dramatis personae* of *Last Poems*.

previous appearances of its peculiar language in Yeats's verse; stone and
statuary symbols had occurred earlier in more equivocal guise. A half-
mocking (and much less overt) epiphany of the poet-as-statue occurs in
'A Living Beauty'; there the poet is cast, not as a Rocky Face, but as a
'weather-worn marble triton among the streams.' Worn out with
making images, he suffers from a divorce between the actual and the
imagined; responsive to the image, 'the pictured beauty', he is indif-
ferent to the real, the delicately and variously human. And the poem
offers this as a cause for dismay. Similarly the language of 'Easter, 1916'
equates the rebels' possession of their 'dream', their ideal image, with
the enchanting their hearts to a stone 'To trouble the living stream':
stone is inimical to the living tissue of experience. And on the one
occasion in Yeats's verse where the language richly predicts 'The
Statues', a disaffection for stone and sculpted stone persists. The opening
chorus of *The Only Jealousy of Emer* invokes ideal beauty in terms that
anticipate the 'calculation, number, measurement' of *Last Poems*:

> How many centuries spent
> The sedentary soul
> In toils of measurement
> Beyond eagle or mole,
> Beyond hearing or seeing,
> Or Archimedes' guess,
> To raise into being
> That loveliness? (*C.Pl.*, 281–282)

But the closing chorus interprets the play's action as a dismissal of this
ideal loveliness in favour of less exalted visions; the lure of the ideal, as
often in Yeats's plays and lyrics, is at odds with effective living. 'A
statue of solitude' endangers the distinctively human:

> He that has loved the best
> May turn from a statue
> His too human breast. (*C.Pl.*, 295)

Marble serves to specify the hostility of unearthly formal beauty.

The originality of 'The Statues', compared with these earlier uses of
its peculiar language, is that the fixity of marble becomes, not the
antagonist of living, but the potential locus of life-enhancing knowledge. The release of this knowledge is accomplished by the exertion
of imaginative energy, by the imaginative possession of the archetype
as discovered in the statue. The tendency of the ideal image to 'keep a
marble or a bronze repose' ('Among School Children'; the idiom per-

sists) is cancelled by a passion-generated act of imagination; the impressment of 'live lips' upon a 'plummet-measured face' is the indicative act of 'imagined love' animating the ideal repose. The hour is 'midnight', always the moment of apocalypse in Yeats. 'Body' and 'soul' embrace in the act of imaginative apprehension, and solitary beds are exchanged for 'some public place'; the 'statue of solitude' no longer enjoys its terrifying aloofness, the 'formality', 'abstraction' of the image becomes relevant for living. Later verses extend the possibilities-for-living. The craft of the poet-as-sculptor, acknowledged in verse two, performs an imaginative function similar to that of the passion-driven boys and girls: 'dreams' are given their 'looking glass' in statues ('there is nothing left', one remembers, 'but statue and dream'), and the statues enjoy potential for swaying a nation's ideals. The 'intended, complete' image can, if recognised, subdue Asiatic variousness, form-lessness, or the complexities of knowledge and appearance—the mere accidents of natural life—and establish the groundwork of an entire civilisation. At the poem's end Yeats answers his previous equivocal response to the 1916 rebels (see 'Easter 1916'); in summoning to imagi-native presence the ideal image, the personal archetype, of Cuchulain, Pearse and his companions were enabled to 'climb to [their] proper dark' out of the accidental formlessness of contemporary living. The actual statue of Cuchulain in the Post Office, imaginatively realised, could serve as the locus for the establishment of a new and ennobling Irish civilisation—the long-cherished aim of Yeats's own dramatisation of the Cuchulain legend. Time and chance would be defeated and Rocky Face might properly rejoice.

If we wished to put this significance another way we might again turn to Northrop Frye. One weakness of Yeats's *A Vision*, he says, is the absence of an 'apocalytpic construct' to set against what the system conceives as 'the opposed and impossible ideals' of unity and individu-ality 'which only superhuman beings can reach'. 'The Statues', I think, offers specifically just such a construct; apocalypse becomes feasible, through imaginative exertion, within the framework of living. Frye draws attention to the sentence with which *A Vision* ends, contrasting the 'real Heracles' at the banquet of the immortal gods with 'Heracles the shadowy image bound to an endless cycle'; to 'mount' (the word is Yeats's own; it is at home among *Last Poems*) to that other Heracles— the real and the free—becomes a possibility for poet and nation. Imagi-native knowledge of the personal archetypes carries its ultimate reward.

*   *   *

Knowledge of the sculpted image, 'The Statues' declares, bestows personal energy, power. Many of the *Last Poems* are occupied with the poet's desire to re-fashion himself (a variant on the rejoicing Rocky Face) into a figure of abundant energy. 'Grant me an old man's frenzy, / Myself must I remake. . . .' (*C.P.*, 347); the unchristened heart exerts itself finally in this new context as 'The Wild Old Wicked Man' or John Kinsella; Crazy Jane momentarily returns; the images desired and invoked are those 'That constitute the wild' (*C.P.*, 367);[10] figures of history, ancient and contemporary, are summoned to characterise some abundant energy of mind or person, Caesar, Helen, Irving, Talma, the O'Rahilly, Casement, Parnell: the last flourishes of the long-meditated delight in personality. Everywhere joy, gaiety, frenzy are invoked and declared; the vital rhythms of 'Three Songs' and some other ballad-like pieces contribute metric and syntactic energy.[11] 'An old man's eagle mind' is imaginatively discovered.

To write poetry is itself to know and to disclose imaginative energy. As John Holloway shows in another chapter of this book, a common factor among many major poems is the giving incarnation to 'energised subjectivity, . . . passionate and powerful self-possession.' In a manner characteristic of *Last Poems* what had once been implicit in the reader's experience of the poem is now directly asserted. One among these poems allegorises the assumption of imaginative power. 'To Dorothy Wellesley' admits allegory because it is addressed to a fellow-poet; Lady Dorothy, with whom Yeats shared in these years 'intellec-tual sensuality', is a surrogate for the poet himself. The poetic experience is explicitly timed at midnight, the moment of visionary knowledge; at its conclusion the poetess climbs to the darkness of her book-lined chamber (the 'proper dark' of 'The Statues') and there gains knowledge of the Proud Furies 'each with her torch on high'.[12] The poem's action imitates the advance of an act of imaginative possession, the poetic process, and the assumption of the appropriate reward in personal energy. The first lines envisage the transmutation of external reality by (precisely) an apprehensive act: the poetess is bidden to grasp in her hand the 'moonless midnight of the trees' and to transform it to the

[10] The images (of lion, virgin, harlot, child, eagle, and another, wind) are linked in the prose with Yeats's 'delight in active men', personal energy. *E. & I.*, 530.

[11] Contemporary letters to Dorothy Wellesley show a simplistic, almost childlike, delight in vigorous rhythms.

[12] Compare 'Her Vision in the Wood', one of the few considerable poems in *Words For Music Perhaps* (*C.P.*, 312).

condition of imagined reality: 'famous old upholsteries'[13] ('As though' is mere poetic tact.) She then possesses the artifice sensuously, re-creates it within her own mind, becomes 'Rammed full with that most sensuous silence of the night.' Her reward consists in a visitation from the 'Proud Furies', instinct of energy, the very antithesis of 'Content' and 'satisfied Conscience'. The poet's dilemma at life's end is answered: 'My temptation', as he tells us, 'is quiet',[14] a temptation overcome by knowledge of 'frenzy', the gift of the Furies. And frenzy is known imaginatively in the poetic act; writing the poem involves a vicarious expenditure of imaginative energy: the verbs ('stretch', 'tighten', 'rammed', 'climb', 'bay') are notably indicative of the effortful nature of the experience. What it meant for Yeats is suggested by a passing note in *Autobiographies*, echoing the sixth and seventh lines of the present poem:

> E—— himself, all muscular force and ardour, makes me think of that line written, as one believes of Shakespeare by Ben Jonson— 'So rammed with life that he can but grow in life with being.' (*Auto.*, 480)

An alluring reward for the expenditure of imaginative energy by the ageing poet: to grow in life vicariously, as Time saps remaining physical strength. Shakespeare, ideally conceived, takes his place, though covertly, beside the other personal archetypes invoked and declared in *Last Poems*.

II

Among the poems of *The Winding Stair* 'Vacillation' asks the question which precipitates the concerns and commitments of *Last Poems*:

> Between extremities
> Man runs his course;
> A brand, or flaming breath,
> Comes to destroy
> All those antinomies
> Of day and night;
> The body calls it death,
> The heart remorse.
> But if these be right
> What is joy? (*C.P.*, 282)

---

[13] Does Yeats mean, perhaps, 'tapestries'?
[14] In 'An Acre of Grass', *C.P.*, 346.

'joy' turns out to be, as we have discovered, the imaginative possession of an image; reconciling or cancelling the antinomies, it makes joy possible. But so far the only antagonist has been 'remorse'; the second adversary remains. Yeats explains in a 1935 letter to Dorothy Wellesley: 'To me the supreme aim [of 'arranging' one's ideas and writing poetry] is an act of faith and reason to make one rejoice in the midst of tragedy'.[15] Yeats was at the date of writing 'still an invalid dreading fatigue'; other letters show him vividly conscious of approaching death. *Last Poems* are concerned to re-make the self and so win joy in the imminent presence of death; to go further: they seek to re-make death itself, to justify the taunt that 'Man has created death' (*C.P.*, 264). Hence the emphasis, new in these poems, on tragedy—on the art form most preoccupied with man's response to his mortality.

Yeats's somewhat personal views of tragedy ask explanation. In common with other literary forms, tragedy is properly given over to 'action' not to 'thought': 'masterpieces, whether of the stage or study, excel in their action, their visibility; who can forget Odysseus, Don Quixote, Hamlet, Lear, Faust, all figures in a peep-show'[16]; tragedy is, to put it simply, the locus of personality. Not of intricate psychology; the tragic heroes are a gallery of figures who exhibit, like the figures, the personal archetypes, of *Last Poems*, some abundant but uncomplicated personal energy. To identify with them, as author or spectator, is to discover joy, the familiar reward: 'Some Frenchman has said that farce is the struggle against a ridiculous object, comedy against a movable object, tragedy against an immovable; and because the will, or energy, is greatest in tragedy, tragedy is the more noble; but I add that "will or energy is eternal delight", and when its limit is reached it may become a pure aimless joy, though the man, the shade [the inferior Heracles?] still mourns his lost object.'[17] For the true tragic hero—the real Heracles—there will be no mourning: 'There may be in this or that detail painful tragedy, but in the whole work none. I have heard Lady Gregory say, rejecting some play in the modern manner sent to the Abbey Theatre, "Tragedy must be a joy to the man who dies!"' (*E. & I.*, 522). The implications of joy are specified: 'The heroes of Shakespeare convey to us through their looks, or through the metaphorical patterns of their speech, the sudden enlargement of their vision, their ecstasy at the approach of death.' (*E. & I.*, 522–523) The metaphor

[15] *Letters on Poetry from W. B. Yeats to Dorothy Wellesley* (1964), p. 12.
[16] *On the Boiler*, p. 33.
[17] *ibid.*, p. 35.

is reversible: 'ecstasy is a kind of death' (*E. & I.*, 71); to conflate, confuse, the two experiences is the outcome of Yeats's heady logic; death will be ecstasy, apocalypse—not an enemy—to the man who conceives of life as tragedy. Meditating on such a fittingly tragic death, that of Hamlet, Yeats tells us: 'This idea of death suggests to me Blake's design . . . of the soul and body embracing.' (*Letters*, 917) We are back at the language appropriate to 'The Statues', where body and soul embrace in knowledge of the sculptor's work. To re-make one's death in the tragic idiom is to discover an ecstasy closely allied to the joy attaching to imaginative possession of the sculpted figure, the joy known to Rocky Face. The writing of poetry, imaginative conquest, becomes subversive of the last reality.

The *personae* of tragedy, with whom the poet may identify, are frequent in *Last Poems*. Yeats elects to 're-make' himself as Timon and Lear ('An Acre of Grass'); Hamlet and Lear, Ophelia and Cordelia 'perform their tragic play' in 'Lapis Lazuli'; Hamlet is named in 'The Statues'. None of these characters had made previous appearances in the lyric verse. In 'Hound Voice' there is a reminiscence of *Lear*;[18] the madness of 'Why should not Old Men be Mad?' again remembers Lear.[19] Cuchulain, as tragic hero, is present in 'The Statues', 'Crazy Jane on the Mountain', 'The Circus Animals' Desertion', 'Cuchulain Comforted'; Parnell, hero of three poems, is described in prose as 'a tragedian';[20] Margot Ruddock, the unnamed heroine of 'A Crazed Girl' was 'a frustrated tragic genius' who found herself in the ecstasy of her frenzied dance upon the shore.[21] All serve within the economy of *Last Poems* as examples of tragic dying, or tragic ecstasy, by imaginative knowledge of whom Yeats may re-make his own death.

'Lapis Lazuli' is the considerable poem in which Yeats specifies the intimate connection between tragic joy and the poet's discovered power. The first two verses effect a redemption of the word 'gay'; contemptuously pronounced by the 'hysterical women'—bound as they are to the world of cyclical accident—it becomes in verse two synonymous with tragic joy, the joy of liberation. Unlike the despised actors of 'The Old Stone Cross', the actors of this poem understand 'what

[18] Compare 'The women that I picked spoke sweet and low' with *Lear* V. iii (of Cordelia): Her voice was ever soft / Gentle and low.'

[19] Behind Lear stands that 'silent and fierce old man' William Pollexfen, another of the book's personal archetypes. See *Auto*, 9.

[20] See the Variorum edition of the poems (ed. Allt and Alspach, 1957), p. 835; the contrast is with 'the great comedian' O'Connell.

[21] See Yeats's introduction (p. ix) to her *The Lemon Tree* (1937).

unearthly stuff / Rounds a mighty scene' (*C.P.*, 366); by successful interpretation of their rôles they achieve ecstasy and apocalyptic knowledge: 'Heaven blazing into the head.' The abrupt syntax, connectives altogether pared away, mimics the immediacy and the power of the discovered knowledge. 'Tragedy wrought to its uttermost' brings about the ecstatic confusion of death the prose describes. But the poet's especial craft has yet to be linked with this victory, his joy, 'gaiety', justified. Like 'A Bronze Head' and 'The Statues', 'Lapis Lazuli' took its origin from the contemplation of a sculpted image; a letter to Dorothy Wellesley speaks of 'a great piece [of lapis lazuli] carved by some Chinese sculptor. . . . Ascetic, pupil, hard stone, eternal theme of the sensual east. The heroic cry in the midst of despair. But no, I am wrong, the east has its solutions always and therefore knows nothing of tragedy. It is we, not the east, that must raise the heroic cry.'[22] The logic moves confidently between sculpted image, tragedy and the 'heroic cry' of poetry; 'Lapis Lazuli' offers an imaginative collocation of the same order. Section three contains properties that directly recall 'The Statues'; Callimachus 'handled marble as if it were bronze' (the characteristic materials), but his images that shaped the thought of a civilization were destroyed by time's action; as in 'The Statues' each new 'gay' civilisation must rebuild its own focal images. The remaining sections recall 'A Bronze Head' and 'To Dorothy Wellesley'. They enact the imaginative possession of the sculpted image, to bring the poet 'gaiety', as Dorothy Wellesley possessed her environment to win her own apocalyptic vision. The short fourth section presents the lapis lazuli carving as it appears to an objective scrutiny; the final section mimics an encroaching act of imaginative possession. At first the stone of the carving remains actual; its 'Every discoloration . . . accidental crack or dent' merely 'seems' water-course or avalanche; but even here the process of re-making is incipient. Then details are added ('doubtless'), details not even registered on the stone by 'accidental' usage; plum and cherry-branch flower at the poet's command. The next phrase brings confession:

I

Delight to imagine them seated there;

The act of imaginative possession is complete. And on its completion the image is made to contradict its marble repose; the scene the last lines depict is one of animation, of request and compliance, music

---

[22] *Letters . . . to Dorothy Wellesley*, p. 8.

and glittering eyes. The outcome is inevitable; the poem comes to rest declaring the poet's achievement, through imaginative exertion, of his apocalyptic reward: the last word is 'gay'.

III

The emphatic stress in Yeats's view of tragedy falls on the hero's rejoicing at the moment of death; to experience tragedy is altogether life-enhancing, exhilarating, death-cancelling. The refrain of 'The Gyres' may therefore appropriately be 'What matter?'; a superb non-chalance invests many *Last Poems*. The other side of the tragic duality in common experience, the deeply painful sense of loss, of wasted potential, is barely noticed: 'there may be in this or that detail painful tragedy, but in the whole work none.' Towards such a position the brilliant logic of Yeats's career—or an important aspect of it—had tended; the writing of poetry and the whole elaborate structure of *A Vision* were to confer just such security, an invulnerable aloofness. A comparison between 'Lapis Lazuli' and 'Nineteen Hundred and Nineteen' will show the process at work: the earlier poem greets the inevitable breaking of 'many ingenious lovely things' with dismay, even despair; 'Lapis Lazuli' knows the same facts with the superb detachment Rocky Face is bidden to discover. But there is a sense in which Yeats as poet has been trapped by a remorseless logic of his own creating; the discovery of the sculpted image and the assumption of the poetic-be-come-real energy may indeed be the inevitably right outcome, the 'ultimate insight', of the dedicated career. But they may operate also to the impoverishment of the poet; to detach the poetic sensibility from painful circumstance makes for a poverty that cannot be compensated by any merely declaratory security. The real 'images' of the great poems are not the specifically summoned ones, tower and winding stair, golden bird or even chestnut tree and dancer, but the infinite variousness of the poet's sensibility as he meditates, the varying deployments of allegiance and mistrust. There are signs of impoverishment in *Last Poems*; something of the assertive propagandist is felt, at his most unacceptable in the flat recommendation of violence for its own sake ('good strong blows are delights to the mind'); rhythm, though capable of niceties possible only to the aged virtuoso, is too often merely insistent. A certain thinness is bred; *Last Poems* almost wholly lacks the richly complex, brilliantly architected structure of many great poems. Yeats had claimed that his Church had an altar but no pulpit; the sheer

H.G.–K

assertiveness of some *Last Poems* would argue the prominent existence
of pulpit at the end of life.

But to rest here would be to miss the opposed allegiances within the
collection. Yeats is too intelligent a self-critic to have been blind to
these new impoverishments; several poems consider explicitly the very
dilemma we have noted. Some present, in contrast to the powerful
aloofness of the Rocky Face, the natural man vividly conscious of
time's injuries. Among these, 'The Municipal Gallery Revisited' looks
at first glance a poem in the familiar idiom. The gallery pictures are the
images to be possessed anew by the poet; they, like others, result from
a work of imaginative re-making:

> [Not] The dead Ireland of my youth, but an Ireland
> The poets have imagined, terrible and gay.

The 'terrible beauty' of 'Easter 1916', to create which Pearse and the
others had been 'transformed utterly', is here memorialised in art;
'terrible and gay' is the condition of tragic joy discovered in 'Lapis
Lazuli'. And beside the poet's imagined Ireland hang portraits of his
friends; the syntax demands that we take the 'permanent or impermanent images' to refer to such portraits; like the other characteristic
poses of this collection, personal archetypes, his 'friends' take their
place as fixed, 'sculpted' images to be imaginatively known. We seem
about to have urged on us once more the advantages of powerful self-
possession. But the idiom is largely distinct from others among *Last
Poems*.[23] The syntax is one of colon and semi-colon; there is leisure to
insert 'I say', 'certainly', leisure for repetition; long-suspended sentences
may ignore even the break between verses (Yeats noted that complete
coincidence between period and stanza brought 'energy'); rhythm is
relaxed and diction plain, undemanding; the speaker's environment is
generously, not to say superfluously, stocked. The general effect is one
of easy gravity, an undesigning wandering amid memories; as against
the telling compression, the abrupt energetic juxtapositions of 'The
Statues' or 'Lapis Lazuli'. Where 'The Gyres' delights in enigma, 'The
Municipal Gallery' seems anxious to lead us on, to explain as fully as
possible. The distinction is absolute; it registers in an unaffected
recording of personal emotion altogether foreign to the aloof detachment of those other poems:

[23] An exception is 'A Bronze Head'; explaining I think Yeats's decision to
cancel the original last stanza.

> Heart-smitten with emotion I sink down,
> My heart recovering with covered eyes . . .

'What matter?' is replaced by a confession of despair at the loss of what was unique, irrecoverable:

> And I am in despair that time may bring
> Approved patterns of women or of men
> But not that self-same excellence again.

The 'approved patterns', the norm that was susceptible of becoming a sculpted pose, are rejected in favour of the variously human. Acknowledgement is made, not of the triumphant Rocky Face, but of the 'heart', the locus of natural feeling.

Other poems in the earlier part of the collection (the group closing with 'Are You Content', first published as *New Poems* in 1938) betray something of the same commitment. Self-judging poems such as 'What Then?' view the poetic triumph, in refrain at least, with deflating irony:

> 'The work is done', grown old he thought . . .
> 'Let the fools rage, I swerved in naught,
> But someting to perfection brought';
> *But louder sang that ghost, 'What then?'* (C.P., 348)

The ambivalent refrain questions not only the value of the achievement but the fate of the poet; the assurance of 'Heaven blazing into the head' appears to recede. The power that attends identification with the personal archetype is similarly undercut in 'Are You Content?' 'Infirm and aged' Yeats might

> demonstrate in my own life
> What Robert Browning meant
> By an old hunter talking with Gods;
> But I am not content. (*C.P.*, 371)

Reference to the essays will disclose an association with Berkeley, a recurrent hero, behind the lines (*E. & I.*, 408–9); but even imaginative identification with that 'angry unscrupulous solitary' does not in this mood content the heart.

The mood incipient in the 1938 *New Poems* is developed in those first published posthumously as *Last Poems* in 1939. In this new group, the most terrifying of 'The Apparitions' becomes Yeats's own 'coat upon a coat-hanger'; death can no longer be re-fashioned to ecstasy, but is regarded with the heart's candour:

His empty heart is full at length,
But he has need of all that strength
Because of the increasing Night
That opens her mystery and fright. (*C.P.*, 387)

In a more considerable way 'High Talk' revalues the poet's craft, the
source of powerful self-possession in other poems. Yeats casts himself as
Malachi Stilt-Jack, the maker of metaphors, of art in the grand manner.
Already implicit in the chosen *dramatis persona* is an ironic valuation:
the walker upon stilts, though an eye-catching figure, is inescapably an
absurd posturing creature on his 'timber toes'; the reaction he provokes
from the onlookers recalls only juvenile practical jokes: 'women shriek'.
And the activity he is committed to is a precarious one, carried out
unnaturally, under strain. The last few lines of the poem record with
desperate seriousness the human predicament from which attention has
been diverted by the stilted figure. Metaphor, the poet's craft, is explicitly abandoned. The setting registers apocalypse: 'night splits and
the dawn breaks loose'; but it brings with it 'terrible novelty', not the
welcome of a conquered territory. Under its brilliant light the natural
man, no longer upon timber toes, 'stalks on', a hunted yet eager and
vital being prompted and terrified by revelation. The apocalyptic
grandeur is suggested by the 'great sea-horses' (symbolic, but by comparison with the stilt-walker part of the natural setting) 'laughing' at
the dawn in ecstasy or terrifying superior knowledge; the poet's
imaginings are seen as paltry contrivances beside such heart-recognised
'mystery and fright'.

The strategy of 'The Circus Animals' Desertion' parallels that of
'High Talk'; the circus phantasmagoria, the connection explicitly made
by the '*stilted* boy', carries with it the same ironic valuation. The circus
animals have merely been 'on show'; their triviality is gestured towards
by the colloquial indifference of 'The Lord knows what'. In essence the
poem is a direct espousal of the 'heart'; in the face of approaching death
poetic triumph is not possible or not relevant; the 'masterful images',
'complete' and self-sufficient, have come to seem a showman's imperti-
nence. 'Character isolated by a deed', the condition precisely of the
powerful *dramatis personae* of earlier *Last Poems*, is set aside. The poet
lies down in preference in 'the foul rag-and-bone-shop of the heart';
the miscellaneous, chance, nature of the contents, their disorderly profusion, stands for the absence of identifiable meaning that attends direct
on-the-pulses experience; the 'raving slut' indicates the kind of un-
mastered violence, the intoxicating vigour, Yeats commonly associates

with such experience. In one of his latest essays Yeats speaks of his admiration for his 'brother's extreme book, "The Charmed Life",' an admiration evoked by 'his pursuit of all that through its unpredictable, unarrangeable reality, least resembles knowledge.'[24] 'The Circus Animals' Desertion', whatever its negative aspects as a 'Dejection Ode', is equally a vote for such heart-reality against the belief in formality, 'calculation, number, measurement' of earlier poems.

'The Man and the Echo' answers 'The Gyres' directly. The setting is again oracular; 'the cleft that's christened Alt' was associated with the Delphic chasm. But where 'The Gyres' is declaratory, assertive, this poem ends on a poignant note; its temper is questioning, the poem's *raison d'être* being an inquest on the self and the poetry. Nor has the poet been transformed to a Rocky Face; his is the natural undefended sensibility condemned to 'lie awake night after night / And never get the answers right'. The answers he receives from the Rocky Voice are confessedly no more than an echo of his questions. To the ultimate question,

> O Rocky Voice
> Shall we in that great night rejoice?

the oracle returns no answer. It is an effect of calculated restraint to refuse even the token reassurance of an acoustic reply. In place of the voice from the cavern with its confident knowledge of one word, 'Rejoice', we have the anguish of not knowing. As in 'High Talk', the poet's triumph seems trivial before the heart's naked experience:

> But hush, for I have lost the theme,
> Its joy or night seem but a dream;
> Up there some hawk or owl has struck,
> Dropping out of sky or rock,
> A stricken rabbit is crying out,
> And its cry distracts my thought.

The anguish of death is overwhelmingly more vivid than poetry's 'theme'; 'joy', the familiar claim, and 'night', the threat, are both impertinent rationalisations beside direct knowledge of death's imminence.

'The Black Tower' was Yeats's last poem. Beside its disquieting uncertainty 'Under Ben Bulben', the 'official' tail-piece, assertive, secure, looks almost brash. 'The Black Tower' in effect makes over for

[24] *On the Boiler*, p. 36.

the last time what remains Yeats's central symbol, the tower. That proud image, with its winding stair conducting to wisdom, is now a tower of refuge only, sombre, beleaguered, suffering the exigencies of want. This poem, like 'The Gyres', records the moment when the gyre changes direction; but not now from a position of untouchable superiority—the poet is deeply involved in the uncertainties the moment brings. Aware of distress, there exists also the possibility of release and new vigour when the dark of the moon comes round at last. The implied link with Yeats's own dying is barely escapable. The poised ambivalence with which the moment of apocalypse is awaited is characteristic of the temper of these latest poems. Terror is declared as well as joy, heart mysteries as well as heaven blazing into the head.

IX

The Plays

PETER URE

★

I

As early as 1900 Yeats was able to express even the past and future
history of the drama in terms of widening and contracting gyres. 'The
drama', he wrote,

> has need of cities that it may find men in sufficient numbers, and cities
> destroy the emotions to which it appeals, and therefore the days of
> the drama are brief and come but seldom. It has one day when the
> emotions of cities still remember the emotions of sailors and
> husbandmen and shepherds and users of the spear and the bow . . .
> and it has another day, now beginning, when thought and scholar-
> ship discover their desire. In the first day, it is the art of the people;
> and in the second day . . . it is the preparation of a priesthood. It
> may be, though the world is not old enough to show us any example,
> that this priesthood will spread their religion everywhere, and make
> their Art the Art of the people. (E. & I., 167–8)

This is an accurate enough sketch of the historical principles that guided
Yeats's own practice as a playwright. Playwrights of the great days
traditionally selected their locations from the metropolis, where palace,
castle, and market jostle for the best sites. The Victorian theatre chose
its locations at random; no style seems to have established itself, and
certainly nothing that could convey to their inhabitants the real sense
of what was happening to their cities. There are records of the absurd
labours that sometimes went into making Shakespeare accurate: *The
Winter's Tale* with Pyrrhic dances contrived from Nuttall's *Classical
and Archaeological Dictionary*, and Mamilius drawing a toy cart based on
a terracotta prototype in the British Museum; 'Mr. Punch has it upon
authority to state that the Bear at present running in Oxford Street in
The Winter's Tale is an archaeological copy from the original bear of

Noah's ark.'[1] When Shaw began *Widowers' Houses*, when, four years later in 1889, Yeats met Maud Gonne at his father's house in Bedford Park and sat down to write *The Countess Cathleen* for her, English playwrights had, for all serious purposes, been for some time locked up in the middle-class drawing-room. Even Shaw did not for some years do much to release them from their bondage. Yeats wrote in 1903 about a performance of Ibsen's *Ghosts*:

> All the characters seemed to be less than life-size; the stage . . . seemed larger than I had ever seen it. Little whimpering puppets moved here and there in the middle of that great abyss. Why did they not speak out with louder voices or move with freer gestures? What was it that weighed upon their souls perpetually? Certainly they were all in prison, and yet there was no prison. (*P. & C.*, 122)

And a year or so later he wrote of the elaboration of the scene and technique in the modern theatre in an essay which is full of his suspicion of the *painted* stage, of the kind of thing which Charles Kean had done so successfully at the Oxford Street Theatre to *The Winter's Tale*:

> The theatre grows more elaborate, developing the player at the expense of the poet, developing the scenery at the expense of the player, always increasing the importance of whatever has come to it out of the mere mechanism of a building or the interests of a class, specialising more and more, doing whatever is easiest rather than what is most noble, and shaping imaginations before the footlights as behind, that are stirred to excitement that belongs to it and not to life. (*P. & C.*, 178)

'Puppets in prison', the 'mechanism of a building or the interests of a class'—clearly, more than one act of liberation was necessary. The first and last and the most important for Yeats was to make the play reach at 'life' by freeing itself more and more from elaboration that only mimicked the surface of life. This, with all its need for definition, for an accurate understanding of what he meant by the 'deeps' and what he meant by the superficies, was the most complex task which Yeats undertook as a playwright, and the one most liable to backfire in unexpected ways, to turn out to be a serpent with its tail in its mouth after all. If that story could be rightly written, we might have the whole truth about Yeats the playwright. We need only to quote his late confession from 'The Circus Animals' Desertion':

[1] Quoted in W. M. Merchant, *Shakespeare and the Artist* (London, 1959), p. 216.

Players and painted stage took all my love,
And not those things that they were emblems of, (*C.P.*, 392)

in order to realise that the fascination of 'theatre-business, management of men' was something that often distracted him from 'life'. His suspicions of the stage as a place where the single vision of the poet had to master, if it could, the wayward behaviour, the quarrels, and the merely minor accomplishments of fragmentary men and hysterical woman were complicated by the deep appeal which all that fuss and fury made to something histrionic and gregarious in himself. He was far less successful in making his various roles—as Irishman, or theatre director, or mage, or courtly lover—serve his plays than he was in forging them all into the poems' unities of being; and the plays are therefore smaller things by far. Yet there is no doubt that his attempt to discover 'life' by means of a refashioned and liberated drama made abundant calls upon his genius, which was not always unresponsive. The complexities of that particular act of liberation may for the moment, though, be put aside while we examine the simpler matter of the 'interests of a class' and its terrible symbol, that stifling drawing-room.

For Yeats was right in foreseeing, at a time when the Abbey Theatre had only just begun, that the devotion to Irish subject-matter, the mere shift of the location from London, with its Anglo-Saxon passion for the abstract and the ideal, its disordered subjection to a kaleidoscope of international, intellectual fashions (as it seemed to him), would solve the problem of the drawing-room. 'Let a man turn his face to us', he wrote, 'and talk of what is near to our hearts, Irish Kings and Irish Legends and Irish Countrymen' (*P. & C.*, 111). It was the last of these three that mattered most in practice, there is no doubt that in bringing with them their inevitable ambience of Dublin streets and Mayo cottages the Irish countrymen put an end to the West End drawing-room so far as the real history of the drama is concerned. 'Our opportunity in Ireland', Yeats wrote in 1905,

is not that our playwrights have more talent—it is possible that they have less than the workers in an old tradition—but that the necessity of putting a life that has not hitherto been dramatised into their plays excludes all those types which have had their origin in a different social order. (*P. & C.*, 143)

The consequential danger—that the plays would become merely propaganda for the Nationalist cause—he foresaw just as acutely and evaded as adroitly. For the time being, at least, it did not happen (though how much of the credit is due to the fact that the Irish theatre was then ultimately overseen by an official of the English Government it would be impolitic to inquire). 'The public life of Athens', Yeats reminded *The United Irishman* and kindred spirits, with that touch of resonant arrogance that is one of the glories of his mind,

> found its chief celebration in the monstrous caricature of Aristo-phanes, and the Greek nation was so proud, so free from morbid sensitiveness, that it invited the foreign ambassadors to the spectacle. (*P. & C.*, 150)

The greatest of Irish comedies, *The Playboy of the Western World*, and the greatest of Irish tragedies (if tragedy it is), *Juno and the Paycock*, are there to assure us that he was prophetically right on all counts. 'Some-body must teach reality and justice.'[2]

These plays are far finer than any that Yeats could achieve. Yet, within this same context of the discovery of new locations, an interest still attaches to his own drawing-room plays, *Where There Is Nothing* and *The Words upon the Window-Pane*. Both are, of course, attempts to *faire tordre le cou* of the drawing-room, to smash or explode it. Nearly thirty years separate them (1902 to 1930), and they have the additional interest of showing how much Yeats had advanced, by 1930, in the rather complex operation of making a dramatic form turn its sword in its own proper entrails. *Where There Is Nothing* begins, if not in a drawing-room, in the equally dismal setting of a croquet lawn, a setting which the hero endeavours to dismantle as he takes his way out on to the tinkers' roads, seeking to become the 'beggarman of all the ages', to 'express himself in "life" '. But, apart from its other defects, which were sufficiently recognised by its author, the play makes too many concessions to the form which it is trying to destroy; its naturalism strives against the hero's exalted vision and turns it all into a rhetoric which awakens distrust and unbelief. In *The Words upon the Window-Pane*, on the other hand, Yeats momentarily shocks us into suspending our disbelief by, precisely, introducing the Furies into the drawing-room—the device that T. S. Eliot was to repudiate and Yeats con-tinually to desire just because he hoped that it 'would transport the audience violently from one plane of reality to another',[3] or, in his own, and not Eliot's, words, would induce 'the sense of spiritual reality [that] comes . . . from some violent shock', since 'Belief comes from

---

[2] *Dramatis Personae* (London, 1936), p. 180.
[3] T. S. Eliot, *On Poetry and Poets* (London, 1957), p. 74.

shock and is not desired.'[4] In the centre of a naturalistic problem play about spiritualism he sets an image of discarnate suffering, and unites us violently to that image not by rhetoric but by a single gesture when the medium, Mrs. Henderson, cries out in Swift's voice and phrase as the curtain falls. Of all Yeats's plays, for an audience still attuned to the naturalistic tradition as reinforced by Eliot, *The Words upon the Window-Pane* is the one that most deserves to be judged in the theatre and will best serve to give an appetite for working through the *Collected Plays*.

And yet the violence which Yeats had in his fashion wrought upon drawing-room expectations was already by 1930 something of an anachronism. The Abbey had taken the course which he expected, growing ever more 'objective with the objectivity of the office and the workshop' (*P. & C.*, 206), its locations chosen from cottage or streets and not from the English house. Synge had produced the perfected form of the 'peasant play', and O'Casey had brought the movement to full maturity by returning it to its megapolitical and Jonsonian centre with the one indisputable masterpiece of the whole repertoire. *Juno and the Paycock* is a great expression of 'the emotions of cities', and the degree of its objectivity, in both the Yeatsian and the ordinary senses, can easily be measured if one consults the appropriate pages in *Inishfallen, Fare Thee Well*. The only play which Yeats set in a city offers a startling contrast to *Juno*, with which it is almost exactly contemporary. Yeats had told Lady Gregory some years earlier, now that the time had come for him to leave the Abbey because the plays had turned towards objectivity, and the players had begun to copy their old grandmothers in Aran, that he sought the theatre's anti-self; and *The Player Queen* may be said to be the anti-self of *Juno*. Its two scenes, an open space at the meeting of streets and the throne-room of a palace, return us to the city of power; but this city is a comic emblem of a civilisation which is collapsing, as the gyre expands, in preparation for a second coming and the birth of a new era; the heroine is an actress who plays queens' parts, but would prefer to be a real queen and so have power over the city. In the process of 'mocking his own thought', thought which had by now contrived to crystallise into almost credal pattern, Yeats's intimations of the anti-mask and the gyres (both of which originate in the 1890s), he has produced, as Mrs. Vendler has said, something resembling 'a chapter from *A Vision* read with an

[4] *Wheels and Butterflies* (London, 1934), p. 120; *A Vision*, 53.

eyebrow cocked'.[5] From the confusion of allegorical cross-currents Mrs. Vendler has teased out those elements in the story which relate to the fortunes of the *poète maudit* Septimus, his wife Decima, and his Daimon of poetic inspiration, the chaste, white Unicorn with whose undying image the poet longs to unite his muse, but never can. The fickle wife cannot, I think, be read, as she is by Mrs. Vendler, purely as an allegory of the Muse; the play ends with her union not with the Daimon (whose coming is farcically and vengefully postponed) but with the Prime Minister and with the role of Queen, and the Unicorn is not only an aesthetic symbol but also the immanent beast-deity which was for Yeats a figuration about the character of a new cultural and religious dispensation. If beneath the characters of *The Player Queen* there obscurely lurks a very old story, about the cursed poet whom his Muse rejected, we must not forget that what Maud Gonne rejected him for was Nationalism and John MacBride the politician. As its location in the city suggests, the play is about kingdoms as well as about the poet; the strong elements in it of neo-classical intrigue, appropriate to this location, have savage undertones of tragedy, deriving not only from glimpses of the city's mob (turbulent and murderous as their city shudders towards a new age) but also from the final extrusion of Septimus from his place at the Queen's table and from the final frustration—we might almost say 'punishment'—of Decima. In devising her fate, Yeats strikes almost the note with which, illiberally, he wrote of Eva Gore-Booth:

> I know not what the younger dreams—
> Some vague Utopia—and she seems,
> When withered old and skeleton-gaunt,
> An image of such politics. (*C.P.*, 263)

II

These themes remind us, leapfrogging, backwards this time, over the space of another thirty years, of the plays of the earliest period, and perhaps most of all of two that are specially significant, *The Countess Cathleen* and *The King's Threshold*, another play about whether the poet's vision has any place in the kingdom. Aleel, whose unchristened heart the Countess rejects in order that she may succour her people, Seanchan in *The King's Threshold*, who makes out of his rejection by

[5] H. H. Vendler, *Yeats's Vision and the Later Plays* (Cambridge, Mass., 1963), p. 128.

the old world a visionary acceptance, joyful in tragedy, of life-in-death and death-in-life, and Septimus in *The Player Queen*, a comic parody of them both, who recognises his kinship with the beggars, as Seanchan had, and has to deal with a tricky Muse who turns her face elsewhere—these persons march sufficiently with the process which, in Yeats's poems, transforms the vague speaker of *The Wind Among the Reeds*, a Pre-Raphaelite voice in the head, into the seer of 'Byzantium' and the scarecrow of 'Among School Children'. To that series, others could be added: the Stroller/Swineherd of *The King of the Great Clock Tower* and *A Full Moon in March* is the proper issue of the *miraculeuse nuit nuptiale* of Forgael and Dectora in *The Shadowy Waters* so many years earlier. *The King's Threshold* has also to be taken more literally and impersonally, for it has one dimension as a Ruskinian plea for the recognition of a necessary link between the kind of society which is worth living in and the cultivation of approved arts:

> But why were you born crooked?
> What bad poet did your mothers listen to
> That you were born so crooked? (*C.Pl.*, 133)

The problem of how the 'wasteful virtues', heroical as well as poetical—for the poet's 'book', as in the dedicatory poem to *Responsibilities*, affirms his kinship with his chivalrous and reckless forebears—may be integrated into the ordered kingdom, the cities of power, is a controlling theme in other plays of the period, most clearly in the first of the Cuchulain series, *On Baile's Strand*. Cuchulain's and Conchubar's dilemma in this play is how to be both strong and wasteful, reasonable and poetical, how to get things into order without losing the impulse to create; how, in short, does the city attain Unity of Being? It was Yeats's own personal and aesthetic dilemma, but it was also interdependently, or so he thought, that of his society. This should remind us that, when he writes in Berkeley's phrase of 'We Irish', speaks of 'the poems of civilisation', or describes the ruin and rebirth of cultures in *A Vision*, he is not merely cultivating metaphors for aesthetic experience. In *On Baile's Strand* Cuchulain's mind is got into disorder by Aoife's evil will; this is an early intimation of Yeats's Conradian theme of what heroes have to fight against, 'the breath of unknown powers that shape our destinies',[6] the ghost, the evil spell, but, for Yeats as not for Conrad, also a longed-for annulment of human intricacies:

---

[6] Conrad, *The Shadow-Line*.

oblivion
Even to quench Cuchulain's drouth,
Even to still that heart. (*C. Pl.*, 293)

Conchubar unawares helps to do Aoife's work for her, and Cuchulain's unity breaks down into madness, leaving the city desolate and un-guarded. Perhaps, since it has lost him, it is a city without poets, too; when last we see it the beggars are running off to steal the chickens from the pot. *On Baile's Strand* records in its hero a failure of the imagination to accomplish the task assigned to it (that of recognising and loving his son); but the play nearest to it in date, *Deirdre*, though on a famous tragic theme, is its counter-truth, for it describes in its heroine a triumph of the loving imagination. Again, a Conrad parallel suggests itself—the difference between Lord Jim and Axel Heyst. Deirdre's mind ends in that state of high imaginative order in which she re-creates her self out of a paradigm of possible roles, and attains, for the space of time necessary to triumph over Conchubar's amorous will and her own fearful horror, unity of being. Of all Yeats's early plays, *Deirdre* is the one in which he came nearest to reaching down to 'life' by contriving a 'ritual of passion' which would, he hoped, induce the condition of tragic reverie where player and spectator draw upon the *anima mundi*, 'that soul which is alike in all men', the dikes between them broken down and drowned—the dikes, that is to say, of 'players and painted stage', the footlights, 'the mere mechanism of a building and the interests of a class'. And, in *Deirdre*, the poets *are* present to commemorate the scene:

Now strike the wire, and sing to it a while,
Knowing that all is happy, and that you know
Within what bride-bed I shall lie this night. (*C.Pl.*, 201)

Enough perhaps has been said to show that these early plays are not merely gestures in support of a cultural enterprise, the Irish National Theatre Company or the Abbey players, but central to the history of a great poet's mind. Yet nobody who wished to argue that any of these plays deserve a continued life within a less specialised context than the history of that mind could possibly be persuasive. The poems in *The Green Helmet* of 1910 are the first that speak out; much more is this true of the plays of the same period. There are powerful fables, a few examples of vigorous words tied to the speaker and responsive to what else is on the stage with him; but all is vitiated by Yeats's very intensity and purity of purpose, which produces guarded and monotonous rhythms, pages of *carefully* organised periods that open out from time to time into figurative writing which curiously adds no extra dimension to the verse—the wallpaper suddenly blazes with a peacock, but it is a flat peacock still, and looks self-conscious amongst the grave arabesques that surround it.

Still, despite their now much-faded appearance, these are plays which were hammered out with a very intent consciousness of the stage at Yeats's command, the things and people on it; they are certainly not just lyrical exercises, and it is sometimes hard to tell, especially when we have in mind the *prima facie* evidence of Yeats's continual revisions in the light of actual experience in the theatre, how much their failure to survive is due to a change of taste and ideas in the theatre audience, which once took these plays and now, having in the meantime sub-mitted to other masters, cannot take them. It is impossible to arrive at any general rules about what is and is not theatrically viable when audiences of our own day can sit enthralled by the soliloquies of actors buried up to their necks in mounds of earth. (Yeats anticipated this device early in his career when he suggested that barrels with castors on them might be used at rehearsals so that actors could forget their bodies and concentrate on their speech.) The playwright is the audience's master, and as he gives place to his successors they alter the notion of what is truly of the theatre, so that the accolade of 'theatrical craftsman' honorifically accorded to a writer by 'practical men of the theatre' is the most vulnerable part even of Shakespeare. Yeats's best theatrical effects are often muffled, though, by the literary wit and high cir-cumlocution of his verse; it will not do to dismiss him as merely another lyric poet who wanted to turn the stage into a sounding-board for his own voice and has been suitably punished; but it is true that, while admitting that dramatic action must 'burn up the author's opinions', he found it hard to recognise that it must, in another sense, burn up a concern for purity of diction and articulated syntax. There were several reasons for the failure. His healthy reaction against the meaningless movements of naturalism, the endless 'dressing of the stage', the perpetual fidget, led him to value stillness and absence of gesture and to stress the primacy of speech—but it could not bear the weight of all that devoted concentration and authorial redaction. He wanted the speech, too, to be vivid but remain still and quiet; yet this quietness was not natural to him: did he not confess at the end of his life that 'Synge, Lady Gregory, and I were all instinctively of the school of Talma', which permits an actor 'to throw up an arm calling down the thunder-bolts of Heaven' (E. & I., 529)? The resistance which he offered, for the sake of his ideology, to the gesture of melodrama resulted in a cautiously constrained and two-dimensional style, a demurely restricted vocabulary resembling the privative arabesques of *The Wind among the Reeds*. Furthermore, he was uneasy about blank verse, the Shakes-pearian, the Renaissance measure; his wish was to get back behind the Renaissance into a world of imagined heroic unities, away from that mid-point of civilisation which he both adored and detested.[7] And yet he was saddled with blank verse, and in retrospect at least tolerated it only when he could 'put it out of joint' in *The Countess Cathleen*, for the Countess was 'vaguely medieval' and so could bear blank verse a little better than a character from heroic saga such as Cuchulain (E. & I., 523–5). Always he seemed when writing blank verse to suffer from those varied constraints.

Again, if we apply the criterion of location, the early plays will seem a muddle—but one with some suggestive alleviations. In his settings Yeats has achieved no personal style, no recognisable locale, but shifts about opportunistically 'like some poor Arab tribesman and his tent'. The cottages and castles are simply naturalistic settings, specimens of the genre *cottage* or *castle*, just as the drawing-room in *The Second Mrs. Tanqueray* is one of a thousand drawing-rooms. Yeats's later attempts to interfere with these settings in the interests of medieval keepings or bold, primary richness of effect—directing, for example, that the first scene in *The Countess Cathleen* should resemble a missal painting or putting his Fool and Blind Man into masks—do not make any fundamental alteration in the feeling that the location itself contributes nothing to the plays except a more or less appropriate background. In *The Shadowy Waters*, however, there is a more promising arrangement: 'The whole picture', Yeats wrote, 'as it were moves together—sky and sea and cloud are as it were actors' (*Letters*, 425). Consider, next, the difference between *On Baile's Strand* and *The King's Threshold*: Baile's strand itself signally fails to contribute anything to the play; but the King's threshold has been turned by Seanchan into an emblem which is also a playing-place; it is central to the inward meaning and the outward action of the play:

> there is a custom,
> An old and foolish custom, that if a man
> Be wronged, or think that he is wronged, and starve

[7] *On the Boiler* (Cuala Press, 1938), p. 27.

Upon another's threshold till he die,
The common people, for all time to come,
Will raise a heavy cry against that threshold,
Even though it be the King's. (*C.Pl.*, 108)

To it everyone must come and towards it all the action of the play
flows, and all the local colour, because it is a place where meanings are
focused and decisions have to be taken, just as the house in *The Alchemist*
is made the centre of a spider's web. There is nothing arbitrary here;
place and story interlock. This surely is a great advantage, because a
unity of elements which might translate itself into real unity of being
must be a criterion for plays on the scale which Yeats normally composed; he had not much time to persuade us into a conviction of the
decorum of his scene or to establish by slow gradations that place and
people and story cohere, but must present such a conviction highly
wrought almost as soon as the curtain rises. Yeats's aesthetic pre-
possessions, his whole endeavour to convert the vast design into the
single image, all suggest that the interlocking of action and location
may provide a clue to the presence of that kind of organic unity which
his theatre appears naturally to demand. And gradually it becomes clear
that one method of distinguishing his more successful plays from the
others is to observe that in them the story is *about* the place, or, to put
it in another way, that the characters have to come to just this place,
and no other anywhere in the world, so that this story may happen.
An analogy from the poems may reinforce the point: in those poems
which he invests with a sense of the sacred and unique character of the
locale—such as 'I walked among the seven woods of Coole' (signifi-
cantly linked to *The Shadowy Waters* as its dedication), other Coole
poems ('The Wild Swans', 'Coole Park, 1929' and so on), 'In Memory
of Major Robert Gregory', 'Easter 1916', 'A Prayer for My Daughter',
'In Memory of Eva Gore-Booth', and a number of others up to 'Under
Ben Bulben'—it is plain that the location is an actor, too. In these
poems, in which the mind is transforming everything into a superhuman dream, it also preserves the places through all that transformation in the first freshness of their nature; Coole, the Tower, the
mountain, and the streets of Dublin survive as felt actualities amidst all
the re-ordering imposed upon them by Yeats's convictions, so that they
seem freely to play their parts in the great mythology. Having studied
that extraordinary Baedeker, we can recognise them if we go to them:

Not such as are in Newton's metaphor,
But actual shells of Rosses' level shore. (*C.P.*, 278)

H.G.–L

Their participation in the total structure of the poems is analogous to the way in which the locations in some of Yeats's later plays contribute to a unity of all their elements.

III

'The scene is any bare space before a wall . . .' This formula, from *At the Hawk's Well*, the first of the plays written under the influence of the Japanese Noh, is explicit or implicit in most of those which succeed it. The patterned screen merely and tentatively suggests; the responsibility for evoking the location, its uniqueness and meaning, is delegated to the characters within the play:

> I call to the eye of the mind
> A well long choked up and dry
> And boughs long stripped by the wind (*C.Pl.*, 208)

or

> The hour before dawn and the moon covered up;
> The little village of Abbey is covered up;
> The little narrow trodden way . . . (*C.Pl.*, 434)

We are already caught into the process by which the voice, as an element inside the work, invites us to see and imagine within a context which it is actively creating, as Coole is created for us in the poems by a mind brooding upon analogies and locational meanings, preserving their freshness and yet organising them into a total vision or conviction. The four Plays for Dancers show this, and show besides most clearly other elements at work, demanding to be wrought together; and all these are present, with varying degrees of completeness, in most of the later plays.

First, in the four Plays for Dancers, there are the Musicians. Because this is a drama seeking a deep of the mind, they are charged not only with the task of setting the outward scene and describing what the protagonists wear and look like and how (if need be) they are to be dated, but also with enunciating a theme as they unfold the curtain— woman's beauty in *The Only Jealousy*, subjectivity and self-absorption in *Calvary*. As Yeats, in later plays, stylised the superficies more and more, this enunciation became the most of what they have to do:

First Attendant. What do we sing?
Second Attendant. 'Sing anything, sing any old thing', said he.
(*C.Pl.*, 621)

The conventions adapted from the Noh were eagerly used to deepen and confirm earlier insights and practice. The poets had often been present to enlarge and deepen perspective in the first plays—Aleel in *The Countess Cathleen*, the Musicians in *Deirdre*, even, in their fashion, the Fool and the Blind Man; but now no attempt is made at a logical explanation of their presence in the scene; they come with the confident authority of an unexamined convention (like a rising curtain or the announcement of a theme in music), and like both these devices they withdraw us from everyday consciousness, and achieve what Yeats liked to call an appropriate distance from life. But 'distance' always suggests 'escape', whereas what the Musicians require of us is an act of concentration: the mind is to become 'a dark well, no surface, depth only' (*Auto.*, 292); we are to plunge down with images which recede from us into a more powerful life, to pass from the superficies to 'life', to 'reality', to the *anima mundi* where masquers and spectators commune in a dance.

The actual dance itself, of which both Yeats and his critics have made so much, is not, as I see it, the most important feature of his plays (many of the later ones, of course, once he had freed himself from the first absorption by the Noh, dispense with it altogether). Nearly all his plays work towards some moment of decision, enlightenment, or revelation, a peripeteia or 'turn'. This, as both Eric Bentley and Ronald Peacock have argued, is the point on which one must insist if one wishes to prove that Yeats is a playwright as well as a poet, and did succeed, as he wanted to, in showing events and not merely talking of them. He understood that his business as a playwright was not to meditate or to soliloquise but to contrive encounters from which a protagonist emerges changed, 'smitten as by the lightning-flash' (the analogy is with artistic experience as Yeats described it),[8] his world or himself revealed to him by new knowledge or the necessity of decision: 'Yeats is not only a dramatist but a classic dramatist'; 'A single, often loose, knot, untied with a single movement—such, for the most part, are his plays.'[9] The Noh plays, with which much of his work has structural affinity, helped Yeats to strengthen and define the climactic moments of revelation and spiritual enlightenment, but such moments are characteristically present in plays written long before he had heard of the Noh; indeed, a list of them would include *all* the early plays—

[8] *Essays* (London, 1924), pp. 503–4.
[9] E. Bentley in *The Permanence of Yeats* (New York, 1950), p. 239; R. Peacock, *The Poet in the Theatre* (London, 1946), p. 99.

Cathleen ni Houlihan itself, long his most famous and popular piece, is one of the best examples. It is these moments, and not the dance, which count, and the dance is not coincident with them, except in a marginal and qualified way. The stress on the dance, which is partly accounted for by Yeats's own emphases, but is more central to his poems and to his symbolist aesthetic than to his work as a playwright, has made these plays seem more remote and inhuman than they are. He scarcely ever, except in *A Full Moon in March*, succeeded in making the dance more than an illustration to the main action of the play; modern producers, chilled at the prospect of having to obtain the services of another Michio Ito or another Ninette de Valois, could well dispense with it altogether, shocking though the suggestion sounds. In *At the Hawk's Well* the dance is more truly vital to the climax than in any of the other plays, but even here it is Cuchulain's decision to *face* the hawk-dancer, in spite of the curse, that leads to his betrayal by his own courage, the ironic point made by the play about the character of the heroic act, 'a sacrifice of himself to himself'.[10] In *The Only Jealousy*, the dance of the Woman of the Sidhe is an accompaniment to a dialogue, and it is in the dialogue that the nature and burden of Cuchulain's choice are made explicit, nor has the dance in this play anything to do with Emer's own moment of decision; indeed, it has not much more importance than the Woman's dress or the armour of the Ghost in *Hamlet*. In *The Dreaming of the Bones* and *Calvary* it has become a bit of subordinate styling. The dance is often an amplification of the gesture and appearance of a character and of his recondite meaning (the Woman of the Sidhe is after all a version of the Image), but the responsibility for untying the knot rests still with the hero and not with the Ghost.

The moment of revelation, when the play blazes into 'miracle', is found in its purest and most theatrically impressive form in *The Resurrection*, when the masked Figure of Christ enters the room and all the long-calculated and converging lines of the play achieve their resolution. When the Greek touches the wounded side of his Idea, the questions that have been worried at during the play and the irrational intimations that have been throbbing beneath its surface are resolved and confirmed in a moment that has the blank and terrifying authority of the eyes of a Byzantine icon:

> *The Greek.* It is the phantom of our master. Why are you afraid? He has been crucified and buried, but only in semblance, and is

10 *Wheels and Butterflies*, p. 75.

among us once more. [*The Hebrew kneels.*] There is nothing here but a phantom, it has no flesh and blood. Because I know the truth I am not afraid. Look, I will touch it. It may be hard under my hand like a statue—I have heard of such things—or my hand may pass through it—but there is no flesh and blood. [*He goes slowly up to the figure and passes his hand over its side.*] The heart of a phantom is beating! The heart of a phantom is beating! [*He screams. The figure of Christ crosses the stage and passes into the inner room.*] (*C.Pl.*, 593)

This moment has all the significance that Yeats would have liked to bestow upon the dance in the Noh form, and none of it is lost because the figure of Christ cannot and, of course, need not dance. The purity of the moment here is due to the fact that *The Resurrection* is a play of ideas; the Greek, the Hebrew, and the other characters are representative figures, surrogates for Yeats's insights into the nature of primary and antithetical civilisations and men. (*The Resurrection*, at least, must be taken on a literal and historical level and not translated into assertions about poetry.) It has been made into a play not only by the shown event but by some sufficiently sharp historical actualisations. But it has no hero; nobody is responsible.

But in those plays where the characters are not surrogates in quite the same way as they are in *The Resurrection*—plays, in short, which are not *primarily* plays of ideas but which do incorporate a moment in which not only ideas but sometimes names and destinies are altered or made clear—we encounter the problem of the hero who does possess and validate a name or an individuality. This is specially true of *At the Hawk's Well*, *The Only Jealousy of Emer*, *The Herne's Egg*, *Purgatory* and *The Death of Cuchulain*. These five works are at the centre of Yeats's achievement as a playwright and probably constitute his chief claim for consideration in that role.

What distinguishes the protagonists in these plays is that each of them has a long personal history and a destiny which is being consciously worked out. Even the young Cuchulain in the first of them, although at the beginning of his history, carries explicitly the burden of its future unfolding. Yeats, of course, was not concerned to create 'character', to discriminate and define individuality, in the way that Shakespeare does; indeed, he valued most those moments in Shakespearian tragedy where character seemed to him to 'sink away', where Cleopatra or Hamlet become exemplars of creative joy and blaze with a noble, powerful and uncommitted energy, like Chapman's heroes at the moments of their deaths and Herculean apotheoses. A consummation such as that drowns the lines and accidents of individuality, which, from this point of view, belong to those superficies (like the 'wheels and pulleys', footlights, elaborate scenery, the 'mere mechanism of a building or the interests of a class') that it is the play's business to recede from into the more powerful life where we share the 'one lofty emotion' and seem to ourselves most completely alive.[11] Not Rembrandt, therefore, but Michelangelo; not the world-considering eyes of Roman portrait-busts, but the blank eyes of the Phidian statues and the masked face of the Noble Dancer. These plays, however, dramatise the encounter between this condition and the human life and history of the hero. He brings to that encounter sexual desire or defiant courage, love and hatred, ignorance and crime, as these have been written in his history and nature. These passions are simply written, for Yeats, as we would expect from his rejection of highly discriminate characterisation, has no wish to distract our attention ('God asks nothing of the highest soul but *attention*') from the vivacity of the encounter by giving the hero much more than a sense of his identity as a human being and the consequently finite nature of his destiny. These are removed from the level of mere generalisation enough to make the encounter express in dramatic terms a favourite antithesis between nature and supernature, impermanent and permanent images, artist and saint, the 'soldier's right' and the ascent to Heaven. And so Yeats uses many personages from the heroic cycles, from sagas that do not define and particularise character in post-Renaissance fashion but keep it simple and primary. Yeats's reasoning seems to have been that, if in the greatest moments of the greatest tragedies all the carefully constructed human circumstances and characterising psychology are burned up or sink away, then, in plays on the scale which he was writing, he could dispense with them almost altogether and proceed in a few strides towards that cherished manifestation. Each of his plays is thus a kind of last act of an Elizabethan play as Elizabethan plays were read by Yeats, and he will borrow from the Greeks the method of incapsulating such history as he needs within the last stride towards the catastrophe. Yeats did not care to notice that in his last acts Shakespeare does preserve the secret traces of individuality in a thousand subtle ways and that his long exposure of his audience to an interpretative rendering of Lear or Othello during the previous acts

[11] This theory is clearly set out in Yeats's most important essay on the drama, 'The Tragic Theatre', written in 1910. There are two versions of it, as the *Preface to Plays for an Irish Theatre* (1911) and in *The Cutting of an Agate* (New York, 1912), the latter being the version reprinted in *Essays* (1924) and *E. & I.*

is, as it were, an invisible asset on which an audience draws in order to modify its experience of the catastrophe. Othello 'roars', Lear's tears scald, Hamlet struggles with Horatio for the poisoned cup, Coriolanus dies in a fit of extremely Marcian rage. Always Shakespeare provides us with something that reminds us of what the heroes are as they become nothing, or prepare for their entrance into the 'condition of fire'. Hamlet and Lear, Yeats said, 'do not break up their lines to weep', but this is just what Shakespeare directs them to do. Yeats forced Shakespeare to fit his own theory, which he fortified with his own highly idiosyncratic experience of Shakespeare, by clapping a conventionalised Greek or Japanese mask on to the deplorably tawdry and real faces of his heroes: conduct perhaps more excusable than Thomas Rymer's, but originating from a not dissimilar suspicion of Shakespeare's vulgar concern with the particular case.

In so far as they stress the antitheses which I have mentioned, these plays are faithful to the way so many of the poems are ordered, and to their manner of both pulling away from and drawing towards the measureless consummation and the undying image: 'Sailing to Byzantium', for example, which represents the sensual music with passionate understanding even while it moves towards the golden artefact, or 'All Souls' Night', which is threaded upon a delight in vivid, human personalities as it passes into

> Such thought, that in it bound
> I need no other thing. (*C.P.*, 259)

In the poems Yeats, being freed from a dramatic theory that had, as he thought, to minimise character for the sake of opening the way into the *anima mundi*, into a 'life' where everything is powerful precisely because it is generalised and archetypal, was able to be much more generous to the human personality. Furthermore, in the poems the antitheses are always more intimate and intense because they pertain to the speaker, the poet in the poem; they do not need ever to be untied or come to an end because they are free from the sequence in time, however short, that plays demand, and are built into the system of stresses and strains that constitute the structure of the poem. This is the ideal unity of the symbolist work, and plays which attempt to imitate it stumble fatally, as Yeats's do, over the need for sequence. A few of Yeats's plays—*Calvary*, especially, and, less rigidly, *The Dreaming of the Bones*—get closest to the symbolist condition, but for that reason have less dramatic power; *Calvary* shows no event. The dilemma is very strange, and Yeats did not solve it. And we might add—since it seems part of the same complex of fatalities—that, because plays have to move on and achieve the resolution of strains, a proof or moral hovers. But it is a contradiction within the form that a work which aspires to the condition of symbolism should be obliged to provide a proof other than the proof of its own existence. A doctrine begins to be offered and asserted outside the work, instead of being protected from scrutiny by safely participating with all the other elements that go to make up the symbolist structure. And one cannot on the whole claim that Yeats's proofs or morals are very useful: if you resist the god you will be reborn as a donkey (*The Herne's Egg*), although it has some respectable antecedents and parallels amongst the religions of the world, is the worst and most obtrusive, unless we are to assume (which is highly probable) that Yeats was here again mocking his own thought.

For, although all the plays represent the heroes' failures of understanding and their consequent exclusion from the condition figured by the springing water in *At the Hawk's Well* or the green tree in *Purgatory*, tragedy is hardly an accurate term for them. To his encounter with the Ghost the hero brings his history of involvement in the crime of death and birth, and that simple tale is seen with mounting irony, until Yeats, when he handles it in *The Herne's Egg*, depicts it as oafish and 'wild'. Neither Cuchulain nor Congal nor the Old Man in *Purgatory* understand the metaphysical aid that offers them changeless beauty or absolution from the 'crime of being born' (and born again). Although we must discriminate between these states when we wish to define Yeats's philosophical mythology, they can, when we are experiencing the plays, be felt simply as the artifice of eternity—a term which is (as Frank Kermode says) reversible. The heroes, therefore, are Blind Men and Fools. They live in a condition of bewilderment and disorder which is described in varying modes, desperate, solemn, and 'heroical-tragical', or brash, energetic and serio-comic. Like the Artist, they dwell 'in the humility of brutes' and cannot renounce Experience; but, like him, they assert their allegiance to the unfinished man and his pain, to those who love 'in brief longing and deceiving hope' (like the people whom Forgael despised in *The Shadowy Waters*), and to those who, as Cuchulain did in 'The Grey Rock', betray the gods. This is the noblest thing in Yeats's plays, though he is apprehending a tragi-comic dilemma rather than improving a moral. This allegiance the heroes bring to their encounter with the superhuman, as Congal does in *The Herne's Egg*:

Congal. If I should give myself a wound,
Let life run away, I'd win the bout.
He said I must die at the hands of a Fool
And sent you hither. Give me that spit!
I put it in this crevice of the rock,
That I may fall upon the point.
These stones will keep it sticking upright.
    [*They arrange stones, he puts the spit in.*]
Congal [*almost screaming in his excitement*]
Fool! Am I myself a Fool?
For if I am a Fool, he wins the bout.
Fool. You are King of Connacht. If you were a Fool
They would have chased you with their dogs.
Congal. I am King Congal of Connacht and of Tara,
That wise, victorious, voluble, unlucky,
Blasphemous, famous, infamous man.
Fool, take this spit when red with blood,
Show it to the people and get all the pennies:
What does it matter what they think?
The Great Herne knows that I have won. (*C.Pl.*, 675–6)

Congal has not 'won', and he is a Fool to think so; but he has brought his name into the lists, the symbol of his history, uniqueness, and heroic quality; self and name are not easy to dissever—' 'Tis a spell, you see, of much power!'[12] In *Purgatory*, which works Yeats's most profound variation on the theme, he extends it to show us how the Old Man is motivated not by the sense of himself as 'an image of heroic self-possession'[13]—the archetypal subjectivity of the hero, making him the proper object of the desire or malice of the gods who wish, as in *The Resurrection*, to 'take complete possession'—but instead by a sense of his degradation and namelessness. This is ambiguously qualified by his kinship and history, or one part of it—for he is the son of a fine lady and a drunken beast. This complex of motives, or, one wants to say, this *character*, drives him to intervene on his mother's behalf in the terrible rationale of a supernatural system. *Purgatory* is as far as Yeats got in modifying his dislike of character in the interests of a Shakespearian concern for the particular case. For that reason, and not only because its verse-line set an example to Eliot,[14] it can be claimed as his best, though not his most characteristic, achievement in the theatre.

Finally, there is a kind of logic about Yeats's long entanglement with

[12] *Coriolanus*, V.ii.93.   [13] Yeats's description of Hamlet, *Auto.*, 47.
[14] Eliot, *On Poetry and Poets*, p. 77.

blank verse in a series of plays on the heroic subject. The first poetic play in which he escaped entirely from blank verse was *The Green Helmet*, a pivotal and probably underrated work. For it, he chose a 'heroic' pre-Renaissance line. Ironically enough, it probably owes most to the slightly longer line of Morris's *Sigurd the Volsung*, a poem which was for Yeats inseparably associated with the heroic subject.[15] In *The Green Helmet* it is a form of verse in which 'everything can be said that has to be said'[16] by both the low and the high characters, the prosaic and the poetical ones, in modes of speech that range from comic bravado to dreaming evocation. Its irregular fourteeners, when split in half, greatly resemble the three- and four-stress lines of the much later plays in which he abandoned blank verse altogether, *The Herne's Egg* and *Purgatory*. Indeed, it might be said that it was the discovery of the Japanese Noh, which seemed to him to translate best into blank verse varied with lyric metres, that prevented for so long any further exploitation of the flexible 'ballad metre' of *The Green Helmet*. It is another irony that this play, whose metre is an index of Yeats's desire to escape from the Renaissance and Shakespearian measure in order to depict a world of imaginative unities that the Renaissance had, he thought, destroyed, should shadow forth just such an act of destruction or liberation. In *The Green Helmet* Cuchulain wants to turn the Red Man's helmet, the prize for valour, into a drinking-cup to be shared by all; but the society depicted in the play is one of 'weasels fighting in a hole'; it cannot accept, as the Red Man very well knows, Cuchulain's vision of a world 'hooped together / Brought under a rule'; Cuchulain is like the dreamers of 'Nineteen Hundred and Nineteen' who thought to achieve a semblance of peace and were cheated by the makers of discord. Although he has striven in the play for another sort of unity, he is obliged therefore to submit to being chosen, to being named as the hero, the great personality, the one who will master his society, take his place as the hero of plays, and enact the role of one of those 'sundry magnifications' which Yeats thought of as emerging out of Unity of Culture and 'general agreement' to flower into the Shakespearian moment. Chaucer's personages began it:

> Chaucer's personages . . . disengaged themselves from Chaucer's crowd, forgot their common goal and shrine, and after sundry magnifications became each in turn the centre of some Elizabethan play. (*Auto.*, 193)

15 See *Wheels and Butterflies*, pp. 75–76.
16 Eliot, *On Poetry and Poets*, p. 74.

Or, as he put it elsewhere:

> In the Spiritual dawn when Raphael painted the Camera della Segnatura, and the Medician Popes dreamed of uniting Christianity and Paganism, all that was sacred with all that was secular, Europe might have made its plan, begun the solution of its problems, but individualism came instead; the egg, instead of hatching, burst. (*E. & I.*, 467–8)

Individualism came instead, 'breaking up the old rhythms of life' (*E. & I.*, 110), and with it 'magnification', the great Shakespearian personality, who is emphatically *not* one of Chaucer's crowd, and with him came blank verse. This, as Yeats put it, was to be 'cast up out of the whale's belly':

> When I speak blank verse and analyse my feelings, I stand at a moment of history when instinct, its traditional songs and dances, its general agreement, is of the past. I have been cast up out of the whale's belly. (*E. & I.*, 524)

Blank verse, which could express all the subtleties of Shakespearian characterisation, superseded the impersonal, chanting metres of Chaucer's crowd. (Yeats, struggling against his fate, used to try and get his players to speak his blank verse in that manner, and perhaps the two-dimensional quality on which I have commented arises from the same compromise.) It is, therefore, oddly fitting that Yeats's own sundry magnifications should speak in blank verse. The unease that their Shakespearian and Jacobean rhythms, faintly heard, aroused in their author and arouse in us is an emblem of their precarious footing and their individuality. 'Impure and lonely', like the artist, they are driven to assert their identities and personal histories and proclaim the charter of the self; yet all the while they remember the whale's belly, the peace of an imagined general agreement, and of a condition where it is the part of the individual to submit to the god and become the god's artefact and not his own,

> oblivion
> Even to quench Cuchulain's drouth,
> Even to still that heart. (*C.Pl.*, 293)

The whole development clearly demonstrates the need for seeing Yeats's aesthetics and his readings of actual history as vitally interdependent guides to his poetic practice.

If Yeats, like the neo-platonic mages who interested those Medician

Popes, had ever devised his City of the Sun, one wonders if it would have contained a theatre. He had certainly hoped that his work as a playwright would deepen the political passion of a nation and would make it more completely alive by returning it to some source of imaginative coherence, creating the 'one mind of enjoyment' to which all things are possible. But as he gradually perceived the sheer unlikelihood of Unity of Culture, there was a change of feeling: 'I did not see', he wrote in 1909, 'until Synge began to write, that we must renounce the deliberate creation of a kind of Holy City in the imagination, and express the individual.' The change freed his poetry and made it possible for it to develop into a supreme accomplishment; but both dramatic theory and dramatic practice lagged behind, looking backwards towards the dream of a great act of imaginative communion between audience, playwright, and player, at the ideal but unreachable shadows of Athens and Urbino behind the crowds in the Abbey and the more restricted group of 'leisured and lettered people' in Lady Cunard's drawing-room. Perhaps the poetry could not have achieved such liberation, had Yeats not been able to maintain the integrity of his artistic endeavour and a continuity with ambitions which he was deeply reluctant to discard by reserving the principal expression of them for the plays. In that way, the weakness of the plays, by comparison with the strength of the poems, might be justified at last.

X

Rhythm and Pattern in 'Autobiographies'

IAN FLETCHER

*

I

THE title of *Autobiographies* is accurate. The single volume contains approaches to the past made at distinct times in differing modes, ranging from the mosaic of *Trembling of the Veil* to the *journal intime* structure of *Estrangement*, a man talking to himself after the day's work and bitterness with a kind of vivid formality. I want to touch only on *Reveries*, *Trembling of the Veil* and *Dramatis Personae*, not because I believe that *Estrangement*, *The Death of Synge* or the 1930 Diary are less important, but because they are less consciously historical, more disjunct, aphoristic, the raw material for composed autobiography.[1]

Of all Yeats's prose *Autobiographies*, though sometimes occasional and often polemical, are the most sustained. The aphoristic and fragmentary sections were possibly intended as prolegomena to that 'new autobiography—1900 to 1926' which Yeats thought of as 'the final test of my intellect, my last great effort', which he kept putting off. There are problems about the three parts of *Autobiographies* that are my concern. *Dramatis Personae* was largely composed from Yeats's letters to Lady Gregory, but the history of the composition of *Reveries* is obscure: it probably went through several drafts. Richard Ellmann informs us

---

[1] The complex relationship between Yeats's poetry and *Autobiographies* lies beyond the confines of this essay. It is, however, a topic that would repay study. An acute reviewer of the 1926 volume commented on the two-way traffic: Section viii of *Hodos Chameliontos* 'touching on the innate nature of ideas drawn from watching caged canaries' suggesting an unwritten poem (possibly sections v and vi of 'Meditations in Time of Civil War'), while 'certain parts are indeed refashionings of experience already passed through the difficult alembic of the verse'. This can be related to that progressive 'self-transcendence'—Yeats's interpretation of the doctrine of Wilde's *Intentions*—which *Autobiographies* was designed to serve.

that an earlier draft of *Trembling of the Veil* was completed in 1916–17.[2] Comment on *Autobiographies* must be provisional.

The first mention of *Reveries* in Yeats's letters belongs to November 1914. From this it is clear that Yeats had been engaged with the book from about the late summer on. The seven years before this date had been both painful and frustrating, and *Reveries* was composed in their shadow: schisms in the Abbey, the mere success of esteem of his own plays, the *Playboy* controversy of 1907, Synge's death in 1909 and the controversy with the Dublin Council and populace over the proposed Lutyens Gallery for Lane's pictures. In 1908 the appearance of Yeats's *Collected Works* must have seemed to the poet to mark off an era, as though his achievement were already in the past. At this time we find him in letters referring to himself as 'belonging to the fabulous ages' and 'becoming mythical even to myself': we find an increasing identification with the past and with his dead friends of the 1890s in particular. Such backward looking was a symptom of general discouragement. His own personal life had become random and in his spiritual life there was a void. By 1914 he had broken his connection with the rump of the Golden Dawn that remained after the schisms of Mathers and Waite. We find him resorting to spiritualism and trying somewhat pathetically to verify the historicity of the spirits who 'came to him through mediums'.

The pressures in such circumstances were towards the organisation of an attitude; documentation and self-clarification; an attempt to stabilise the present—an aim that makes its first positive appearance in his volume of poems *The Green Helmet* of 1910. It is here that the process of mythologising himself and his friends begins. Recent history is frozen, stylised. Maud Gonne becomes the emblem of his present despair—a *femme fatale*, still making a traditional appearance as an Irish Helen, but now associated directly with Dublin: 'Was there another Troy for her to burn?'

It is rather in *Poems Written in Discouragement* of 1913 and in *Responsibilities* that the mythologising becomes explicit and past and present are consciously poised against one another. Addressing in the opening poem of *Responsibilities* his burgess ancestors of the late eighteenth and early nineteenth centuries, Yeats writes:

---

[2] The only fragments I have seen give a more naturalistic account of Yeats's waking to sex and an anecdote about Lionel Johnson writing a Latin poem on absinthe.

Although I have come close on forty-nine,
I have no child, I have nothing but a book,
Nothing but that to prove your blood and mine. (C.P., 113)

In this volume the events of the last seven years are mythologised: the epigrams of the *Green Helmet* edge into dramatic lyric. Synge, Lady Gregory, John O'Leary and Hugh Lane are poised against the Dublin of the present which fumbles in a greasy till by the light of a holy candle. Aristocrat, noble Fenian and poet equally represent a heroic and defeated past.

Placing himself in history and tradition was indeed one of Yeats's 'responsibilities' at this time, but it conflicted with a 'responsibility' to the present: he needed to associate himself with Lady Gregory and Hugh Lane; the enemy being a textbook burgess capitalist such as William Murphy or those petty-burgess Paudeen enemies of Synge and Lane. His own impeccably burgess ancestors have to be dignified with 'the wasteful virtues' that 'earn the sun', credited with spontaneity and 'personality'. But what we can accept in *Responsibilities* as dramatic speech (even so amusingly defiant a line as 'Blood that has not passed through any huckster's loin') will be harder to accept in a prose account; we accuse the historian of self-interest. In the poems the 'personal ego' (J. B. Yeats's phrase) has evaporated, a role in contemporary history can be enforced and acted out.

In the Preface to *Reveries*, dated Christmas 1914, Yeats wrote:

> I have changed nothing to my knowledge; and yet it must be that I have changed many things without my knowledge; for I am writing after many years and have consulted neither friend, nor letter, nor old newspaper, and describe what comes oftenest into my memory.

But the past remains the possession of others and he fears that 'some surviving friend may remember something in a different shape and be offended with my book'. The frankness is partly ingenuous: he is attempting to transcend his past self by presenting a selective image of that self, and he wishes to trust what has survived by impressing itself most deeply, though he is aware that memory not only shapes the past but actually imposes meanings. And re-enacting the past not only changes the past, it changes the present.

A recently published letter of 20 November 1914 to Lady Gregory indicates how Yeats wished to see himself:

That is a wonderful letter of my father's. It came at the right moment for I am writing an account of Dowden (I shall wind up with the Rhymers' Club). I think we shall live as a generation as the Young Irelanders did. We shall not be detached figures. I think it is partly with that motive I am trying for instance to improve my sisters' and publish my father's letters. Your biography when it comes will complete the image.

Here Yeats explicitly associates himself with his friends, the tragic actors of *Responsibilities*, as 'a generation', and associates his friends as a group with Young Ireland. As D. J. Gordon has put it, 'an acute, exacerbated sense of his own historicity comprehended the historicity of others, sharpened and nourished by the awareness that he and his friends were part of the history of modern Ireland'. Implicitly he also associates himself with the Rhymers' Club—another 'generation' whose defeat substantiates and extends the defeat of the artists of J. B. Yeats's and Yeats's own 'tragic' generation. The pressure here is towards over-coming a tragic determinism.

Lady Gregory was still very much alive, while the Rhymers (with the exception of Symons, whose career had been broken by madness) were dead and so historically perfect. Poetry demonstrated its classic superiority over history: it could mythologise the living as though they were not themselves still part of an emerging historical process. This mode was not to be abandoned. Yeats continued to write poems, consciously conceived as historical acts, on persons and on the places associated with them. Writing these, he was deliberately creating a version of the modern history of Ireland, 'an Ireland the poets have imagined terrible and gay', a version he wished to transmit as a docu-ment to posterity. But as the letter to Lady Gregory shows, Yeats was not averse to documentation of another kind. It is in this light that his father's unfinished and his own achieved autobiography must be seen. And while he was engaged on *Reveries*, Lady Gregory was concluding her chapter of autobiography, *Our Irish Theatre*, with its selective extracts from Yeats's letters and its heroic portraiture of O'Leary and Synge.

Yeats's original plan had been to conclude *Reveries* with an account of the Rhymers' Club; that the Rhymers were much in his mind at this time we know from *Responsibilities*, where Johnson and Dowson are given tragic status. Like the Young Ireland writers, the more prominent Rhymers possessed a much greater historical than aesthetic importance, even though the Rhymers' devotion to art was altogether opposed to Young Ireland's subordination of art to rhetoric and politics.

Young Ireland had been an attempt on the part of a few to realise a nation's soul, in contrast to O'Connell's flattery of the mob. The Rhymers also attempted, in a different way, to realise in themselves the historical spirit, and they rejected popular culture. Both groups survive as groups rather than as individuals: the Rhymers partly because they were to be memorialised by Yeats in much the same way as Gavan Duffy had memorialised the Young Ireland figures in *Young Ireland* and *1845–1849*. Yeats's intention was to follow Duffy as the historian of a generation that had realised itself historically because 'it thought the same thought' and created its own history. And Duffy's historical record had itself been an attempted reshaping of history.

Yeats's portrait of Duffy looks forward to the graceful malice of *Dramatis Personae*. It presents him as the anti-type of O'Leary among the Young Ireland generation, living on like some Latimerian fish to abash the new age. It is one version of history competing actively with another, though the ground disputed is narrowly literary:

> Sir Charles Gavan Duffy arrived. He brought with him much manuscript, the private letters of a Young Irish poetess, a dry but informing unpublished essay by Davis, and an unpublished novel by William Carleton into the middle of which he had dropped a hot coal, so that nothing remained but the borders of every page.

A fussy short sentence is swallowed by a long sentence, whose gyre concludes with the exquisitely emblematic case of the burning coal and so acts out Duffy's dry-fingered antiquarianism; his incapacity to sustain whatever was genuinely creative in Anglo-Irish literature. Yeats's position in the quarrel with Duffy may have owed something to Arnold, but it was immediately influenced by the beliefs of the Rhymers.

The Rhymers—as Yeats saw them—were, unlike Young Ireland, concerned not merely with personal art but with collapse and dis-integration, and they wished to enact this in themselves sacrificially. Yeats's association of Young Ireland with the Rhymers, and of J. B. Yeats's generation of artists and poets with his own, is not simply because (contingently or not) they formed part of his own drama. It sprang from the need to find what Yeats termed 'rhythm' in history (a rhythm of heroic failure). As his early interest in Joachim de Flora's Four Ages showed, this had been one of his preoccupations in the 1890s.[3] Such 'rhythm' had to be recognised in the multiplicity of the

---

[3] See also 'The Adoration of the Magi' and G. Melchiori, *The Whole Mystery of Art* (1960), pp. 60–63, for documentation.

self before it could be recognised in history; it determines the structure
of *Trembling of the Veil* rather than that of *Reveries.*

Reveries is concerned with heroes and sacred places. The book's
polarities are Ireland and England: Sligo, Dublin and London. Yeats
as child and young man is involved in his father's uneasy shifts between
these places: a rootlessness symbolic of the modern imaginative artist (it
predicts the rootlessness of Simeon Solomon or Dowson), and also of
the decline of true nationalism. Places for Yeats have a quality of *mana*
that owes little to patient visual detail (it is hardly' Pre-Raphaelite'). It
is the *interaction* of places and persons that he particularly evokes. 'He
was probably always moved more by the human image than the
painter's.'[4] Yet he still saw that human image partly in terms of the
painter's eye. From his father, he had caught an eye for pose and gesture,
for the unselfconscious stance that reveals the intimate self, the ground
of this perception being that gathering of the 'moment' in J. B. Yeats's
impressionist portraiture.

With Yeats, physical image creates narrative, is both cause and
symptom: what actually happens becomes metaphorical. In *Autobiographies* people tend to be arrested in moments that reveal 'a fragment
of the divine life', an instant which has the effect of a complete statement, both stylised and spontaneous. Yeats owes this, however, less to
his father's portraits than to his letters.

Just as *Dramatis Personae* wins immediacy from the dialogue *outre
tombe* with George Moore, *Reveries* wins immediacy from its dialogue
with Yeats's father:

> Someone to whom I read [*Reveries*] said to me the other day 'If
> Gosse had not taken the title you should call it "Father and Son".'
> I am not going to ask your leave for the bits of your conversation I
> quote.

Father and son influenced one another and one of John Butler Yeats's
gifts, that of aphorism, was clearly passed on. Between 1912 and 1914
he wrote his son a number of remarkable letters which had much to
say on the subject of 'personality', the essential self freed from accidents
of time and habit; on the necessary solitude of the artist and the need
for dramatising one's experience to avoid a purely personal art. 'Personality' for J. B. Yeats was 'love':

[4] From D. J. Gordon's speech at the opening of 'W. B. Yeats: Images of a
Poet', a Reading University Exhibition at the Whitworth Gallery, Manchester,
May 1961.

neither right nor wrong—for it transcends intellect and morality, and while it keeps to being pure personality we love for it is *one* with our very selves, and with the all *pervasive* Divine.[5]

In precisely these terms the 'personalities' of Yeats's *Autobiographies* are presented as parts of his 'very self'. At a moment of indecision Yeats was using his father as a mentor, as he had previously used other mentors (Johnson, Ricketts, etc.).

Practising his father's advice to dramatise experience, Yeats began with J. B. Yeats himself. His father's crisis, a crisis in romantic art and literature, is presented in *Reveries* through an argument in terms of 'personality' between Pre-Raphaelite imagination, intensity, on the one hand, and Positivism and an Impressionism defined as 'Realism' on the other. J. B. Yeats's betrayal of Pre-Raphaelite principles is associated with the treason of his other friends.

The material here is derived from J. B. Yeats's letters. The elder Yeats's friends were a pathetic rather than a tragic generation. Some, to be sure—Page, Wilson, Potter—die without a choice being offered. They are solitaries, without an audience. Others like Nettleship or Dowden survive by compromise. All are caught in emblematic gestures that lead one from the work to 'personality'. The crippled genius of Nettleship enacts its own mutilation: the enormous cup he drinks from contains—cocoa, so that Edwin Ellis's remark that Nettleship 'drank his genius away' has vibrations the speaker barely intended. Dowden's ironic calm and O'Leary's moral genius, passionate, Roman, Hebraic, confront one another.

Dowden may be taken as characteristic of Yeats's problems. His subject had died only a year before, and J. B. Yeats had been Dowden's 'intimate enemy', but after Dowden's death Yeats was not prepared to adopt his father's gentlemanly attitude. J. B. Yeats wrote that it was better to be illogical than inhuman, and accused his son of presenting

[5] J. B. Yeats's rhetoric is skilfully vague. This seems to point to some rather Emersonian transcendentalism. It is interesting to note that Susan Mitchell defined the older Yeats's portraits of women in terms that may well have been in W. B. Yeats's mind when he made his famous polemical comparison between Strozzi and Sargent: 'John Butler Yeats had the rare quality that he not only made his women pretty, any artist can do that, but he made them lovable, manifesting some interior beauty in their souls. Incomparable executants like Sargent and William Orpen have not this faculty: they exhibit all a woman's character, but no spiritual life looks out of the faces that are so superbly drawn.'

Dowden deliberately and exclusively from a personal and didactic point of view; of submitting Dowden to a contrived biographical pattern. After the publication of *Reveries* W. B. Yeats returned to the question, admitting that he was nervous about the Dowden section, but arguing that it could not be omitted, since the book was 'a history of the revolt, which perhaps unconsciously you taught me, against certain Victorian ideals'. And as though admitting his father's accusation of being inhuman, Yeats observed in the following year that 'in my account of Dowden I had to picture him as a little unreal, set up for contrast behind the real image of O'Leary'. The juxtaposition is not really dramatic, but drama enters in the presentation of the divided self common to both Dowden and O'Leary. O'Leary's noble head, his intransigence, his sense of political morality as style and his love of literature are poised against the flatness of the autobiography on which he lavished such effort. Dowden's romantic face and his earlier poetry that hints at passion, though passion renounced, are poised against his over-reliance on intellect.

J. B. Yeats's relationship with Dowden has a subdued parallel in his son's relationship with J. F. Taylor, obscure great orator, ugly, solitary, flashing into high speech; a disappointed though pertinacious lover of women. The image of Taylor is important in several ways. It enacts that opposition between poetry and oratory that J. B. Yeats believed was inevitable; but explains Taylor's greatness by presenting him in *O altitudo* moments as altogether solitary, unaware of the blind crowd, a poet. Taylor is also a man divided in himself—his jealousy of Yeats's friendship with O'Leary is more than a Young Ireland Fenian distrust of the new 'literary' nationalism. The encounter is presented less definitively than it would have been in *Trembling of the Veil*. Taylor's motives, his inner life, remain unpredictable, mysterious. He is viewed from a distance, and this precisely catches the 'point of view' of the young Yeats of the late 1880s and 1890s, a young man who was a late comer to an Irish scene which he found already peopled by powerful figures. He shows himself here as always intensely aware of the difference between his own generation and theirs. The enmity between himself and Taylor is constructive: to choose one's intimate enemies objectifies one's limitations.

Such stringency hardly seems reflected in the record. The prose of *Autobiographies* is often thought of as Paterian, lushly mantic, salted with some good Irish stories. Yet if *Reveries* owes anything to Pater, that influence is less of cadence and vocabulary than attitude, and of an attitude that reinforces the influence of Yeats's father. In *Style*, Pater had distinguished between the debris of fact and the writer's personal sense of fact. Analogously he had distinguished the 'moment' as the unit of experience, isolated, absolute, flexible, in protest against the 'positive' fiction of a stable world. The creative role of contemplation and, particularly, memory in Pater's work and his influence on Proust and Virginia Woolf are well known. For Pater, memory constitutes an identity which can be redeemed from time by re-enacting moments of sensuous significance: '. . . the finer sort of memory, bringing its object to mind with great clearness, yet, as sometimes happens in dreams, raised a little above its self and above ordinary retrospect' (*The Child in the House*). In Pater's words, this is a substitution of the 'typical' for the 'actual'; memory operates discontinuously, if vividly, and is recognised by the sense of loss. But substitution of 'typical' for 'actual' is distancing, and few of Pater's evocations of childhood have any eager directness of detail or sense of the jaggedness of recall. Similarly, Yeats's account of family, schools, holidays, adolescent awakening to sex and ideals is distanced by a meditative style—as Mr. Ellmann has pointed out, anger is 'adroitly excluded'. But the arrangement of *Reveries* with its sharp sections (rather than the 'chapters' Yeats termed them) is intended to enact discontinuousness. The sections vary in length (xviii and xx by contrast with xi) resembling (in intention at least) that lyrical dissolution of event in Romantic historians where rapid sections and sentences echo the pulse of what is re-enacted and the historian's excitement in re-enaction. Yeats's rhythm of anti-climactic reflection in *Reveries* is naturally slow and even. (He uses the Carlylean historic present only for the first page or two of *Reveries*, in Section xv of *Ireland after Parnell* and in Section xx of *Trembling of the Veil* to evoke the 'crack up' of the '90s.) His early memories leave the impression of being recorded solely because they are remembered; but each 'spot of memory' relates to such themes as: I, the poet, William Yeats, Ireland, romantic past and sordid present.

We have seen that what is acceptable as dramatic speech in *Responsibilities* might become suspect in autobiography. In prose Yeats stresses heroism, nobility of personality rather than aristocratic value connected with property; despite a mild flourish of ancestors in the third section, *Reveries* are surprisingly devoid of social context. What emerges is Yeats's sense of being 'Irish' in the English Babylon.

In *Reveries*, many of the connections, as in *Responsibilities*, are carried by syntax. Style in courage and platonic courtesy is mediated through asyndeton, punctilious subjunctives,[6] magniloquent 'buts', yet the sentence-structure is rarely overelaborate. Where we find elaboration of rhythm it is, like the imagery, functional, as in this passage on George Eliot where style itself rebukes:

> She seemed to have a distrust or a distaste for all in life that gives one a springing foot. Then, too, she knew so well how to enforce her distaste by the authority of her mid-Victorian science or by some habit of mind of its breeding, that I, who had not escaped the fascination of what I loathed, doubted while the book lay open whatsoever my instinct knew of splendour. (p. 88)

The second is an unusually long sentence for *Reveries*. The histrionic pauses, contours almost of the breathing mind, the anxious poise between authority and instinct, the final freed tune with its faint Pauline echo fully realise the inwardness of the experience. (The experience has perhaps little to do finally with George Eliot.)

'Now that I have written it out', Yeats wrote in his preface, 'I may even begin to forget it all.' A middle-aged bore, bowed down with the weight of 'a precious, an incommunicable past', he may stop button-holing strangers. But the deeper meaning suggests the cathartic; final responsibility to the past involves not rejection, but transcendence: liberation from guilt, self-pity, historical necessity, the inescapable folly of art, multiplicity and indirection, that 'wilderness of mirrors', whether of Wilde's competing gifts or magian temptations. Writing is the act of self-criticism that detaches the poet from the composed image, even if the composure issues from anticlimax, 'a preparation for something that never happens'.

In *Reveries*, Yeats's past self is realised, painfully encountering and addressing others, socially clumsy, morally naïve. This book ends not with the Rhymers' Club but with Yeats's return to London in 1887, giving the volume a severer shape. He stands at the beginning of his career as an Irish poet, at the moment when he realises himself as an exile, and in this light the final judgement on himself in 1914 is ironic rather than self-pitying. The title *Reveries* is not an escape into the past, it signifies an attempt to distinguish pattern. At the point of painful disengagement from spoiled aspirations the conditions have been fulfilled for the narrator's 'epiphany': a synthesis, as often in Yeats, has been proclaimed at the point where it is rejected.

---

[6] George Moore in *Ave* claims to have introduced Yeats to the subjunctive; it is more likely to have been Lionel Johnson.

II

Writing to his father on 26 December 1914, Yeats indicated that when he carried his memoirs beyond 1887 he would be liable to further difficulties of the type already encountered in treating of Dowden:

> they would have besides to be written in a different way. While I was immature I was a different person and I can stand apart and judge. Later on, I should always, I feel, write of other people. I dare say I shall return to the subject but only in fragments. (Letters, 589)

Often one of his best critics, Yeats has defined the limitations of *Trembling of the Veil*. Far more ambitious, eloquent and richly detailed than *Reveries*, *Trembling of the Veil* is tonally and structurally puzzling. The second draft was composed during the period of the Anglo-Irish and Irish Civil wars, when Yeats was clarifying the material of *A Vision*. The period described lies between 1887 and 1897, the death in 1891 of the political Messiah, Parnell, marking an important division. Formally 'Four Years' is the most satisfying section; the remainder was written to contract (60,000 words) and Yeats more than once expressed uneasiness as to whether the years between 1891 and 1897 could be stretched to the agreed length.

Writing to Olivia Shakespear on 22 December 1921, he observed that the book was likely to seem inadequate, since 'I study every man I meet at some moment of crisis—I alone have no crisis'. And in another letter of 28 February 1934 he reveals that the problem of omission was still with him when he came to compose *Dramatis Personae*: 'I am just beginning on Woburn buildings . . . alas the most significant image of those years must be left out.' The reference is to the *enmenagement* with Mrs. Shakespear in 1896 or that of 1903. And since the unrecorded crises are the heart of much of his later poetry, the loss is severe. If there is little sense of the author's presence in *Trembling of the Veil*, little self-criticism and self-clarification, the abstention is clearly deliberate.

In addition to reticence about his deepest emotional experiences, there were other difficulties. 'Whenever I have included a living man I have submitted my words for his correction. This is specially important . . . I want to show that though I am being published by Moore's publisher I do not accept Moore's practice.' That he still had doubts is indicated by this passage from a letter to Mrs. Shakespear: '[The book] needs the wild mystical part to lift it out of gossip, and the mystical part will not be as clear as it should be for lack of diagrams.' 'Mysticism' was beyond Moore, that 'precious thing' that Moore, like a passing dog, 'defiled'.

It is Moore's version of history which Yeats's autobiographies challenge. In *Trembling of the Veil* Yeats uses something of Moore's approach not to the living but to the dead. The distinction lies between Moore's malice and Yeats's didacticism; the similarity lies in the thematic and apologetic elements. As Arthur Schumaker has pointed out, *Hail and Farewell* uses distinct thematic devices derived from Wagner's *Ring*, all leading to the climax where Moore discovers himself as Siegfried 'given the task of reforging broken weapons of thought and restoring Ireland to thought and responsibility'. His stated intention was to represent the past moment as a passing *now*: 'To take a certain amount of material and model it much as [one] would do in a novel.' The persons in Moore's trilogy become types of human character, representative of a fallen Ireland; transitions are concealed, meditation modulates into speech, chronology is fluid; manipulation of the past is added to selection of event and, as is not the case with *Trembling of the Veil*, there is a high incidence of direct speech. The similarities to Yeats's work, and the contrasts, are plain.

Another passage from a letter to Mrs. Shakespear reveals how in *Autobiographies* even energising hatred of the dead was to be muted. Tenderness to the living can be exemplified by Yeats's treatment of Johnson, who was Mrs. Shakespear's cousin and to whom she had been deeply attached: he was to be shown 'as the noble tragic figure that he was . . . those who follow me are likely to take their key from what I have written'. But the effect was to puzzle rather than convince. Charles Ricketts found the memoirs in general persuasive, but the presentation of Johnson surprising:

> It is singular that he should have impressed himself on you, doubtless it was the attraction of the *opposite*, he struck me then, and in recollection, as a typical 'Fruit sec' of his class, time and training. I caught him making a lamentable howler in a translation of Baudelaire. He said or did something else which I have forgotten and never created that bogus atmosphere with which he impressed you.[7]

Where *Reveries* had been the record of self-discovery through others, in *Trembling of the Veil* all sequence of cause and effect is fractured by a

[7] From a letter in the possession of Mrs. W. B. Yeats. Yeats seems to have had the impression that Johnson might have admired his work, but did not like him.

new teleology, the invasion of the 'supernatural', the most violent force in history. Gossip and mysticism collide, but do not coalesce. Another sophisticated form of determinism results, though not the positivists' mere aggregation of fact against which the whole structure of *Trembling of the Veil* is a protest. The relatively firm chronology, the questing quality of *Reveries*, is dissolved and the book given a sense of omen fulfilled: the validation of his own insights and those of his generation of poets and occultists, 'the things wild people half scholars and rhapsodical persons wrote about, when you and I were young'. With Parnell's death in 1891 *Four Years* comes to an end; 1892, the year Yeats began from in his *Oxford Book of Modern Verse*, the year of the *First Book of the Rhymers' Club*, ushered in the poetry of what he came to see as the last phase of the historical cycle. The insights of his friends and their rejection of the vulgar dream of progress was to be more violently corroborated than either he or they had anticipated.

Yeats shared with his generation a sense of history that expressed itself as an acute, even exacerbated sense of contemporaneity, of the moment defined only in its relationship to past and future. Scholarship, revolution and the natural sciences had conspired to induce in late-nineteenth-century artists and intellectuals what was often an anguished sense of the moment as isolable, definable, an unstable ridge between abysses. It is in the nineteenth century that the sense of belonging to a decade, to a generation, was developed. Not until the 1890s could Lord Henry Wootton have said to Dorian Gray 'fin de siècle' and have received the antiphonal answer 'fin du globe'. Such tremors are common to ends of centuries, but the 1890s have more in common with the year 1000—a year of perfect numbers—or with the year 1600, than with the shrugging dismissal of, say, Dryden's *Secular Masque*. As the blank zeros of the calendar figure approached, the temporal uncertainties of the century merged in a diffuse, an irrational chiliasm.

The sense of Apocalypse, of the new age heralded by some terrible annunciation, was substantiated by Madame Blavatsky, Mathers and the Symbolists. Against this was posed the possibility of unity of culture: the symbol, to be achieved like Stalinism in one country, Ireland. But the historical pattern faltered into anticlimax: the 'Tragic Generation' immersed themselves in the flux, dying 'as soon as their constitutions would permit', and the attempt to achieve unity of culture through Societies, through the more literate Unionists and Land-owners, and finally—transcending tragic individualism—through a Symbolist theatre, failed. The Easter Rising forced Yeats to redefine the past, in Morton Zabel's words 'to discover the laws of character, of creative power and of history'. The last three sections of *Trembling of the Veil* break off into a 'bundle of fragments', into the incoherence of an historic present without a future tense, which requires *A Vision* for its clarification.

'In art rhythm is everything', Arthur Symons had declared in a Symbolist manifesto published in *The Dome* of 1898. Yeats assumed Symons's phraseology of 'pattern' and 'rhythm' and applied them (in an article published also in the *Dome*) to the Symbolist designs of Althea Gyles and subsequently to poetry and to Symbolist 'total' theatre and history.[8] The words themselves imply 'image' (rather than naturalist 'subject'), the non-rational, the visionary. The Symbolist reaction towards trance is accompanied by a reaction against the tyranny of fact: a supernatural 'rhythm' against which personality (the individual in tragic passion) defines itself.

The search for both 'rhythm' and 'pattern', recurrence in time and space (the artist's isolation and the dilemma of a generation) manifests itself in the search for a cyclical view of history. This Yeats began to wish to substitute for the notion of history as chaos or as chiliastic. He was already reaching towards this in the 1890s, though the members of the Tragic Generation are without it. When he came to write *Trembling of the Veil* such a view becomes a category for the interpretation of personalities, individualities. The Tragic Generation merely re-enact more violently and self-consciously the experiences of J. B. Yeats and his friends.

Yeats's 1890s are hardly those of history, or of literary history. To the sober historian the imposition of Death Duties in 1894 appears more significant than the trials of Wilde in the following year; the continuous economic depression of 1890–6 than the sputtering history of the Rhymers. Yet Yeats focuses on two of the major characteristics of the decade: Ireland, and the climax of the revolt against Victorianism,

---

[8] The terms I have borrowed from Northrop Frye's *Anatomy of Criticism*. For Mr. Frye, *Finnegans Wake* is 'a great circular organisation of mutating categories'. Recurrence is generally spoken of as 'rhythm' when it moves along in time and 'pattern' when it is spread out in space. From Mr. Frye's criteria, *Autobiographies* might perhaps be judged as overmimetic, not sufficiently mythicised. As an example of rhythm, there is the role of Simeon Solomon. He poignantly associates the two generations by his occasional visits, 'a ragged figure as of some fallen dynasty', to the haunts of the Rhymers. Solomon's poverty and vice foreshadow Dowson's and Wilde's last years and Johnson's vision of himself as reduced to borrowing half-crowns from friends.

the so-called normality that was sick. We get the flavour of a London that was now dominating the provinces, imposing its own centralised cultural pattern; and we even have some vague sense of the brooding, almost iconic figure of Victoria herself, ageless, it seemed, the dignified if dowdy incarnation of a people's dream. But Yeats's 1890s may still seem altogether too narrow, since we now associate the decade's revolt with figures who seem more relevant to the twentieth century, with Ibsen, Zola, Shaw, Butler and Gissing, rather than with the denizens of the Cheshire Cheese. Yet the *fin de siècle* mood was startlingly diffused: in James's *Altar of the Dead*, in Wells's early fables, for example. And the themes of *Trembling of the Veil*, the sense of isolation and alienation and the confrontation of artist and audience, remain valid comment beyond Yeats's circle.

For Yeats's '90s include (if somewhat obliquely) many pressures common to all schools. There are, for example, the temptations of placating and securing an audience through the new publicity media, 'the interview and letter to the press'; what Yeats calls Moore's 'immediate sensational contact with public opinion'. Again, we find the Imperialists' self-destructive energies of aggression realised in the image of Henley and his 'regatta' of young men. Much of Yeats's comment is gossip, but it remains if not actual, typical: his image of Beardsley as Huysmanish saint conforms to the image John Gray gave when he edited Beardsley's letters. Johnson (in *Mors Janua Vitae* and *Mystic and Cavalier*) and Wilde had both mythologised themselves. With Dowson, however, the case was different. Yeats followed Symons, who had presented Dowson in 1900 as a conventional *poète maudit*, 'a demoralised Keats', though understandably Symons makes little attempt to associate Dowson with his contemporaries. Dowson, however, had also done his mythologising and this ran counter to Symons, and to Yeats's association of the 'Tragic Generation' with the protest against Positivism. Submitting to the Huxley-Tindall world-view, Dowson's ethic of 'drift' was culled from the negative side of Schopenhauer's philosophy: a willed will-lessness.

Yeats had then every excuse for mythologising his friends, for, like all young poets, they mythologised one another, and Yeats was performing a service similar to Gautier's history of Romanticism, where the generation of 1830 is aggrandised by gossip. The Tragic Generation insisted on suffering and dying mythologically: they were always trying to invent themselves, such was their sense of the individual's isolation in history, their distrust of 'generalisation'. And Yeats's mythologising begins as always from physical appearance: Henley, the paralysed viking; Johnson, the suave ambiguous Hellenistic head over the figurine body tapering away to vanishing-point; the uneasily bewigged Davidson; suggesting verdicts on lives and art.

Moreover, the process by which the notion of a 'Tragic Generation' was elaborated can be studied. Yeats had mythologised Johnson during Johnson's lifetime in a brief essay in Brooke's and Rolleston's *A Treasury of Irish Poetry* (1900).[9] He associated Johnson with Villiers's Axël in his tower, wavering in solitude between two dreams: of Ireland and the Catholic Church. But Johnson was a special case—his life had by that time passed already into a 'mythic' phase, a living death of illness, terror, remorse, whisky and isolation. Yeats had not associated Johnson with a generation. In 1908 Symons suffered the nervous collapse that virtually ended his career and in 1909 Davidson walked into the sea. In a lecture given at the Memorial Hall, Manchester, on 31 October 1910 Yeats reveals that by this time he was placing his own generation historically, but in a manner that was strictly limited. His account anticipates strikingly the account of the Rhymers' programme given in *Trembling of the Veil*. He begins with the Renaissance discovery of Academic Form (against which Pre-Raphaelitism had rebelled) and proceeds to the rejection of 'subject' in painting and its parallel in poetry. It is the version of 'dissociation of sensibility' which Yeats offers elsewhere. The hero-villain Milton is 'the Raphael of traditional morality' and the expression of classical morality alternately ennobled and dulled Wordsworth's genius and chilled Tennyson's *Idylls*. The 1890s witnessed 'the revolt of my own fiery generation' and 'the man who first proclaimed it was the younger Hallam who invented the phrase "the aesthetic school in poetry" '. The new type of poet was one who did not aspire to teach, eschewing popular morality and easy anecdote, but simply gave one 'his vision'.

Yeats, his lecture goes on, had come to recognise that 'we have thrown away the most powerful of all things in literature—personal utterance'. What he had thought of as a purely personal insight was, he now saw, 'the thought of his generation . . . One thing I had not foreseen and that was if you make your art of your personality you will have a very troubled life. Goethe said, "We know ourselves by action only; never by contemplation." The moment you begin the

---

[9] p. 467. But see also p. xxii of the first edition of *A Book of Irish Verse*, edited by Yeats in 1895: 'the arts that consume the personality in solitude . . . the immortal [arts], which could but divide him from the hearts of men'.

expression of yourself as an artist your life in some mysterious way is full of tumult.' It was a lesson explicit already in Hallam's essay on Tennyson which had been reprinted by one of the Rhymers, Le Gallienne, in 1893. 'To me it meant Irish leagues and movements and all kinds of heterogeneous activities which were not good for my life, as it seemed to me at the time. To the others it meant dissipation; that generation was a doomed generation . . . I believe it was that they made their nature passionate by making their art personal.' And of Johnson and Dowson, Yeats spoke in terms that closely resemble those in *Trembling of the Veil*, concluding that when he thought of that 'doomed generation I am not sure whether it was sin or sanctity which was found in their brief lives'.[10]

It is an interpretation which has not been strictly touched by notions of 'personality'. The tone is far more tentative than that of *Trembling of the Veil*, where Yeats is more assured about sin and sanctity, while the doctrine looks back to *Ideas of Good and Evil*. Of Dowson Yeats had written that his art 'was curiously faint and shadowy. I believe that the art of any man who is sincerely seeking for the truth, seeking for beauty, is very likely to be faint and hesitating. The art that is entirely confident, or the speaking and writing . . . entirely confident, is the work of the kind of man who is speaking with other men's thoughts.' That hint as to false certainty provides the only crystallisation of what the Rhymers—in Yeats's presentation of them—were reacting against; not anecdote, but the formalism of English Parnassians such as Gosse, Dobson and Lang. In an article published in the *Providence Journal* of 1892 Yeats had attacked the foreign forms of these Parnassians, though the main target was the false 'objectivity' of attempting to rid a poem of any taint of its author. The attack on exotic forms seems to consort with the churchwarden pipes, ale and Dr. Johnson's Cheshire Cheese.

Yeats's presentation of himself in *The Tragic Generation* sharply illustrates the process to which his material was being subjected, and perhaps some of the limitations, even the inadequacies, which this treatment resulted in. In the 1910 lecture, as in *Autobiographies*, Yeats claims that he founded the various societies with which he was connected in the 1890s to make substantive the moral of the artist losing

---

[10] These excerpts from the text of Yeats's lecture I have taken from the occultist magazine, *The Path*, I, 6, pp. 105–10. Yeats's version of Hallam's review of Tennyson is misleading. Yeats suggests here that Pre-raphaelitism, his own generation and Augustus John, all share a 'rhythm' of revolt against Academic Form.

himself in toil that is not sedentary (Yeats's unhappy emotional life at
this time had affinities with the passive Dowson's). It remains difficult,
however, to determine whether his inaccuracies are due to stylisation
or simple forgetfulness. But two examples are certainly central. Yeats
obscures the origins of the Rhymers' Club which he claims to have
founded with Rhys in 1891 and which, in fact, gradually cohered out
of informal readings at 20 Fitzroy Street, 'Whiteladies', the house
Arthur Mackmurdo had bought in 1889. For Yeats, this process is not
sufficiently dramatic. If on the one hand his own account is false to the
young man of *Reveries*, feeling his way, on the other it dramatises,
legitimately perhaps, that young man's latent decisiveness: he presided
over the moment of coherence. There is little sense in *Trembling of the
Veil* of the Rhymers' miscellaneous muster, ranging in age from the
fifties down. Consequently, the Rhymers tend to be confused with the
'Tragic Generation'. The 'pattern' that Yeats is distinguishing applies
not merely to the Rhymers and to Henley, but to naturalists like
Crackanthorpe, whose unhappy love affair and suicide make him
severely exemplary.

Similarly, although there was a preliminary meeting of the Irish
Literary Society at the Yeats house in Bedford Park, Yeats's assertion
that he was the Society's founder was challenged by the secretary,
Michael Macdonagh, in an unpublished account of the Society's
archives, and Yeats's claim is not supported by the Society's early
historian, W. P. Ryan. To be sure, Yeats admits that the Society
cohered out of the Southwark Club, but it is clear that he is presenting
himself in a way that is not altogether usual in this section of *Autobiographies*.

For other reasons, Yeats's relationships with women in the 1890s
are subjected to 'pattern'. The counterpart of the male artist is the 'new'
woman who tends to assume male characteristics: Althea Gyles (the
red-headed girl in AE's settlement in Dublin and one of Smithers's
repertoire of mistresses), Florence Farr, Maud Gonne. Apart from the
luminosity of her first visit to Bedford Park, Maud Gonne scarcely
appears as the object of Yeats's 'barren passion'. That she should appear
at all is perhaps remarkable, though she is confined to her agitator's
role, particularly to the male role of orator (there is no account of her
interest in the occult). Metaphor carries a narrative force when she is
glimpsed *en passant* with her regalia of bird-cages and canaries (though
once with a Donegal hawk) rather as she appears with a more conventional monkey in Sarah Purser's oil. Cruelty and triviality are

hinted—Yeats's usual defensive assertion of the Fatal Woman theme.

Yet the very elaboration of *Trembling of the Veil* defeats its own purpose. It muffles the book's climax. What we seem to be fundamentally concerned with is the relation between artist and audience. This is resolved most nakedly by the artist's counter-attack through the theatre. In the theatre the dramatist encounters that audience under conditions of sharp excitement. When he belongs to a generation self-consciously in revolt, the hostility between himself (making a customary first-night appearance) and his audience is almost ritually enacted (the disapprobation of plays was distinctly less inhibited then). Moore in *Ave* tells us that Yeats believed that the author should be present at first nights: only by watching the effect of his play could he learn his trade.

The Tragic Generation opens with a theatrical episode—the staging of Todhunter's *Sicilian Idyll* at the Bedford Park Club House.

It was Todhunter's practice that had given Yeats his earliest model for emulation, as we gather from an unpublished letter of 24 April 1885 to Todhunter from J. B. Yeats:

> I am most grateful to you for your kind letter and your interest in Willie—but did not write because I suppose painting devours everything—yet I have been wanting to tell you that Willie on his side watches with an almost breathless interest your course as dramatic poet—and has been doing so for a long time—he has read everything you have written most carefully.
>
> —he finished when at Howth your Rienzi at a single sitting—'the' sitting ending at 2 o'clock in the morning . . .
>
> That Willie is a poet I have long known—what I am really interested in is seeing the dramatic idea emerge and I think before this present drama . . . of his has finished, you will see evidence of his dramatic instinct.[11]

The whole account of Todhunter in *Trembling of the Veil* is manipulated with such firm economy that nothing sways the reader from the definitive image of Todhunter sitting in his box at the Avenue Theatre, surrounded by his family, enduring the crass cries of gallery and pit, without gesture though with dull courage, as his *Comedy of Sighs* staggers to its fiasco.

'Petulant and unstable, he was incapable of any emotion that could give life to a cause.' Todhunter refuses to act out the drama of the passionate artist confronting the enemies of art; artistically he dies in

---

[11] Manuscript in Reading University Library.

his bed. Successful at Bedford Park, Todhunter had been tempted to conquer the commercial theatre, but to conquer the managers he abandoned poetry for Ibsen, or more precisely, Pinero. Of Todhunter's *Helena of Troas* (1886) Yeats wrote that 'I had thought (it) as unactable as unreadable', though in 1892, following second-hand accounts of its production: 'its sonorous verse united to the rhythmical motions of the white-robed chorus, and the solemnity of burning incense, produced a semi-religious effect new to the modern stage'.

Nothing could more firmly relate to the theme of symbolism triumphing over positivism and naturalism. What seems to have struck Yeats most was the 'mood' of E. W. Godwin's production in 1886, 'acting, scenery and verse were all a perfect unity'. But the account of Todhunter has to submit to its climax. His experience at the Avenue Theatre in 1894 predicts that of Synge, though it was Yeats himself and his father who actually faced the audience when the *Playboy* challenged their clichés. There is a brisk contrast with Wilde (or Shaw) cajoling the audience with the play and mocking them in person. When James faced a hostile crowd on the first night of *Guy Domville*, history obliged with an exemplary episode: the solitary artist extending the dramatic ritual by appearing as scapegoat (Dickens's public readings which so shortened his life provide the anti-type).

The most famous of the scapegoats was, of course, Wilde. In Yeats's account of him the artist's life becomes itself a play; though Wilde's genius balked at tragedy, 'that elaborate playing with tragedy was an attempt to escape from emotion by its exaggeration'. The trial is only obliquely mentioned, but for Yeats it was clearly Wilde's last and greatest play. Wilde played it as comedy, but its note turned tragic, and when he was convicted 'the harlots in the street outside danced upon the pavement', a tousled maenadic parody of the tragic chorus, or the Furies on the roof-top of Agamemnon's palace.

G. S. Fraser has best defined Yeats's attitude to Wilde as one of 'Platonic tolerance':

Thrasymachus and Protagoras are archetypal figures of intellectual comedy, they are there in the dialogues to be destroyed, yet they represent something in human nature—the bully or the sophist in all of us—that is indestructible. Yeats's Oscar Wilde is (given another scene, another set of weapons) as indestructible an archetype as Plato's Alcibiades. His life should be a great tragedy, or a horrid melodramatic warning; but his temperament is irrepressibly that of what Yeats, in another connection, called 'the great comedian'. And his Mask dominates his Body of Fate. . . . What should be appalling becomes farcical, and what should be ignoble farce is magnificently lent style.[12]

Of this the brothel episode in Dieppe is the most graphic instance. Dowson and Wilde pool funds to teach Wilde 'a more wholesome taste'. A crowd attends them to the brothel and awaits the event. Wilde appears:

> He said in a low voice to Dowson, 'The first these ten years, and it will be the last. It was like cold mutton'—always, as Henley had said, 'a scholar and a gentleman', he now remembered that the Elizabethan dramatists used the words 'cold mutton'—and then aloud so that the crowd might hear him, 'But tell it in England, for it will entirely restore my character.' (*Auto.*, 328).

The episode is conceived dramatically and Wilde disappears with an exit-line that is both pathetic and funny.

The section on *The Tragic Generation* which began with the account of *A Comedy of Sighs* ends with the meeting with Synge and with Yeats and Symons witnessing Jarry's *Ubu Roi*[13] at Lugne Poe's symbolist *Théatre de l'oeuvre*. In Jarry's play, from a distance of twenty years, he can see only comedy and the return of the objective cycle. The reduction of human beings to marionettes, where the self-conscious and the primitive come full circle, the point where 'the painter's brush consumes his dreams', provides a faltering finish before the onset of 'the Savage God', confirming the circular and determinist structure of the whole book.

III

On 28 February 1934 Yeats referred to 'the drama I am building up in my Lady Gregory'. The material taken from his own letters was to be transformed into an epitaph on the conflict of personalities that preceded the founding of the Abbey Theatre and into an exaltation of Lady Gregory as aristocrat and prose artist over Moore and Martyn. Himself the only survivor, Yeats approached the past in a manner at once detached and involved: 'things reveal themselves passing away'. The years between 1897 and 1902 assumed coherence: 'It is curious

---

[12] Yeats employs the phrase in his poem 'Parnell's Funeral'. Tim Healy is reported to have called Parnell 'a tragic comedian' soon after the *débâcle*, probably remembering Lassalle and Meredith's novel.

[13] See A. Symons, *Studies in Seven Arts* (1906), pp. 371–7.

H.G.–N

how one's life falls into definite sections—in 1897 a new scene was set, new actors appeared.' But the dramatic metaphor at once pays tribute to the excitement of those years and distances them: Yeats himself, or rather his idea of himself, is a puppet among puppets. If the national theatre is to be judged, he wrote, 'what [Moore] is and what I am will be weighed and very little what we have said and done'.

Yet much of *Dramatis Personae* is concerned with what Moore said and did. Through a pretended auditor, it is a dialogue with Moore. Before composing it, Yeats was reading Moore 'that I may write'; and the writing was designed to overgo Moore in his own art, impressionist autobiography, an art based on Paterian 'style', self-transparency. 'Style' is indivisible, and what one says or does or writes flows from what one is.

Moore's side of the dialogue had begun in 1898 with *Evelyn Innes*, dedicated to Yeats and Symons, 'two writers with whom I am in sympathy'. Moore cast Yeats as the poet and magician Ulick Dean, and a letter to Olivia Shakespear suggests that Yeats was both pleased and amused. *Hail and Farewell* appeared long after the quarrel between the two men. In *Ave* Moore hesitates between two images of Yeats. The poet's operatic appearance suggests an image close to Katharine Tynan's: 'an Irish parody of the poetry I had seen all my life strutting its rhythmic way in the alleys of the Luxembourg gardens, preening its rhymes by the fountains, excessive in habit and gait'.[14] The other image suggests latent strength, and Yeats's slippery dialectic is accorded appreciation. Yeats did not take ridicule kindly and the breach between himself and Moore was final, though Moore carried his ingenuousness into old age and complained that when Yeats came to London he never visited Ebury Gardens.

Although *Dramatis Personae* attempts to surpass Moore in his own art, Yeats is no Messiah. Under the relaxed surface, however, the book focuses Yeats's version of history, the game or play which every literary achievement imposes more firmly on the past, even if it is a past that has now a splendid irrelevance.

We begin with the three Galway 'great houses', Coole, Roxborough, Tulyra (and by implication we think of Moore Hall in County Mayo). The relaxed quality of *Dramatis Personae* owes something perhaps to the fact that Yeats had already written the poems that celebrate Lady Gregory and the part she and Coole played in modern Irish history.

14 Katharine Tynan had published without Yeats's permission extracts from his letters of the '80s and '90s in her *Twenty five Years* (1913).

There is none of the 'spilled poetry' and spilled mythology of parts of *Trembling of the Veil*. Yet *Dramatis Personae* itself clarifies the ground for 'The Municipal Gallery Revisited' and supremely the 'painted stage' of 'The Circus Animals' Desertion'. In *Dramatis Personae*, after judging Moore and Martyn, Yeats implicitly judges himself.

The judgements on Moore and Martyn are full of malicious insight. Yeats proceeds to use them, as Moore had used Martyn and Yeats, for copy. A mutual contempt binds Moore and Martyn and a common self-esteem. Martyn, the saint, warms himself with his own sanctity in the presence of the sinner, Moore, and the sinner feels more self-importantly wicked in the presence of the saint. The judgement is framed through a peasant saying which reduces both men to a very ordinary humanity. Indeed, both Moore and Martyn reduce themselves to the peasant. Yeats's note here is one of malice discovered through the questing rhythms of talk—Martyn's mother is of dubious class and Moore's education was not at Urbino but in the stables. Physical appearance promotes, as usual, mythologising: Moore's face is carved out of that sour and vulgar vegetable, the turnip. The most inconsequential narrative serves the theme: 'One evening . . . I heard a voice resounding as if in a funnel, someone in a hansom cab was denouncing its driver, and Moore drove by.' This is sinewy talk: frustration and aggression are suggested by the simile, and the final resonant anticlimax turns Moore into a one-man juggernaut, 'not a man, but a mob'. Moore's lack of style, of the aristocratic values, is tangentially but convincingly demonstrated by his treatment of cabmen and waiters. Yeats's 'style' emerges simply through talk and once only by reference to 'my great-grandmother Corbet, the mistress of Sandymount', where the resonance is well-manneredly casual. Yeats's values are again obliquely asserted. His insistence on Moore's gross frankness about women recalls his own reticence; the frankness is even dismissed as compensation for ugliness: 'he never kisses and always tells'. His own love for Maud Gonne, Yeats distances as he distances his mystical circus animals, 'which I have discussed too much elsewhere'. His own platonising view of one man, one woman, whether wife, mistress or obsession, he treats without pomp. The auditor is invited to distinguish.

There are connections with the method of *Trembling of the Veil*. History assumes a metaphoric role in the account of the emblematic fire at Tulyra which divides the present from its roots in the past and reinforces the image of Martyn as mule. Indeed, the presentation of Martyn is queerly harsh compared with Moore's genial contempt. Differences in politics and the schism of the Theatre of Ireland in 1907 may have rankled, and Martyn's rather public conscience irritated Yeats as it had irritated Moore.[15] Counterpointing Moore's account in *Ave*, Yeats's account of Gill's dinner to himself and Martyn is conducted through the familiar dialectic of 'images'. Moore speaks first, inaudibly, badly, succeeded by Taylor, who is below his best. But physical description distinguishes the two men. Taylor's body, as the tense phrases record, 'was angular, rigid with suppressed rage, his gaze fixed upon some object, his clothes badly made, his erect attitude suggested a firm base'— a firm base in the Ireland whose provinciality condemned him to obscurity. Moore, the failed cosmopolite, is hit off in one comprehensive sentence: 'Moore's body was insinuating, upflowing, circulative, curvicular, pop-eyed.' The lack of physical definition is brilliantly suggested by the use of near-synonyms, each purporting to catch at the oddity, the absence of style, and after the rise into the mock-pompous 'circulative' and 'curvicular' the word 'pop-eyed' forces its way artlessly out and the image collapses into finality. Both Taylor and Moore are placed by the image of O'Grady who speaks with such a drunken majestic sweetness that his Unionist opponent applauds the Nationalist sentiments. 'Their torch smoked, their wine had dregs, his element burned or ran pure.' O'Grady's oratory is the purest symbolism, includes but transcends logic.[16]

For both Yeats and Moore final judgement on their respective styles, their respective self-transparency, is a literary judgement. Moore had learned the necessity for style in the later 1880s under the influence of Pater,[17] but the books that most satisfied their author, *Heloise and Abelard* and *The Brook Kerith*, though written after *Hail and Farewell*, had their roots in the trilogy and in *The Lake*. Yeats's shrewdest stroke is the suggestion that the painful limpidities of the later Moore were based on some 'silly youthful experiments' of his own. (Susan Mitchell's suggestion that Moore owed to Yeats the notion of revising and re-revising his earlier work is instantly plausible.) Yeats does not under-

[15] For the Theatre of Ireland, see M. Nic Shiubhlaigh, *The Splendid Years* (Dublin, 1955), pp. 73–107 in particular.

[16] The description, like the description of Taylor's oratory in *Reveries*, seems to owe something to J. B. Yeats's account of Isaac Butt *chanting* his sentences when speaking in the Four Courts on some case that appealed to him. See *Passages from the Letters of John Butler Yeats*, ed. Ezra Pound (1917), p. 34.

[17] With rather gruesome results in *A Mere Accident* and *Mike Fletcher*, where aestheticism and naturalism jostle uneasily.

estimate Moore's force, but praise is polemical. Moore's work is a triumph of will, not the effect of grace, and the effort shows. Apparent magnanimity is frequent in *Dramatis Personae*. Episode is balanced against episode and Yeats's side of the *Where There is Nothing* encounter, with its sputter of threats and telegrams, is prepared by the reference to Moore's plagiarism that reveals both shamelessness and courage.

The structure of *Dramatis Personae* moves towards the exaltation of Lady Gregory,[18] and Yeats's own talk is taken up into her translation of Grania's lullaby over Diarmuid in that 'musical caressing English which never goes far from the idiom of the country people she knows so well'. This has been ushered in by the compunction of the last reference to Moore ('I look back with some remorse'), by the brief account of Hyde's ease of style in the Irish language and a reflection on Synge, the inheritor. Our thoughts are swayed deliberately to 'Coole' and 'Coole and Ballylee'; and by the comic sparagmos of the tinkers after the performance of Yeats's and Lady Gregory's *Unicorn from the Stars* to the *Playboy* and its consequences both on stage and off, to riots and the superior fictions that cause them.[19] The subject of the lament, Diarmuid and Grania, indicates that more than a requiem over the episode of the National Theatre is intended, for its subject symphonically associates Lady Gregory with Yeats and with Moore, since all were concerned in writing a play of that title that was finished to no one's satisfaction and whose comic history is recorded in Moore's *Ave*. It remains a final comment on *Dramatis Personae* also, on the fiction that does not deceive its author, but whose unity of tone makes it the most artfully achieved of Yeats's essays in self-transcendence.

[18] In *Dramatis Personae*, the absence of self-conscious 'rhythm' involves a corresponding absence of omission and distortion. The connections of Sir Robert and Lady Gregory with Egyptian Nationalism are probably casually omitted and Lady Gregory's role as dramatist is muted.

[19] The tinkers appear in *Our Irish Theatre*. Lady Gregory recalls that a magistrate called one of them 'Paul Ruttledge', the hero of *Unicorn from the Stars*. Hearing that they had been put in a book, the tinkers reacted in riot.

Index